MORAL MAN

AND

IMMORAL SOCIETY

By Reinhold Niebuhr

THE STRUCTURE OF NATIONS AND EMPIRES
PIOUS AND SECULAR AMERICA
THE SELF AND THE DRAMAS OF HISTORY
CHRISTIAN REALISM AND POLITICAL PROBLEMS
THE IRONY OF AMERICAN HISTORY
FAITH AND HISTORY
THE CHILDREN OF LIGHT AND THE
CHILDREN OF DARKNESS
THE NATURE AND DESTINY OF MAN
BEYOND TRAGEDY

REINHOLD NIEBUHR ON POLITICS:
*His Political Philosophy and Its Application
to Our Age as Expressed in His Writings.*
Edited by Harry R. Davis and Robert C. Good

MORAL MAN

AND

IMMORAL SOCIETY

A Study in Ethics and Politics

By

REINHOLD NIEBUHR

CHARLES SCRIBNER'S SONS · NEW YORK

TO
U. M. N.

CONTENTS

PREFACE

Moral Man and Immoral Society was published in 1932, which is to say more than a quarter of a century ago. Naturally many of its references are dated. The most obvious ones are those referring to the post-war policies of America, to the Labour Party of Ramsay MacDonald, to the League of Nations and to the then unsolved problem of England and India.

But despite these dated references I consented to the republication of the book because I still believe that the central thesis of the book is important and I am still committed to it. The central thesis was, and is, that the Liberal Movement both religious and secular seemed to be unconscious of the basic difference between the morality of individuals and the morality of collectives, whether races, classes or nations. This difference ought not to make for a moral cynicism, that is, the belief that the collective must simply follow its own interests. But if the difference is real, as I think it is, it refutes many still prevalent moralistic approaches to the political order.

I have since elaborated the thesis, first stated in *Moral Man and Immoral Society,* in various facets in various volumes. I have changed my mind about many things, but I am inclined to think that all of our contemporary experience validates rather than refutes the basic thesis of this volume.

May, 1960   REINHOLD NIEBUHR

INTRODUCTION

THE thesis to be elaborated in these pages is that a sharp distinction must be drawn between the moral and social behavior of individuals and of social groups, national, racial, and economic; and that this distinction justifies and necessitates political policies which a purely individualistic ethic must always find embarrassing. The title "Moral Man and Immoral Society" suggests the intended distinction too unqualifiedly, but it is nevertheless a fair indication of the argument to which the following pages are devoted. Individual men may be moral in the sense that they are able to consider interests other than their own in determining problems of conduct, and are capable, on occasion, of preferring the advantages of others to their own. They are endowed by nature with a measure of sympathy and consideration for their kind, the breadth of which may be extended by an astute social pedagogy. Their rational faculty prompts them to a sense of justice which educational discipline may refine and purge of egoistic elements until they are able to view a social situation, in which their own interests are involved, with a fair measure of objectivity. But all these achievements are more difficult, if not impossible, for human societies and social groups. In every human group there is less reason to guide and to check impulse, less capacity for self-transcendence, less ability to comprehend the needs of others and therefore more unrestrained egoism than the individuals, who compose the group, reveal in their personal relationships.

The inferiority of the morality of groups to that of individuals is due in part to the difficulty of establishing a rational social force which is powerful enough to cope with the natural impulses by which society achieves its cohesion; but in part it is merely the revelation of a collective egoism, compounded of the egoistic impulses of individuals, which achieve a more vivid expression and a more cumulative effect when they are united in a common impulse than when they express themselves separately and discreetly.

Inasfar as this treatise has a polemic interest it is directed against the moralists, both religious and secular, who imagine that the egoism of individuals is being progressively checked by the development of rationality or the growth of a religiously inspired goodwill and that nothing but the continuance of this process is necessary to establish social harmony between all the human societies and collectives. Social analyses and prophecies made by moralists, sociologists and educators upon the basis of these assumptions lead to a very considerable moral and political confusion in our day. They completely disregard the political necessities in the struggle for justice in human society by failing to recognise those elements in man's collective behavior which belong to the order of nature and can never be brought completely under the dominion of reason or conscience. They do not recognise that when collective power, whether in the form of imperialism or class domination, exploits weakness, it can never be dislodged unless power is raised against it.

If conscience and reason can be insinuated into the resulting struggle they can only qualify but not abolish it.

The most persistent error of modern educators and moralists is the assumption that our social difficulties are due to the failure of the social sciences to keep pace with the physical sciences which have created our technological civilisation. The invariable implication of this assumption is that, with a little more time, a little more adequate moral and social pedagogy and a generally higher development of human intelligence, our social problems will approach solution. "It is," declares Professor John Dewey, "our human intelligence and our human courage which is on trial; it is incredible that men who have brought the technique of physical discovery, invention and use to such a pitch of perfection will abdicate in the face of the infinitely more important human problem. What stands in the way (of a planned economy) is a lot of outworn traditions, moth-eaten slogans and catchwords that do substitute duty for thought, as well as our entrenched predatory self-interest. We shall only make a real beginning in intelligent thought when we cease mouthing platitudes. . . . Just as soon as we begin to use the knowledge and skills we have, to control social consequences in the interest of a shared, abundant and secured life, we shall cease to complain of the backwardness of our social knowledge. . . . We shall then take the road which leads to the assured building up of social science just as men built up physical science when they actively used techniques and tools and numbers in physical experimentation."[1] In spite of Professor Dewey's great interest in

1 John Dewey, *Philosophy and Civilization* (New York: Minton, Balch), p. 329.

and understanding of the modern social problem there is very little clarity in this statement. The real cause of social inertia, "our predatory self-interest," is mentioned only in passing without influencing his reasoning, and with no indication that he understands how much social conservatism is due to the economic interests of the own-ing classes. On the whole, social conservatism is ascribed to ignorance, a viewpoint which states only part of the truth and reveals the natural bias of the educator. The suggestion that we will only make a beginning in intel-ligent thought when we "cease mouthing platitudes," is itself so platitudinous that it rather betrays the confusion of an analyst who has no clear counsels about the way to overcome social inertia. The idea that we cannot be so-cially intelligent until we begin experimentation in so-cial problems in the way that the physical scientists ex-perimented fails to take account of an important differ-ence between the physical and the social sciences. The physical sciences gained their freedom when they over-came the traditionalism based on ignorance, but the tra-ditionalism which the social sciences face is based upon the economic interest of the dominant social classes who are trying to maintain their special privileges in society. Nor can the difference between the very character of so-cial and physical sciences be overlooked. Complete ra-tional objectivity in a social situation is impossible. The very social scientists who are so anxious to offer our gen-eration counsels of salvation and are disappointed that an ignorant and slothful people are so slow to accept their wisdom, betray middle-class prejudices in almost everything they write. Since reason is always, to some de-

gree, the servant of interest in a social situation, social injustice cannot be resolved by moral and rational suasion
alone, as the educator and social scientist usually believes.
Conflict is inevitable, and in this conflict power must be
challenged by power. That fact is not recognized by most
of the educators, and only very grudgingly admitted by
most of the social scientists.

If social conflict be a part of the process of gaining social justice, the idea of most of Professor Dewey's disciples that our salvation depends upon the development of
"experimental procedures"[2] in social life, commensurate
with the experimentalism of the physical sciences, does
not have quite the plausibility which they attribute to it.
Contending factions in a social struggle require morale;
and morale is created by the right dogmas, symbols and
emotionally potent oversimplifications. These are at least
as necessary as the scientific spirit of tentativity. No class
of industrial workers will ever win freedom from the
dominant classes if they give themselves completely to the
"experimental techniques" of the modern educators. They
will have to believe rather more firmly in the justice and
in the probable triumph of their cause, than any impartial science would give them the right to believe, if they
are to have enough energy to contest the power of the
strong. They may be very scientific in projecting their social goal and in choosing the most effective instruments
for its attainment, but a motive force will be required to
nerve them for their task which is not easily derived
from the cool objectivity of science. Modern educators

2 *Cf. inter alia,* John Childs, *Education and the Philosophy of Experimentalism,* p. 37.

are, like rationalists of all the ages, too enamored of the function of reason in life. The world of history, particularly in man's collective behavior, will never be conquered by reason, unless reason uses tools, and is itself driven by forces which are not rational.

The sociologists, as a class, understand the modern social problem even less than the educators. They usually interpret social conflict as the result of a clash between different kinds of "behavior patterns," which can be eliminated if the contending parties will only allow the social scientist to furnish them with a new and more perfect pattern which will do justice to the needs of both parties. With the educators they regard ignorance rather than self-interest as the cause of conflict. "Apparently," declares Kimball Young, "the only way in which collective conflicts, as well as individual conflicts, can be successfully and hygienically solved is by securing a redirection of behavior toward a more feasible environmental objective. This can be accomplished most successfully by the rational reconditioning of attitudes on a higher neuro-psychic or intellectual symbolic plane to the facts of science, preferably through a free discussion with a minimum of propaganda. This is not an easy road to mental and social sanity but it appears to be the only one which arrives at the goal."[3] Here a technique which works very well in individual relations, and in certain types of social conflict due to differences in culture, is made a general panacea. How is it to solve the problem between England and India? Through the Round-Table Conference? But how much would England have

[3] Kimball Young, *Social Attitudes*, p. 72.

granted India at the conference if a non-co-operation campaign, a type of conflict, had not forced the issue?

A favorite counsel of the social scientists is that of accommodation. If two parties are in a conflict, let them, by conferring together, moderate their demands and arrive at a *modus vivendi*. This is, among others, the advice of Professor Hornell Hart.[4] Undoubtedly there are innumerable conflicts which must be resolved in this fashion. But will a disinherited group, such as the Negroes for instance, ever win full justice in society in this fashion? Will not even its most minimum demands seem exorbitant to the dominant whites, among whom only a very small minority will regard the inter-racial problem from the perspective of objective justice? Or how are the industrial workers to follow Professor Hart's advice in dealing with industrial owners, when the owners possess so much power that they can win the debate with the workers, no matter how unconvincing their arguments? Only a very few sociologists seem to have learned that an adjustment of a social conflict, caused by the disproportion of power in society, will hardly result in justice as long as the disproportion of power remains. Sometimes the sociologists are so completely oblivious to the real facts of an industrial civilisation that, as Floyd Allport for instance, they can suggest that the unrest of industrial workers is due not to economic injustice but to a sense of inferiority which will be overcome just as soon as benevolent social psychologists are able to teach the workers that "no one is charging them with inferiority except themselves."[5] These omniscient social scientists will

[4] Hornell Hart, *The Science of Social Relations.*
[5] Floyd Allport, *Social Psychology,* pp. 14–27.

also teach the owners that "interests and profits must be tempered by regard for the worker." Thus "the socialisation of individual control" in industry will obviate the necessity of "socialistic control." Most of the social scientists are such unqualified rationalists that they seem to imagine that men of power will immediately check their exactions and pretensions in society, as soon as they have been apprised by the social scientists that their actions and attitudes are anti-social. Professor Clarence Marsh Case, in an excellent analysis of the social problem, places his confidence in a "reorganisation of values" in which, among other things, industrial leaders must be made to see "that despotically controlled industry in a society that professes democracy as an article of faith is an anachronism that cannot endure."[6] It may be that despotism cannot endure but it will not abdicate merely because the despots have discovered it to be anachronistic. Sir Arthur Salter, to name a brilliant economist among the social scientists, finishes his penetrating analysis of the distempers of our civilisation by expressing the usual hope that a higher intelligence or a sincerer morality will prevent the governments of the future from perpetrating the mistakes of the past. His own analysis proves conclusively that the failure of governments is due to the pressure of economic interest upon them rather than to the "limited capacities of human wisdom." In his own words, "government is failing above all because it has become enmeshed in the task of giving discretionary, particularly preferential, privileges to competitive industry."[7] In spite

[6] Clarence Marsh Case, *Social Process and Human Progress*, p. 233.
[7] Sir Arthur Salter, *Recovery*, p. 341.

of this analysis Sir Arthur expects the governments to redeem our civilisation by becoming more socially minded and he thinks that one method which will help them to do so is to "draw into the service of the public the great private institutions which represent the organised activities of the country, chambers of commerce, banking institutions, industrial and labor organisations." His entire hope for recovery rests upon the possibility of developing a degree of economic disinterestedness among men of power which the entire history of mankind proves them incapable of acquiring. It is rather discouraging to find such naïve confidence in the moral capacities of collective man, among men who make it their business to study collective human behavior. Even when, as Professor Howard Odum, they are prepared to admit that "conflict will be necessary" as long as "unfairness in the distribution of the rewards of labor exists," they put their hope in the future. They regard social conflict as only an expedient of the moment "until broader principles of education and cooperation can be established."[8] Anarchism, with an uncoerced and voluntary justice, seems to be either an explicit or implicit social goal of every second social scientist.

Modern religious idealists usually follow in the wake of social scientists in advocating compromise and accommodation as the way to social justice. Many leaders of the church like to insist that it is not their business to champion the cause of either labor or capital, but only to admonish both sides to a spirit of fairness and accommodation. "Between the far-visioned capitalism of Owen

[8] Howard W. Odum, *Man's Quest for Social Guidance*, p. 477.

[xix]

Young and the hard-headed socialism of Ramsay Mac-Donald," declares Doctor Justin Wroe Nixon, "there is probably no impassable gulf. The progress of mankind . . . depends upon following the MacDonalds and Youngs into those areas."[9] Unfortunately, since those lines were written the socialism of MacDonald has been revealed as not particularly hard-headed, and the depression has shown how little difference there really is between Mr. Young's "new capitalism" and the older and less suave types of capitalism.

What is lacking among all these moralists, whether religious or rational, is an understanding of the brutal character of the behavior of all human collectives, and the power of self-interest and collective egoism in all intergroup relations. Failure to recognise the stubborn resistance of group egoism to all moral and inclusive social objectives inevitably involves them in unrealistic and confused political thought. They regard social conflict either as an impossible method of achieving morally approved ends or as a momentary expedient which a more perfect education or a purer religion will make unnecessary. They do not see that the limitations of the human imagination, the easy subservience of reason to prejudice and passion, and the consequent persistence of irrational egoism, particularly in group behavior, make social conflict an inevitability in human history, probably to its very end.

The romantic overestimate of human virtue and moral capacity, current in our modern middle-class culture, does not always result in an unrealistic appraisal of present so-

[9] Justin Wroe Nixon, *An Emerging Christian Faith*, p. 294.

[xx]

cial facts. Contemporary social situations are frequently appraised quite realistically, but the hope is expressed that a new pedagogy or a revival of religion will make conflict unnecessary in the future. Nevertheless a considerable portion of middle-class culture remains quite unrealistic in its analysis of the contemporary situation. It assumes that evidences of a growing brotherliness between classes and nations are apparent in the present moment. It gives such arrangements as the League of Nations, such ventures as the Kellogg Pact and such schemes as company industrial unions, a connotation of moral and social achievement which the total facts completely belie. "There must," declares Professor George Stratton, a social psychologist, "always be a continuing and widening progress. But our present time seems to promise distinctly the close of an old epoch in world relations and the opening of a new. . . . Under the solemn teaching of the War, most of the nations have made political commitments which are of signal promise for international discipline and for still further and more effective governmental acts."[10] This glorification of the League of Nations as a symbol of a new epoch in international relations has been very general, and frequently very unqualified, in the Christian churches, where liberal Christianity has given itself to the illusion that all social relations are being brought progressively under "the law of Christ." William Adams Brown speaks for the whole liberal Christian viewpoint when he declares: "From many different centres and in many different forms the crusade for a

[10] George M. Stratton, *Social Psychology and International Conduct*, pp. 355-361.

[xxi]

unified and brotherly society is being carried on. The ideal of the League of Nations in which all civilised people shall be represented and in which they shall cooperate with one another in fighting common enemies like war and disease is winning recognition in circles which have hitherto been little suspected of idealism. . . . In relations between races, in strife between capital and labor, in our attitudes toward the weaker and more dependent members of society we are developing a social conscience, and situations which would have been accepted a generation ago as a matter of course are felt as an intolerable scandal."[11] Another theologian and pastor, Justin Wroe Nixon, thinks that "another reason for believing in the growth of social statesmanship on the part of business leaders is based upon their experience as trustees in various philanthropic and educational enterprises."[12] This judgment reveals the moral confusion of liberal Christianity with perfect clarity. Teachers of morals who do not see the difference between the problem of charity within the limits of an accepted social system and the problem of justice between economic groups, holding uneven power within modern industrial society, have simply not faced the most obvious differences between the morals of groups and those of individuals. The suggestion that the fight against disease is in the same category with the fight against war reveals the same confusion. Our contemporary culture fails to realise the power, extent and persistence of group egoism in human relations. It may be possible, though it is never easy, to

[11] William Adams Brown, *Pathways to Certainty*, p. 246.
[12] Justin Wroe Nixon, *An Emerging Christian Faith*, p. 291.

[xxii]

establish just relations between individuals within a group purely by moral and rational suasion and accommodation. In inter-group relations this is practically an impossibiliity. The relations between groups must therefore always be predominantly political rather than ethical, that is, they will be determined by the proportion of power which each group possesses at least as much as by any rational and moral appraisal of the comparative needs and claims of each group. The coercive factors, in distinction to the more purely moral and rational factors, in political relations can never be sharply differentiated and defined. It is not possible to estimate exactly how much a party to a social conflict is influenced by a rational argument or by the threat of force. It is impossible, for instance, to know what proportion of a privileged class accepts higher inheritance taxes because it believes that such taxes are good social policy and what proportion submits merely because the power of the state supports the taxation policy. Since political conflict, at least in times when controversies have not reached the point of crisis, is carried on by the threat, rather than the actual use, of force, it is always easy for the casual or superficial observer to overestimate the moral and rational factors, and to remain oblivious to the covert types of coercion and force which are used in the conflict.

Whatever increase in social intelligence and moral goodwill may be achieved in human history, may serve to mitigate the brutalities of social conflict, but they cannot abolish the conflict itself. That could be accomplished only if human groups, whether racial, national or economic, could achieve a degree of reason and sympathy which would permit them to see and to understand the interests of others as vividly as they understand their own, and a moral goodwill which would prompt them to affirm the rights of others as vigorously as they affirm their own. Given the inevitable limitations of human nature and the limits of the human imagination and intelligence, this is an ideal which individuals may approximate but which is beyond the capacities of human societies. Educators who emphasise the pliability of human nature, social and psychological scientists who dream of "socialising" man and religious idealists who strive to increase the sense of <u>moral responsibility</u>, can serve a very useful function in society in humanising individuals within an established social system and in purging the relations of individuals of as much egoism as possible. In dealing with the problems and necessities of radical social change they are almost invariably confusing in their counsels because they are not conscious of the limitations in human nature which finally frustrate their efforts.

The following pages are devoted to the task of analysing the moral resources and limitations of human nature, of tracing their consequences and cumulative effect in the life of human groups and of weighing political strategies in the light of the ascertained facts. The ultimate purpose of this task is to find political methods which will offer the most promise of achieving an ethical social goal for society. Such methods must always be judged by two criteria: 1. Do they do justice to the moral resources and possibilities in human nature and provide for the exploitation of every latent moral capacity in man? 2. Do they take account of the limitations of human nature, particularly those which manifest themselves in man's collective behavior? So persistent are the moralistic illusions about politics in the middle-class world, that any emphasis upon the second question will probably impress the average reader as unduly cynical. Social viewpoints and analyses are relative to the temper of the age which gives them birth. In America our contemporary culture is still pretty firmly enmeshed in the illusions and sentimentalities of the Age of Reason. A social analysis which is written, at least partially, from the perspective of a disillusioned generation will seem to be almost pure cynicism from the perspective of those who will stand in the credo of the ninteenth century.

MORAL MAN

AND

IMMORAL SOCIETY

CHAPTER ONE

MAN AND SOCIETY: THE ART OF LIVING TOGETHER

THOUGH human society has roots which lie deeper in history than the beginning of human life, men have made comparatively but little progress in solving the problem of their aggregate existence. Each century originates a new complexity and each new generation faces a new vexation in it. For all the centuries of experience, men have not yet learned how to live together without compounding their vices and covering each other "with mud and with blood." The society in which each man lives is at once the basis for, and the nemesis of, that fulness of life which each man seeks. However much human ingenuity may increase the treasures which nature provides for the satisfaction of human needs, they can never be sufficient to satisfy all human wants; for man, unlike other creatures, is gifted and cursed with an imagination which extends his appetites beyond the requirements of subsistence. Human society will never escape the problem of the equitable distribution of the physical and cultural goods which provide for the preservation and fulfillment of human life.

Unfortunately the conquest of nature, and the consequent increase in nature's beneficences to man, have not eased, but rather accentuated, the problem of justice. The same technology, which drew the fangs of nature's enmity of man, also created a society in which the intensity and extent of social cohesion has been greatly increased, and in which power is so unevenly distributed, that justice has become a more difficult achievement. Perhaps it is man's sorry fate, suffering from ills which have their source in the inadequacies of both nature and human society, that the tools by which he eliminates the former should become the means of increasing the latter. That, at least, has been his fate up to the present hour; and it may be that there will be no salvation for the human spirit from the more and more painful burdens of social injustice until the ominous tendency in human history has resulted in perfect tragedy.

Human nature is not wanting in certain endowments for the solution of the problem of human society. Man is endowed by nature with organic relations to his fellowmen; and natural impulse prompts him to consider the needs of others even when they compete with his own. With the higher mammals man shares concern for his offspring; and the long infancy of the child created the basis for an organic social group in the earliest period of human history. Gradually intelligence, imagination, and the necessities of social conflict increased the size of this group. Natural impulse was refined and extended until a less obvious type of consanguinity than an immediate family relationship could be made the basis of social solidarity. Since those early days the units of human cooperation have constantly grown in size, and the areas of significant relationships between the units have likewise increased. Nevertheless conflict between the national units remains as a permanent rather than a passing character-istic of their relations to each other; and each national unit finds it increasingly difficult to maintain either peace or justice within its common life.

While it is possible for intelligence to increase the range of benevolent impulse, and thus prompt a human being to consider the needs and rights of other than those to whom he is bound by organic and physical relationship, there are definite limits in the capacity of ordinary mortals which makes it impossible for them to grant to others what they claim for themselves. Though educators ever since the eighteenth century have given themselves to the fond illusion that justice through voluntary co-operation waited only upon a more universal or a more adequate educational enterprise, there is good reason to believe that the sentiments of benevolence and social goodwill will never be so pure or powerful, and the rational capacity to consider the rights and needs of others in fair competition with our own will never be so fully developed as to create the possibility for the anarchistic millennium which is the social utopia, either explicit or implicit, of all intellectual or religious moralists.

All social co-operation on a larger scale than the most intimate social group requires a measure of coercion. While no state can maintain its unity purely by coercion neither can it preserve itself without coercion. Where the factor of mutual consent is strongly developed, and where standardised and approximately fair methods of adjudicating and resolving conflicting interests within an organised group have been established, the coercive factor in social life is frequently covert, and becomes apparent only in moments of crisis and in the group's policy toward recalcitrant individuals. Yet it is never absent. Divergence of interest, based upon geographic and functional differences within a society, is bound to create different social philosophies and political attitudes which goodwill and intelligence may partly, but never completely, harmonise. Ultimately, unity within an organised social group, or within a federation of such groups, is created by the ability of a dominant group to impose its will. Politics will, to the end of history, be an area where conscience and power meet, where the ethical and coercive factors of human life will interpenetrate and work out their tentative and uneasy compromises. The democratic method of resolving social conflict, which some romanticists hail as a triumph of the ethical over the coercive factor, is really much more coercive than at first seems apparent. The majority has its way, not because the minority believes that the majority is right (few minorities are willing to grant the majority the moral prestige of such a concession), but because the votes of the majority are a symbol of its social strength. Whenever a minority believes that it has some strategic advantage which outweighs the power of numbers, and whenever it is sufficiently intent upon its ends, or desperate enough about its position in society, it refuses to accept the dictates of the majority. Military and economic overlords and revolutionary zealots have been traditionally contemptuous of the will of majorities. Recently Trotsky advised the German communists not to be dismayed by the greater voting strength of the fascists since in the inevitable revolution the power of industrial workers, in charge of the nation's industrial process, would be found much more significant than the social power of clerks and other petty bourgeoisie who comprised the fascist movement.

There are, no doubt, rational and ethical factors in the democratic process. Contending social forces presumably use the forum rather than the battleground to arbitrate their differences in the democratic method, and thus differences are resolved by moral suasion and a rational adjustment of rights to rights. If political issues were really abstract questions of social policy upon which unbiased citizens were asked to commit themselves, the business of voting and the debate which precedes the election might actually be regarded as an educational programme in which a social group discovers its common mind. But the fact is that political opinions are inevitably rooted in economic interests of some kind or other, and only comparatively few citizens can view a problem of social policy without regard to their interest. Conflicting interests therefore can never be completely resolved; and minorities will yield only because the majority has come into control of the police power of the state and may, if the occasion arises, augment that power by its own military strength. Should a minority regard its own strength, whether economic or martial, as strong enough to challenge the power of the majority, it may attempt to wrest control of the state apparatus from the majority, as in the case of the fascist movement in Italy. Sometimes it will resort to armed conflict, even if the prospects of victory are none too bright, as in the instance of the American Civil War, in which the Southern planting interests, outvoted by a combination of Eastern industrialists and Western agrarians, resolved to protect their peculiar interests and privileges by a forceful dissolution of the national union. The coercive factor is, in other words, always present in politics. If economic interests do not conflict too sharply, if the spirit of accommodation partially resolves them, and if the democratic process has achieved moral prestige and historic dignity, the coercive factor in politics may become too covert to be visible to the casual observer. Nevertheless, only a romanticist of the purest water could maintain that a national group ever arrives at a "common mind" or becomes conscious of a "general will" without the use of either force or the threat of force. This is particularly true of nations, but it is also true, though in a slighter degree, of other social groups. Even religious communities, if they are sufficiently large, and if they deal with issues regarded as vital by their members, resort to coercion to preserve their unity. Religious organisations have usually availed themselves of a covert type of coercion (excommunication and the interdict) or they have called upon the police power of the state.

The limitations of the human mind and imagination, the inability of human beings to transcend their own interests sufficiently to envisage the interests of their fellowmen as clearly as they do their own makes force an inevitable part of the process of social cohesion. But the same force which guarantees peace also makes for injustice. "Power," said Henry Adams, "is poison"; and it is a poison which blinds the eyes of moral insight and lames the will of moral purpose. The individual or the group which organises any society, however social its intentions or pretensions, arrogates an inordinate portion of social privilege to itself. The two most obvious types of power are the military and the economic, though in primitive society the power of the priest, partly because he dispenses supernatural benefits and partly because he establishes public order by methods less arduous than those of the soldier, vies with that of the soldier and the landlord. The chief difference between the agrarian civilisations, which lasted from the rise of ancient Babylon and Egypt to the fall of European feudalism, and the commercial and industrial civilisations of today is that in the former the military power is primary, and in the latter it has become secondary, to economic power. In agrarian civilisations the soldier becomes the landlord. In more primitive periods he may claim the land by his own military prowess. In later periods a grateful sovereign bestowed land upon the soldiers who defended his realm and consolidated his dominion. The soldier thus gained the economic security and the social prestige which could be exploited in further martial service to his sovereign. The business man and industrial overlord are gradually usurping the position of eminence and privilege once held by the soldier and the priest. In most European nations their ascendancy over the landed aristocrat of military traditions is not as complete as in America, which has no feudal traditions. In present-day Japan the military caste is still so powerful that it threatens to destroy the rising power of the commercial groups. On the pre-eminence of economic power in an industrial civilisation and its ability to make the military power its tool we shall have more to say later. Our interest at the moment is to record that any kind of significant social power develops social inequality. Even if history is viewed from other than equalitarian perspectives, and it is granted that differentials in economic rewards are morally justified and socially useful, it is impossible to justify the degree of inequality which complex societies inevitably create by the increased centralisation of power which develops with more elaborate civilisations. The literature of all ages is filled with rational and moral justifications of these inequalities, but most of them are specious. If superior abilities and services to society deserve special rewards it may be regarded as axiomatic that the rewards are always higher than the services warrant. No impartial society determines the rewards. The men of power who control society grant these perquisites to themselves. Whenever special ability is not associated with power, as in the case of the modern professional man, his excess of income over the average is ridiculously low in comparison with that of the economic overlords, who are the real centres of power in an industrial society. Most rational and social justifications of unequal privilege are clearly afterthoughts. The facts are created by the disproportion of power which exists in a given social system. The justifications are usually dictated by the desire of the men of power to hide the nakedness of their greed, and by the inclination of society itself to veil the brutal facts of human life from itself. This is a rather pathetic but understandable inclination; since the facts of man's collective life easily rob the average individual of confidence in the human enterprise. The inevitable hypocrisy, which is associated with all of the collective activities of the human race, springs chiefly from this source: that individuals have a moral code which makes the actions of collective man an outrage to their conscience. They therefore invent romantic and moral interpretations of the real facts, preferring to obscure rather than reveal the true character of their collective behavior. Sometimes they are as anxious to offer moral justifications for the brutalities from which they suffer as for those which they commit. The fact that the hypocrisy of man's group behavior, about which we shall have much more to say later, expresses itself not only in terms of self-justification but in terms of moral justification of human behavior in general, symbolises one of the tragedies of the human spirit: its inability to conform its collective life to its individual ideals. As individuals, men believe that they ought to love and serve each other and establish justice between each other. As racial, economic and national groups they take for themselves, whatever their power can command.

The disproportion of power in a complex society which began with the transmutation of the pastoral to the agrarian economy, and which destroyed the simple equalitarianism and communism of the hunting and nomadic social organisation, has perpetuated social injustice in every form through all the ages. Types of power have changed, and gradations of social inequality have varied, but the essential facts have remained unchanged. In Egypt the land was divided into three parts, respectively claimed by the king, the soldiers and the priests. The common people were landless. In Peru, where a rather remarkable despotic communism developed, the king owned all the land but gave the use of one third to the people, another third to the priests and kept one third for himself and his nobles. Needless to say, the commoners were expected to till not only their third but the other two thirds of the lands. In China, where the emperor maintained the right of eminent domain for many centuries, defeating the experiment in feudalism in the third century A.D., and giving each family inalienable rights in the soil which nominally belonged to him, there has probably been less inequality than in any other ancient empire. Nevertheless slavery persisted until a very recent day. In Japan the emperor gave the land to feudal princes, who again sublet it to the inferior nobility. The power of the feudal clans, originating in martial prowess and perpetuated through land ownership, has remained practically unbroken to this day, though the imperial power was ostensibly restored in the latter part of the last century, and growing industry has developed a class of industrial overlords who were partly drawn from the landed aristocracy. In Rome the absolute property rights of the *pater familias* of the patrician class gave him power which placed him on top of the social pyramid. All other classes, beginning with his own women and children, then the plebeians and finally the slaves, took their places in the various lower rungs of the social ladder. The efforts of the Gracchi to destroy the ever growing inequality, which resulted from power breeding more power, proved abortive, as did the land reforms of Solon and Lycurgus in Greece. Military conquest gave the owners of the Roman *latifundia* hundreds of slaves by the labor of which they reduced the small freeholders to penury. Thus the decay of the Roman Empire was prepared; for a state which has only lords and slaves lacks the social cement to preserve it from internal disintegration and the military force to protect it from external aggression.

All through history one may observe the tendency of power to destroy its very *raison d'être*. It is suffered because it achieves internal unity and creates external defenses for the nation. But it grows to such proportions that it destroys the social peace of the state by the animosities which its exactions arouse, and it enervates the sentiment of patriotism by robbing the common man of the basic privileges which might bind him to his nation. The words attributed by Plutarch to Tiberius Gracchus reveal the hollowness of the pretensions by which the powerful classes enlist their slaves in the defense of their dominions: "The wild beasts in Italy had at least their lairs, dens and caves whereto they might retreat; whereas the men who fought and died for that land had nothing in it save air and light, but were forced to wander to and fro with their wives and children, without resting place or house wherein they might lodge. . . . The poor folk go to war, to fight and to die for the delights, riches and superfluities of others."[1] In the long run these pretensions are revealed and the sentiment of patriotism is throttled in the breasts of the disinherited. The privileged groups who are outraged by the want of patriotism among modern proletarians could learn the cause of proletarian internationalism by a little study of history. "It is absurd," says Diodorus Siculus, speaking of Egypt, "to entrust the defence of a country to people who own

[1] Plutarch, *The Parallel Lives*, see "Tiberius Gracchus," *Loeb Classical Library*, Vol. X.

nothing in it,"[2] a reflection which has applicability to other ages and other nations than his own. Russian communists of pure water pour their scorn upon European socialists, among whom patriotism outweighed class loyalty in the World War. But there is a very simple explanation for the nationalism of European socialists. They were not as completely, or at least not as obviously, disinherited as their Russian comrades.

The history of slavery in all ancient civilisations offers an interesting illustration of the development of social injustice with the growing size and complexity of the social unit. In primitive tribal organisation rights are essentially equal within the group, and no rights, or only very minimum rights are recognised outside of the group. The captives of war are killed. With the growth of agriculture the labor of captives becomes useful, and they are enslaved rather than destroyed. Since rightless individuals are introduced into the intimate life of the group, equality of rights disappears; and the inequality remains even after the slaves are no longer regarded as enemies and have become completely organic to the life of the group. The principle of slavery once established, is enlarged to include debt slaves, victims of the growing property system. The membership of the debt slaves in the original community at first guarantees them rights which the captive slaves do not enjoy. But the years gradually wipe out these distinctions and the captive slaves are finally raised to the status of debtor slaves. Thus the more humane attitudes which men practice within their social groups gains a slight victory over the more brutal attitudes towards individuals in

2 Quoted by C. J. M. Letourneau, *Property; Its Origin and Development*, p. 277.

other groups. But the victory is insignificant in comparison with the previous introduction of the morals of intergroup relations into the intimate life of the group by the very establishment of slavery. Barbarism knows little or nothing of class distinctions. These are created and more and more highly elaborated by civilisation. The social impulses, with which men are endowed by nature are not powerful enough, even when they are extended by a growing intelligence, to apply with equal force toward all members of a large community. The distinction between slave and freeman is only one of the many social gradations which higher societies develop. They are determined in every case by the disproportion of power, military and economic, which develops in the more complex civilisations and in the larger social units. A growing social intelligence may be affronted by them and may protest against them, but it changes them only slightly. Neither the prophets of Israel nor the social idealists of Egypt and Babylon, who protested against social injustice, could make their vision of a just society effective. The man of power, though humane impulse may awaken in him, always remains something of the beast of prey. He may be generous within his family, and just within the confines of the group which shares his power and privilege. With only rare exceptions, his highest moral attitude toward members of other groups is one of warlike sportsmanship toward those who equal his power and challenge it, and one of philanthropic generosity toward those who possess less power and privilege. His philanthropy is a perfect illustration of the curious compound of the brutal and the moral which we find in all human behavior; for his generosity is at once a display of his power and an expression of his pity. His generous impulses freeze within him if his power is challenged or his generosities are accepted without grateful humility. If individual men of power should achieve more ethical attitudes than the one described, it remains nevertheless typical for them as a class; and is their practically unvarying attitude when they express themselves not as individuals but as a group.

The rise of modern democracy, beginning with the Eighteenth Century, is sometimes supposed to have substituted the consent of the governed for the power of royal families and aristocratic classes as the cohesive force of national society. This judgment is partly true but not nearly as true as the uncritical devotees of modern democracy assume. The doctrine that government exists by the consent of the governed, and the democratic technique by which the suffrage of the governed determines the policy of the state, may actually reduce the coercive factor in national life, and provide for peaceful and gradual methods of resolving conflicting social interests and changing political institutions. But the creeds and institutions of democracy have never become fully divorced from the special interests of the commercial classes who conceived and developed them. It was their interest to destroy political restraint upon economic activity, and they therefore weakened the authority of the state and made it more pliant to their needs. With the increased centralisation of economic power in the period of modern industrialism, this development merely means that society as such does not control economic power as much as social well-being requires; and that the economic, rather than the political and military, power has become the significant coercive force of modern society. Either it defies the authority of the state or it bends the institutions of the state to its own purposes. Political power has been made responsible, but economic power has become irresponsible in society. The net result is that political power has been made more responsible to economic power. It is, in other words, again the man of power or the dominant class which binds society together, regulates its processes, always paying itself inordinate rewards for its labors. The difference is that owners of factories, rather than owners of land, exert the power, and that it is more purely economic and less military than that which was wielded by the landed aristocrats. Needless to say, it is not completely divorced from military power. It may on occasion appropriate the police and the army of the state to defend its interests against internal and external foes. The military power has become the hired servant and is no longer the progenitor of economic ownership.

There will be opportunity to discuss these modern developments in the growth and use of power in society at greater length in another chapter. At the same time it will be possible to do justice to those aspects of the democratic creed which transcend the interests of the commercial and industrial classes and add a permanent contribution to the history of social life. At present it must suffice to discount a still widely held conviction that the democratic movement has given society a permanent solution for its vexing problems of power and justice.

Society is perennially harassed not only by the fact that

the coercive factors in social life (which the limitations of human intelligence and imagination make inevitable) create injustice in the process of establishing peace; but also by the tendency of the same factors, which make for an uneasy peace within a social group, to aggravate inter-group conflict. Power sacrifices justice to peace within the community and destroys peace between communities. It is not true that only kings make war. The common members of any national community, while sentimentally desiring peace, nevertheless indulge impulses of envy, jealousy, pride, bigotry, and greed which make for conflict between communities. Neither is it true that modern wars are caused solely by the modern capitalistic system with its disproportion of economic power and privilege. Without an almost miraculous increase in human intelligence it will not be easy to resolve the conflicts of interest between various national communities even after the special privilege and the unequal power, which now aggravate international conflicts, have been destroyed. Nevertheless the whole history of mankind bears testimony to the fact that the power which prevents anarchy in intra-group relations encourages anarchy in intergroup relations. The kings of old claimed the loyalty and the sacrifices of their subjects in conflicts with other tyrants, in which the interests of the state and the welfare of the people were completely subordinated to the capricious purposes of the monarch. No personal whim, which a human being might indulge, is excluded from the motives. which have prompted monarchs to shed the blood of their unhappy subjects. Pride, jealousy, disappointed love, hurt vanity, greed for greater treasures, lust for power over larger dominions, petty animosities between royal brothers or between father and son, momentary passions and childish whims, these all have been, not the occasional but the perennially recurring, causes and occasions of international conflict. The growing intelligence of mankind and the increased responsibility of monarchs to their people have placed a check upon the caprice, but not upon the self-interest, of the men of power. They may still engage in social conflict for the satisfaction of their pride and vanity provided they can compound their personal ambitions with, and hallow them by, the ambitions of their group, and the pitiful vanities and passions of the individuals who compose the group. The story of Napoleon belongs to modern and not to ancient history. He could bathe Europe in blood for the sake of gratifying his overweening lust for power, as long as he could pose as the tool of French patriotism and as the instrument of revolutionary fervor. The fact that the democratic sentiment, opposed to the traditional absolutisms of Europe, could be exploited to create a tyranny more sanguinary and terrible than those which it sought ostensibly to destroy; and that the dream of equality, liberty and fraternity of the French Revolution could turn so quickly into the nightmare of Napoleonic imperialism is a tragic revelation of the inadequacies of the human resources with which men must try to solve the problems of their social life. The childish vanity of the German Emperor, who wanted a large navy so that he could stand on equal footing with his royal English uncle at naval manœuvres, helped to make the World War inevitable.[3] He would not have been permit

3 See *Memoirs of Prince Von Bülow*, Vol. III, p. 204.

ted to indulge this vanity however had it not seemed compatible with the prejudices of his people and the economic necessities of a growing empire. Theodore Roosevelt belonged to a little junta which foisted the Spanish-American War upon the American people. The ambition and vanity which prompted him could be veiled and exalted because the will-to-power of an adolescent nation and the frustrated impulses of pugnacity and martial ardor of the pitiful little "men in the street" could find in him symbolic expression and vicarious satisfaction. The need of the modern industrial overlord for raw materials and markets, and rivalry over control of the undeveloped and unexploited portions of the earth are the occasion of modern wars. Yet the ambitions and greed of dominant economic groups within each nation are not the only cause of international conflict. Every social group tends to develop imperial ambitions which are aggravated, but not caused solely, by the lusts of its leaders and privileged groups. Every group, as every individual, has expansive desires which are rooted in the instinct of survival and soon extend beyond it. The will-to-live becomes the will-to-power. Only rarely does nature provide armors of defense which cannot be transmuted into instruments of aggression. The frustrations of the average man, who can never realise the power and the glory which his imagination sets as the ideal, makes him the more willing tool and victim of the imperial ambitions of his group. His frustrated individual ambitions gain a measure of satisfaction in the power and the aggrandisement of his nation. The will-to-power of competing national groups is the cause of the international anarchy which the moral sense of mankind has thus far vainly striven to overcome. Since some nations are more powerful than others, they will at times prevent anarchy by effective imperialism, which in our industrial period has become more covert than overt. But the peace is gained by force and is always an uneasy and an unjust one. As powerful classes organise a nation, so powerful nations organise a crude society of nations. In each case the peace is a tentative one because it is unjust. It has been achieved only partially by a mutual accommodation of conflicting interests and certainly not by a rational and moral adjustment of rights. It will last only until those, who feel themselves too weak to challenge strength, will become, or will feel themselves, powerful enough to do so. It is not necessary to discount the moral influence of the League of Nations completely or to deny that it represents certain gains in the rational and moral organisation of society, to recognise that the peace of contemporary Europe is maintained by the force of French arms and that it will last only as long as the ingenuities of French statesmanship can maintain the combination of political and military forces which holds the people, who feel themselves defrauded by the Versailles Treaty, in check. Significantly the same power, which prompts the fear that prevents immediate action, also creates the mounting hatred which guarantees ultimate rebellion.

Thus society is in a perpetual state of war. Lacking moral and rational resources to organise its life, without resort to coercion, except in the most immediate and intimate social groups, men remain the victims of the individuals, classes and nations by whose force a momentary

coerced unity is achieved, and further conflicts are as certainly created. The fact that the coercive factor in society
is both necessary and dangerous seriously complicates the
whole task of securing both peace and justice. History is
a long tale of abortive efforts toward the desired end of
social cohesion and justice in which failure was usually
due either to the effort to eliminate the factor of force entirely or to an undue reliance upon it. Complete reliance
upon it means that new tyrants usurp the places of eminence from which more traditional monarchs are cast
down. Tolstoian pacifists and other advocates of non-
resistance, noting the evils which force introduces into
society, give themselves to the vain illusion that it can be
completely eliminated, and society organised upon the
basis of anarchistic principles. Their conviction is an illusion, because there are definite limits of moral goodwill
and social intelligence beyond which even the most vital
religion and the most astute educational programme will
not carry a social group, whatever may be possible for individuals in an intimate society. The problem which society faces is clearly one of reducing force by increasing
the factors which make for a moral and rational adjustment of life to life; of bringing such force as is still necessary under responsibility of the whole of society; of destroying the kind of power which cannot be made socially
responsible (the power which resides in economic ownership for instance); and of bringing forces of moral self-
restraint to bear upon types of power which can never be
brought completely under social control. Every one of
these methods has its definite limitations. Society will
probably never be sufficiently intelligent to bring all

power under its control. The stupidity of the average man will permit the oligarch, whether economic or political, to hide his real purposes from the scrutiny of his fellows and to withdraw his activities from effective control. Since it is impossible to count on enough moral goodwill among those who possess irresponsible power to sacrifice it for the good of the whole, it must be destroyed by coercive methods and these will always run the peril of introducing new forms of injustice in place of those abolished. There is, for instance, as yet no clear proof that the power of economic overlords can be destroyed by means less rigorous than communism has employed; but there is also no proof that communistic oligarchs, once the idealistic passion of a revolutionary period is spent, will be very preferable to the capitalistic oligarchs, whom they are to displace. Since the increasing complexity of society makes it impossible to bring all those who are in charge of its intricate techniques and processes, and who are therefore in possession of social power, under complete control, it will always be necessary to rely partly upon the honesty and self-restraint of those who are not socially restrained. But here again, it will never be possible to insure moral antidotes sufficiently potent to destroy the deleterious effects of the poison of power upon character. The future peace and justice of society therefore depend upon, not one but many, social strategies, in all of which moral and coercive factors are compounded in varying degrees. So difficult is it to avoid the Scylla of despotism and the Charybdis of anarchy that it is safe to hazard the prophecy that the dream of perpetual peace and brotherhood for human society is one which will never be fully realised. It is a vision prompted by the conscience and insight of individual man, but incapable of fulfillment by collective man. It is like all true religious visions, possible of approximation but not of realisation in actual history. The vitality of the vision is the measure of man's rebellion against the fate which binds his collective life to the world of nature from which his soul recoils. The vision can be kept alive only by permitting it to overreach itself. But meanwhile collective man, operating on the historic and mundane scene, must content himself with a more modest goal. His concern for some centuries to come is not the creation of an ideal society in which there will be uncoerced and perfect peace and justice, but a society in which there will be enough justice, and in which coercion will be sufficiently non-violent to prevent his common enterprise from issuing into complete disaster. That goal will seem too modest for the romanticists; but the romanticists have so little understanding for the perils in which modern society lives, and overestimate the moral resources at the disposal of the collective human enterprise so easily, that any goal regarded as worthy of achievement by them must necessarily be beyond attainment.

CHAPTER TWO

THE RATIONAL RESOURCES OF THE INDIVIDUAL
FOR SOCIAL LIVING

SINCE the ultimate sources of social conflicts and injustices are to be found in the ignorance and selfishness of men, it is natural that the hope of establishing justice by increasing human intelligence and benevolence should be perennially renewed. Religious idealists have usually emphasised selfishness rather than ignorance as the root of social injustice, and have given themselves to the hope, that a purer religion would increase the benevolence and decrease the egoism of the human spirit. Rationalists inclined to believe that injustice could be overcome by increasing the intelligence of men. They held, either that men were selfish because they were too ignorant to understand the needs of others, or that they were selfish because the victims of their egoism were too ignorant to defend themselves against their exactions. Or they believed that the injustices of society were due to a perpetuation of ancient and hereditary abuses, which were sanctioned by irrational superstitions and would be abolished by reason.

The belief that the growth of human intelligence would automatically eliminate social injustice really dates from the eighteenth century and the Enlightenment. The Age of Reason saw social injustice and medieval traditions and superstitions so intimately related to each other, that it was natural to conclude that the elimination of the one would result in the abolition of the other. Condorcet, one of the most fervent apostles of the Age of Reason, expressed the faith of his generation, when he declared that universal education and the development of the printing press would inevitably result in an ideal society in which the sun would shine "on an earth of none but freemen, with no masters save reason; for tyrants and slaves, priests and their hypocritical tools will all have disappeared."

This faith of the Enlightenment is still the creed of the educators of our day and is shared more or less by philosophers, psychologists and social scientists. The sorry plight of our civilisation has qualified it only in the slightest degree. The traditions and superstitions, which seemed to the eighteenth century to be the very root of injustice, have been eliminated, without checking the constant growth of social injustice. Yet the men of learning persist in their hope that more intelligence will solve the social problem. They may view present realities quite realistically; but they cling to their hope that an adequate pedagogical technique will finally produce the "socialised man" and thus solve the problems of society.

Since there are always unrealised potentialities in human life, which remain undeveloped, if hope does not encourage their development, the optimism of the rationalists and educators is not without value. If their optimism should be too unqualified, it need not result in serious error, when they deal with the facts of individual life. Education can no doubt solve many problems of society, and can increase the capacity of men to envisage the needs of their fellows and to live in harmonious and equitable relations with them. In individual relations a great confidence in the undeveloped potentialities of the human spirit may be the means of developing them. We

"hope, till hope creates
From its own wreck the thing it contemplates."

An optimistic appraisal of human potentialities may therefore create its own verification. But individual limitations have a cumulative effect in human societies, and the moral attitudes, which tend to diminish them, are decreasingly adequate, when they are directed toward masses of men and not to individuals. Any error in the appraisal of the moral resources of individuals is accentuated when it is made the basis of political theory and practice. It is necessary therefore to deal circumspectly with the facts, if the confusion which always exists in the area of life where politics and ethics meet, is to be resolved.

Human beings are endowed by nature with both selfish and unselfish impulses. The individual is a nucleus of energy which is organically related from the very beginning with other energy, but which maintains, nevertheless, its own discreet existence. Every type of energy in nature seeks to preserve and perpetuate itself and to gain fulfillment within terms of its unique genius. The energy of human life does not differ in this from the whole world of nature. It differs only in the degree of reason which directs the energy. Man is the only creature which is fully self-conscious. His reason endows him with a capacity for self-transcendence. He sees himself in relation to his environment and in relation to other life. Reason enables him, within limits, to direct his energy so that it will flow in harmony, and not in conflict, with other life. Reason is not the sole basis of moral virtue in man. His social impulses are more deeply rooted than his rational life. Reason may extend and stabilise, but it does not create, the capacity to affirm other life than his own. Nature endows him with a sex impulse which seeks the perpetuity of his kind with the same degree of energy with which he seeks the preservation of his own life. So basic is this impulse that Freudian psychology is able to interpret the *libido* entirely in its terms. Even if we should adopt the more plausible theory of Adler, that the *libido* expresses itself chiefly in terms of the will-to-power, or that of Jung, which makes the *libido* an undifferentiated energy from which sexuality,[1] the will-to-power and their various derivatives arise, it is obvious that man does not express himself in terms of pure self-assertion, even before conscious purpose begins to qualify egoistic impulse. His natural impulses prompt him not only to the perpetuation of life beyond himself but to some achievement of harmony with other life. Whatever the theory of instincts which we may adopt, whether we regard them as discreet and underived, or whether we think they are sharply defined only after they are socially conditioned, it is obvious that man not only shares a gregarious impulse with the lower creatures but that a specific impulse of pity bids him fly to aid of stricken members of his community. Rationalistic moralists, as for instance

[1] *Cf. inter alia* C. G. Jung, *Two Essays on Analytic Psychology*, Chaps. 2 and 4.

Stoics and Kantians, who derive man's moral capacities purely from his reason and consequently set the mind at war with the impulses, are therefore always driven to the absurdity of depreciating the moral quality of social impulses, which are undeniably good but obviously rooted in instinct and nature. Thus the Stoics abhorred pity and Kant scorned sympathy if it did not flow from a sense of duty.

Reason, inasfar as it is able to survey the whole field of life, analyses the various forces in their relation to each other and, gauging their consequences in terms of the total welfare, it inevitably places the stamp of its approval upon those impulses which affirm life in its most inclusive terms. Practically every moral theory, whether utilitarian or intuitional, insists on the goodness of benevolence, justice, kindness and unselfishness. Even when economic self-seeking is approved, as in the political morality of Adam Smith, the criterion of judgment is the good of the whole. The utilitarians may insist that the goodness of altruism is established by its social utility, and they may distinguish themselves from more rigorous moralists by assigning social utility and moral worth to egoism as well. But, in spite of these differences, the function of reason for every moralist is to support those impulses which carry life beyond itself, and to extend the measure and degree of their sociality. It is fair, therefore, to assume that growing rationality is a guarantee of man's growing morality.

The measure of our rationality determines the degree of vividness with which we appreciate the needs of other life, the extent to which we become conscious of the real character of our own motives and impulses, the ability to harmonise conflicting impulses in our own life and in society, and the capacity to choose adequate means for approved ends. In each instance a development of reason may increase the moral capacity.

The intelligent man, who exploits available resources for knowledge of the needs and wants of his fellows, will be more inclined to adjust his conduct to their needs than those who are less intelligent. He will feel sympathy for misery, not only when it comes immediately into his field of vision, but when it is geographically remote. A famine in China, a disaster in Europe, a cry for help from the ends of the earth, will excite his sympathy and prompt remedial action. No man will ever be so intelligent as to see the needs of others as vividly as he recognises his own, or to be as quick in his aid to remote as to immediately revealed necessities. Nevertheless it is impossible for an astute social pedagogy to increase the range of human sympathy. Social agencies in large urban communities, where individual need is easily obscured in the mass, have evolved stereotyped methods of individualising need by the choice of significant and vivid single examples of general social conditions. Thus they keep social sympathy, which might perish amid the indirect relationships of a large city, alive. The failure of even the wisest type of social pedagogy to prompt benevolences as generous as those which a more intimate community naturally evolves, suggests that ethical attitudes are more dependent upon personal, intimate and organic contacts than social technicians are inclined to assume. The dependence of ethical attitudes upon personal contacts and direct relations contributes to the moral chaos of a civilisation, in which life is related to life mechanically and not organically, and in which mutual responsibilities increase and personal contacts decrease.

The ability to consider, or even to prefer, the interests of others to our own, is not dependent upon the capacity for sympathy. Harmonious social relations depend upon the sense of justice as much as, or even more than, upon the sentiment of benevolence. This sense of justice is a product of the mind and not of the heart. It is the result of reason's insistence upon consistency. One of Immanuel Kant's two moral axioms: "Act in conformity with that maxim and that maxim only which you can at the same time will to be universal law" is simply the application to problems of conduct of reason's desire for consistency. As truth is judged by its harmonious relation to a previously discovered system of truths, so the morality of an action is judged by the possibility of conforming it to a universal scheme of consistent moral actions. This means, in terms of conduct, that the satisfaction of an impulse can be called good only if it can be related in terms of inner consistency with a total harmony of impulses. Unreason may approve the satisfaction of an impulse in the self and disapprove the same impulse in another. But the reasonable man is bound to judge his actions, in some degree, in terms of the total necessities of a social situation. Thus reason tends to check selfish impulses and to grant the satisfaction of legitimate impulses in others.[2]

It is a question whether reason is ever sufficiently pow-

2 For a careful analysis of this function of reason in morality, see L. T. Hobhouse, *The Rational Good.*

erful to achieve, or even to approximate, a complete harmony and consistency between what is demanded for the self and what is granted to the other; but it works to that end. Its first task is to harmonise the various impulses of the self and to bring order out of the chaos of impulses with which nature has endowed man. For nature has not established the same degree of order in the human as in the lower creature. In the animal, impulses are related to each other in a pre-established harmony. But instincts are not as fully formed in human life, and natural impulses may therefore be so enlarged and extended that the satisfaction of one impulse interferes with the satisfaction of another. "All mind," declares Santayana, "is naturally synthetic. . . . In the mindful person the passions have spontaneously acquired a responsibility toward each other; or if they still allow themselves to make merry separately—for liveliness in the parts is a good without which the whole would be lifeless—yet the whole possesses, or aspires to possess, a unity of direction in which all parts may conspire, even if unwittingly."[3] It is naturally easier to bring order into the individual life than to establish a synthesis between it and other life. The force of reason is frequently exhausted in the first task and never essays the second. Yet the rational man is bound to recognise the claims made by others and to see the necessity of arriving at some working harmony for the total body of human impulse. Reason ultimately makes for social as well as for internal order.

The force of reason makes for justice, not only by placing inner restraints upon the desires of the self in the in-

[3] George Santayana, *The Genteel Tradition at Bay*, p. 61.

terest of social harmony, but by judging the claims and assertions of individuals from the perspective of the intelligence of the total community. An irrational society accepts injustice because it does not analyse the pretensions made by the powerful and privileged groups of society. Even that portion of society which suffers most from injustice may hold the power, responsible for it, in reverence. A growing rationality in society destroys the uncritical acceptance of injustice. It may destroy the morale of dominant groups by making them more conscious of the hollowness of their pretensions, so that they will be unable to assert their interests and protect their special privileges with the same degree of self-deception. It may furthermore destroy their social prestige in the community by revealing the relation between their special privileges and the misery of the underprivileged.[4] It may also make those who suffer from injustice more conscious of their rights in society and persuade them to assert their rights more energetically. The resulting social conflict makes for a political rather than a rational justice. But all justice in the less intimate human relations is political as well as rational, that is, it is established by the assertion of power against power as well as by the rational comprehension of, and arbitration between, conflicting rights. The justice which results from such a process may not belong in the category of morally created social values, if

[4] Robert Briffault, in his *Rational Evolution* (pp. 209–10), makes a convincing analysis of this function of reason in the attainment of justice. His thesis is summed up in his words: "No resistance to power is possible while the sanctioning lies, which justify that power, are accepted as valid. While that first and chief line of defense is unbroken there can be no revolt. Before any injustice, any abuse or oppression can be resisted, the lie upon which it is founded must be unmasked, must be clearly recognized for what it is."

morality be defined purely from the perspective of the individual. From the viewpoint of society itself it does represent a moral achievement. It means that the total society, and each constituent group, judges social relations not according to custom and tradition, but according to a rational ideal of justice. The partial perspective of each group makes the achievement of social harmony without conflict impossible. But a rational ideal of justice, operates both in initiating, and in resolving, conflict.

The development of reason and the growth of mind makes for increasingly just relations not only by bringing all impulses in society into reference with, and under the control of, an inclusive social ideal, but also by increasing the penetration with which all factors in the social situation are analysed. The psychological sciences discover and analyse the intricate web of motivation, which lies at the base of all human actions. The social sciences trace the consequences of human behavior into the farthest reaches of social life. They are specialised and yet typical efforts of a growing human intelligence, to come into possession of all facts relevant to human conduct. If the psychological scientist aids men in analysing their true motives, and in separating their inevitable pretensions from the actual desires, which they are intended to hide, he may increase the purity of social morality. If the social scientist is able to point out that traditional and customary social policies do not have the results, intended or pretended by those who champion them, honest social intentions will find more adequate instruments for the attainment of their ends, and dishonest pretensions will be unmasked.

Thus, for instance, a *laissez faire* economic theory is maintained in an industrial era through the ignorant belief that the general welfare is best served by placing the least possible political restraints upon economic activity. The history of the past hundred years is a refutation of the theory; but it is still maintained, or is dying a too lingering death, particularly in nations as politically incompetent as our own. Its survival is due to the ignorance of those who suffer injustice from the application of this theory to modern industrial life but fail to attribute their difficulties to the social anarchy and political irresponsibility which the theory sanctions. Their ignorance permits the beneficiaries of the present anarchic industrial system to make dishonest use of the waning prestige of *laissez faire* economics. The men of power in modern industry would not, of course, capitulate simply because the social philosophy by which they justify their policies had been discredited. When power is robbed of the shining armor of political, moral and philosophical theories, by which it defends itself, it will fight on without armor; but it will be more vulnerable, and the strength of its enemies is increased.

When economic power desires to be left alone it uses the philosophy of *laissez faire* to discourage political restraint upon economic freedom. When it wants to make use of the police power of the state to subdue rebellions and discontent in the ranks of its helots, it justifies the use of political coercion and the resulting suppression of liberties by insisting that peace is more precious than freedom and that its only desire is social peace. A rational analysis of social facts easily punctures this pretension also. It proves that the police power of the state is usually used prematurely; before an effort has been made to eliminate the causes of discontent, and that it therefore tends to perpetuate, injustice and the consequent social disaffections. Social intelligence may, in short, eliminate many abortive means to socially approved ends, whether they have been proposed honestly or dishonestly, and may therefore contribute to a higher measure of social morality. If psychological and social scientists overestimate the possibilities of improving social relations by the development of intelligence, that may be regarded as an understandable *naïveté* of rationalists, who naturally incline to attribute too much power to reason and to recognise its limits too grudgingly. Men will not cease to be dishonest, merely because their dishonesties have been revealed or because they have discovered their own deceptions. Wherever men hold unequal power in society, they will strive to maintain it. They will use whatever means are most convenient to that end and will seek to justify them by the most plausible arguments they are able to devise. Nevertheless there are possibilities of increasing social justice through the development of mind and reason. It may extend social impulses beyond the immediate objectives which nature prompts; it may insist upon harmony in the whole field of vital impulses; and it may reveal all the motives which prompt human action and all the consequences which flow from it so that honest error and dishonest pretensions are reduced. The development of social justice does depend to some degree upon the extension of rationality. But the limits of reason make it inevitable that pure moral action, particularly in the intricate, complex and collective relationships, should be an impossible goal. Men will never be wholly reasonable, and the proportion of reason to impulse becomes increasingly negative when we proceed from the life of individuals to that of social groups, among whom a common mind and purpose is always more or less inchoate and transitory, and who depend therefore upon a common impulse to bind them together.

If reason projects goals more inclusive, and socially more acceptable, than those which natural impulse prompts, the question arises how an adequate dynamic toward the more inclusive objective is gained. In the theory of social philosophers, for whom Professor John Dewey may be regarded as a typical and convenient example, the dynamic is simply the total impulsive character of life. Life according to this school is energy; and its dynamic character provides that it will move forward. If reason cuts straight and broad channels for the stream of life, it will flow in them. Without reason life spends itself in the narrow and tortuous beds, which have been cut by ages of pre-rational impulse, seeking immediate outlets for its energy. This theory hardly does justice to the complexities of human behavior and to the inevitable conflicts between the objectives determined by reason and those of the total body of impulse, rationally unified but bent upon more immediate goals than those which man's highest reason envisages. Men may achieve a rational unity of impulse around the organising centre of the possessive instinct or the will-to-power, and yet have a faint sense of obligation to achieve social objectives, which transcend, or are in conflict with, their will-to-power.

The theory of the sociological naturalists, Spencer and Westermarck and a host of others, maintains that the voice of conscience which supports the more inclusive objectives of reason is really the fear of the group, and that the sense of moral obligation is either the overt or the covert pressure of society upon the individual. Such a theory does not do justice to those types of human behavior in which the individual defies his group. It is sometimes maintained that such defiance must be interpreted as resulting from a sense of loyalty to some community, other than the one to which the non-conformist individual belongs most immediately and most obviously. Such an interpretation vitiates the position it is intended to support. For defiance of a community, which is in control not only of the police power but of the potent force of public approval and disapproval, in the name of a community, which exists only in the moral imagination of the individual (as the community of mankind for instance) and has no means of exerting pressure upon him, obviously points to a force of conscience, more individual than social. The individual character of conscience does not preclude the determination of most moral judgments by the opinions of the group. Most individuals lack the intellectual penetration to form independent judgments and therefore accept the moral opinions of their society. Even when they do form their own judgments there is no certainty that their sense of obligation toward moral values, defined by their own mind, will be powerful enough to overcome the fear of social disapproval. The social character of most moral judgments and the pressure of society upon an individual are both facts to be reckoned with; but neither explains the peculiar phenomenon of the moral life, usually called conscience.

It is impossible, within the purposes of this study, to consider the nature of the sense of moral obligation as fully as it deserves. But it is important to point out that men do possess, among other moral resources, a sense of obligation toward the good, as their mind conceives it. This moral sense does not give content to moral judgments. It is a principle of action which requires the individual to act according to whatever judgments of good and evil he is able to form. It can be equated neither with the total dynamic character of life, nor with the individual's fear of the disapproval or discipline of his group. Reason provides the opportunity for its expression by creating the possibility of conflict between immediate impulses and the inclusive objectives of reason. Yet the sense of obligation cannot be equated with the rational character of life any more than it can be identified with its dynamic character. If reverence for law is the essence of this moral sense, as Kant maintained, it must be observed that reason may provide the law but does not, of itself, furnish the reverence. Broad, seeking to do justice to its dynamic quality, places it in the category of impulse, but gives it a *sui generis* character. Among many human desires, there is a unique desire, "the desire to do right."[5] This is a fairly convincing explanation of the moral sense, though the definition of the sense of "ought" as a desire, even though a unique desire, is still too general to do full justice to it.

[5] *Cf.* C. D. Broad, *Five Types of Ethical Theory*, pp. 282–83.

Whatever its peculiar character, the important fact, for our purposes, is that men do seem to possess, among other moral resources, a sense of obligation toward the good, however they may define it. While it may give force to moral judgments, which must be regarded as mistaken from a rational perspective, its general tendency is to support reason against impulse. Historically it is related to both the rational and the impulsive elements in human nature. While it is not underived, it is at least as unique as the capacity for conceptual knowledge. Like conceptual knowledge it may be strengthened and enlarged by discipline, and may deteriorate by lack of use.

Professor Gilbert Murray, in his *Rise of the Greek Epic,* gives a telling example from Greek history of the force of this element of conscience in human behavior:

If you take people—who have broken away from all their old sanctions, and select from among them some strong turbulent chief who fears no one, you will think that such a man is free to do whatever enters his head. And then as a matter of fact you find that among his lawlessness there will crop up some possible action which somehow makes him feel uncomfortable. If he has done it he "rues" the deed, and is haunted by it. If he has not done it he refrains from doing it. And this is not because any one forces him, nor yet because any particular result will accrue to him afterwards. But simply because he feels *Aidos*. No one can tell where the exact point of honor will arise. When Achilles fought against Eëtion's city, "he sacked all the happy city of the Cilician men, high-gated Thebe, and slew Eëtion; but he spoiled him not of his armour. He had *Aidos* in his heart for that; but he burned him there as he lay in his rich-wrought armour, and heaped a mound above him."—That is *Aidos* pure and clean. Achilles had nothing to gain, nothing to lose. Nobody would have said a word if he had taken Eëtion's richly wrought armour. It would have been quite the natural thing to do. But he happened to feel *Aidos* about it.[6]

The cynic might observe that conscience did not prevent the annihilation of a foe but only the perpetration of an indignity upon his corpse. Conscience is a moral resource in human life, but it is not as powerful as those moralists assume, who would save mankind by cultivating the sense of duty. It is more potent when it supports one impulse against another than when it sets itself against the total force of the individual's desires. It operates more effectively when it consolidates and stabilises socially valuable impulses, as those associated with the family life for instance, than when it attempts to carry impulse beyond the objectives determined by the forces of nature. "Deduct from repentance all that is not purely moral and we must admit that conscience is not so strong *de facto* as perhaps it ought to be *de jure*," declares Leslie Stephens. "Indeed I should say that most men find nothing easier than to suppress its stings, when some immediately bad consequence, or the contempt and abhorrence of their neighbors, does not constantly instill the venom. This is as far as possible from proving that an increased strength of conscience is not highly desirable, and that, even in the existing state of things, its influence is not of the last importance. . . . The sense of duty, faint and flickering as it is in most men, is sufficient to keep the social order from disruption."[7] It is dubious whether

[6] Gilbert Murray, *Rise of the Greek Epic* (New York: Oxford University Press), p. 80.
[7] Leslie Stephens, *The Science of Ethics*, p. 306.

the development of reason, though it increases the opportunities for the exercise of conscience, strengthens the force of conscience itself. In that task religion is more potent than reason. Its relation to conscience must be considered later.

The possibilities of increasing both the rational and the more uniquely moral resources of individuals is so real that it is not surprising that those who study the possibilities should frequently indulge the hope of solving the problems of society by this method. They easily fail to recognise the limits of morality in human life. The possibility of extending reason does not guarantee that it can be extended far enough to give a majority of individuals a comprehension of the total social situation in which they stand. The ability of reason to check impulse does not inevitably provide a sufficient check to prevent the conflict of impulses, particularly the conflict of collective impulses in society.

In analysing the limits of reason in morality it is important to begin by recognising that the force of egoistic impulse is much more powerful than any but the most astute psychological analysts and the most rigorous devotees of introspection realise. If it is defeated on a lower or more obvious level, it will express itself in more subtle forms. If it is defeated by social impulse it insinuates itself into the social impulse, so that a man's devotion to his community always means the expression of a transferred egoism as well as of altruism. Reason may check egoism in order to fit it harmoniously into a total body of social impulse. But the same force of reason is bound to justify the egoism of the individual as a legitimate element in the total body of vital capacities, which society seeks to harmonise. It is difficult to prevent such social justifications of self-assertion from being made prematurely and from destroying the check upon selfish impulse which reason has established from the inner perspective. Rationalism in morals may persuade men in one moment that their selfishness is a peril to society and in the next moment it may condone their egoism as a necessary and inevitable element in the total social harmony. The egoistic impulses are so powerful and insistent that they will be quick to take advantage of any such justifications. The utilitarian movement of the nineteenth century had the laudable purpose of persuading men to achieve a decent harmony between selfish and social impulse by diverting egoistic impulse to the most inclusive possible social objectives. It was significant that it merely provided the rising middle class with a nice moral justification for following its own interests.

Reason may not only justify egoism prematurely but actually give it a force which it does not possess in non-rational nature. Human self-consciousness is the fruit of reason. Men become conscious of themselves as they see themselves in relation to other life and to their environment. This self-consciousness increases the urge to preserve and to extend life. In the animal the instincts of self-preservation do not extend beyond the necessities provided by nature. The animal kills when it is hungry and fights or runs when it is in danger. In man the impulses of self-preservation are transmuted very easily into desires for aggrandisement. There is a pathetic quality in human self-consciousness which accentuates this tendency. Self-consciousness means the recognition of finiteness within infinity. The mind recognises the *ego* as an insignificant point amidst the immensities of the world. In all vital self-consciousness there is a note of protest against this finiteness. It may express itself in religion by the desire to be absorbed in infinitude. On the secular level it expresses itself in man's effort to universalise himself and give his life a significance beyond himself. The root of imperialism is therefore in all self-consciousness.

Once the effort to gain significance beyond himself has succeeded, man fights for his social eminence and increased significance with the same fervor and with the same sense of justification, with which he fights for his life. The economy of nature has provided that means of defense may be quickly transmuted into means of aggression. There is therefore no possibility of drawing a sharp line between the will-to-live and the will-to-power. Even in the emotions, attitudes of defense and aggression are so compounded that fear may easily lead to courage, and the necessity of consolidating the triumph won by courage may justify new fears.

France, seeking to maintain her hegemony in Europe, speaks with monotonous reiteration of her need of security. She typifies the human spirit with its curious mixture of fear of extinction and love of power. Power, once attained, places the individual or the group in a position of perilous eminence so that security is possible only by the extension of power. Thus nature's harmless and justifiable strategies for preserving life, are transmuted in the human spirit into imperial purposes and policies. So inextricably are the two intertwined, that the one may always be used to justify the other in conscious and unconscious deception.

Perhaps the imperial supremacy of the white races in the contemporary world depends much more upon the higher degree of self-consciousness of the "Faustian" soul than upon their development of the techniques of war, their skill in government and their development of economic power. Waldo Frank, explaining the victory of the Spaniards over the great civilisation of Peru, attributes it to the cult of the individual soul: "The Spaniard believed in his own person. The most real reality of his world was his individual soul and his individual body which, though it must die, would rise again in the last days. . . . Whatever his religion, all experience is referred to the will, all his life is ruled by it, all time is made for it. . . . To meet the Spaniard there were no *persons* in Peru. There was only the ayllu. And the will of the ayllu, though persistent was not aggressive. . . . The ayllu did not yearn beyond the condor's flight nor beneath the shallow root of the maize. . . . It was a will delimited by the apparent surface of nature. . . . The Indian could not grasp, could not believe what he beheld. The notion of mortal man sailing across a trackless sea dismayed him. . . . Still more inconceivable was the lust and will of these men. Their every deed of daring, bestiality and devotion (indissolubly mixed in the conquistador) had a dimension which the Indian mind could not reach."[8] This astute analysis of the difference between the white man and the Indian man of nature is broadly ap-

[8] Waldo Frank, *America Hispana*, pp. 54–57.

plicable to the difference between man and nature. The very forces which lift man above nature give natural impulses a new and a more awful potency in the human world. Man fights his battles with instruments in which mind has sharpened nature's claws; and his ferocities are more sustained than those of the natural world, where they are prompted only by the moods and the necessities of the moment. The beast of prey ceases from its conquests when its maw is crammed; but man's lusts are fed by his imagination, and he will not be satisfied until the universal objectives which the imagination envisages are attained. His protest against finiteness makes the universal character of his imperial dreams inevitable. In his sanest moments he sees his life fulfilled as an organic part of a harmonious whole. But he has few sane moments; for he is governed more by imagination than by reason and imagination is compounded of mind and impulse.

The rational forces, which seek to bring this energy, in which self-consciousness has focused the primal dynamic of all life in one particular point, seem weak indeed, when compared with the force arrayed against them. They are all the more inadequate for having no impartial perspective, from which to view, and no transcendent fulcrum, from which to affect human action, They always remain bound to the forces they are intended to discipline. The will-to-power uses reason, as kings use courtiers and chaplains to add grace to their enterprise. Even the most rational men are never quite rational when their own interests are at stake. "What man," said Helvetius, ". . . if with a scrupulous attention he searches all the recesses of his soul, will not perceive that his virtues and vices are wholly owing to different modifications of personal interest? . . . For after all interest is always obeyed; hence the injustice of all our judgments."[9]

This insinuation of the interests of the self into even the most ideal enterprises and most universal objectives, envisaged in moments of highest rationality, makes hypocrisy an inevitable by-product of all virtuous endeavor. It is, in a sense, a tribute to the moral nature of man as well as a proof of his moral limitations; for it is significant that men cannot pursue their own ends with the greatest devotion, if they are unable to attribute universal values to their particular objectives. But men are no more able to eliminate self-interest from their nobler pursuits than they are able to express it fully without hiding it behind and compounding it with honest efforts at or dishonest pretensions of universality. Even a conscious attempt to eliminate dishonest and ambiguous motives is no perfect guarantee against hypocrisy; for there is no miracle by which men can achieve a rationality high enough to give them as vivid an understanding of general interests as of their own.

Jeremy Bentham, who gave himself to the hope that men could be weaned from their immediate desires, if only they could be brought to realise that a broad social interest was not in conflict but in ultimate harmony with a wise egoism, found to his disappointment that a prudent self-interest was an achievement almost as rare as unselfishness. When impulse presses toward immediate goals it cannot always be deterred, even though reason try to persuade it that its real ends may be attained in

[9] Helvetius, *De L'Esprit, or Essays on the Mind,* Essay II, Chap. 2.

more ultimate and inclusive terms. Writing in 1822, after many of his reform movements had failed to claim the popular support he had anticipated, Bentham confessed: "Now for some years past all inconsistencies, all surprises have vanished. . . . A clue to the interior of the labyrinth has been found. It is the principle of self-preference. Man, from the very constitution of his nature, prefers his own happiness to that of all other sentient beings put together."[10] The judgment may be a little too pessimistic, expressing a reaction from too romantic hopes, but it is nearer the truth than the early hope of the utilitarians that reason could resolve the conflict between self-interest and social interest.

Even when the individual is prompted to give himself in devotion to a cause or community, the will-to-power remains. In the family for instance, it may express itself in part within the family circle and in part through the family. Devotion to the family does not exclude the possibility of an autocratic relationship toward it. The tyranny of the husband and father in the family has yielded only very slowly to the principle of mutuality. And it is significant that women have never been able to overcome the vestigial remnants of male autocracy in modern social life without using other than purely rational weapons against it. It was not until they could avail themselves of the weapon of economic power and independence that they were able to gain a complete victory. Nor could they remove various economic disabilities from which they suffered without first securing political power in the state. In the long agitation which preceded suffrage re-

[10] Jeremy Bentham, *Works*, Vol. X, p. 80.

form, the men significantly used the same arguments against their own women, which privileged groups have always used in opposition to the extension of privilege. They insisted that women were not capable of exercising the rights to which they aspired, just as dominant classes have always tried to withhold the opportunity for the exercise of rational functions from underprivileged classes and then accused them of lacking capacities, which can be developed only by exercise.

Even if perfect mutuality should be attained within the family circle, the family may still remain a means of self-aggrandisement. The solicitous father wants his wife and children to have all possible advantages. His greater solicitude for them than for others grows naturally out of the sympathy, which intimate relations prompt. But it is also a projection of his own *ego*. Families may, in fact, be used to advertise a husband's and father's success and prosperity. Both the ascetics and the collectivists, who have regarded the family with a critical eye, are not quite as perverse as they seem from the viewpoint of conventional morality. The ascetics regarded family loyalty as a distraction from perfect devotion to God and the modern communists are inclined to view it as a peril to community loyalty; and there is a measure of truth in their conceptions. The truth is that every immediate loyalty is a potential danger to higher and more inclusive loyalties, and an opportunity for the expression of a sublimated egoism.

The larger social groups above the family, communities, classes, races and nations all present men with the same twofold opportunity for self-denial and self-aggrandisement; and both possibilities are usually exploited. Patriotism is a high form of altruism, when compared with lesser and more parochial loyalties; but from an absolute perspective it is simply another form of selfishness. The larger the group the more certainly will it express itself selfishly in the total human community. It will be more powerful and therefore more able to defy any social restraints which might be devised. It will also be less subject to internal moral restraints. The larger the group the more difficult it is to achieve a common mind and purpose and the more inevitably will it be unified by momentary impulses and immediate and unreflective purposes. The increasing size of the group increases the difficulties of achieving a group self-consciousness, except as it comes in conflict with other groups and is unified by perils and passions of war. It is a rather pathetic aspect of human social life that conflict is a seemingly unavoidable prerequisite of group solidarity. Furthermore the greater the strength and the wider the dominion of a community, the more will it seem to represent universal values from the perspective of the individual. There is something to be said for Treitschke's logic, which made the nation the ultimate community of significant loyalty, on the ground that smaller units were too small to deserve, and larger units too vague and ephemeral to be able to exact, man's supreme loyalty. Treitschke was wrong only in glorying in this moral difficulty.

Try as he will, man seems incapable of forming an international community, with power and prestige great enough to bring social restraint upon collective egoism. He has not even succeeded in disciplining anti-social

group egoism within the nation. The very extension of
human sympathies has therefore resulted in the creation
of larger units of conflict without abolishing conflict. So
civilization has become a device for delegating the vices
of individuals to larger and larger communities. The device gives men the illusion that they are moral; but the
illusion is not lasting. A technological civilisation has created an international community, so interdependent as to
require, even if not powerful or astute enough to achieve,
ultimate social harmony. While there are halting efforts
to create an international mind and conscience, capable
of coping with this social situation, modern man has progressed only a little beyond his fathers in extending his
ethical attitudes beyond the group to which he is organic
and which possesses symbols, vivid enough to excite his
social sympathies. His group is larger than that of his
fathers, but whatever moral gain may be ascribed to that
development is partially lost by the greater heterogeneity
and the diminished mutuality of this larger group. The
modern nation is divided into classes and the classes ex-
hibit a greater disproportion of power and privilege than
in the primitive community. This social inequality leads
not only to internal strife but to conflict between various
national communities, by prompting the more privileged
and powerful classes to seek advantages at the expense of
other nations so that they may consolidate the privileges
which they have won at the expense of their own na-
tionals. Thus modern life is involved in both class and international conflict; and it may be that class privileges
cannot be abolished or diminished until they have reduced the whole of modern society to international and

intra-national chaos. The growing intelligence of mankind seems not to be growing rapidly enough to achieve mastery over the social problems, which the advances of technology create.

CHAPTER THREE

THE RELIGIOUS RESOURCES OF THE INDIVIDUAL
FOR SOCIAL LIVING

THE hopes and expectations of an ideal society, through the development of the moral capacities of individual men, have proceeded from and been encouraged by the religious, as well as the rational, idealists. The belief that a revival of religion will furnish the resources by which men will extricate themselves from their social chaos is a perennial one, and it expresses itself even in an age in which the forces of religion are on the defensive against a host of enemies and detractors. It justifies a thorough examination of the relation of religion to the moral life, particularly since an increasing number of sensitive spirits, whose chief interest is in the social problem, regard religion as a hindrance rather than a help in redeeming society from its ills.

If the recognition of selfishness is prerequisite to the mitigation of its force and the diminution of its anti-social consequences in society, religion should be a dominant influence in the socialisation of man; for religion is fruitful of the spirit of contrition. Feeling himself under the scrutiny of an omniscient eye, and setting his puny will into juxtaposition with a holy and omnipotent will, the religious man is filled with a sense of shame for the impertinence of his self-centred life. The sentiment of contrition runs as a persistent motif of humility through all classical religious literature, and expresses itself in all religious life. It may become so stereotyped and formalised that its inner vitality is lost, but even then it pays tribute to an inner necessity of the religious life.

Essentially religion is a sense of the absolute. When, as is usually the case, the absolute is imagined in terms of man's own highest ethical aspirations, a perspective is created from which all moral achievements are judged to be inadequate. Viewed from the relative perspectives of the historic scene, there is no human action which cannot be justified in terms of some historic purpose or approved in comparison with some less virtuous action. The absolute reference of religion eliminates these partial perspectives and premature justifications. There is no guarantee against the interpretation of the absolute in terms of faulty moral insights; and human vice and error may thus be clothed by religion in garments of divine magnificence and given the prestige of the absolute. Yet there is a general development in the high religions toward an interpretation of the divine as benevolent will, and a consequent increase of condemnation upon all selfish actions and desires. In investing the heart of the cosmos with an ethical will, the religious imagination unites its awe before the infinitude and majesty of the physical world with its reverence for the ethical principle of the inner life. The inner world of conscience, which is in constant rebellion against the outer world of nature, is made supreme over the world of nature by the fiat of religion. Thus the Bechuana regarded thunder as the accusing voice of God and cried: "I have not stolen, I have not stolen, who among us has taken the goods of another?"[1] And Jesus, in the sublime *naïveté* of the religious imagination at its best, interprets the impartiality of nature toward the evil and the good, which secular reason might regard as its injustice, as a revelation of the impartial love of God. The religious imagination, seeking an ultimate goal and point of reference for the moral urges of life, finds support for its yearning after the absolute in the infinitude and majesty of the physical world. The omnipotence of God, as seen in the world of nature, invests his moral character with the quality of the absolute and transfigures it into holiness. Since supreme omnipotence and perfect holiness are incompatible attributes, there is a note of rational absurdity in all religion, which more rational types of theologies attempt to eliminate. But they cannot succeed without sacrificing a measure of religious vitality.

The religious conscience is sensitive not only because its imperfections are judged in the light of the absolute but because its obligations are felt to be obligations toward a person. The holy will is a personal will. Philosophers may find difficulty in transferring the concept of personality, loaded as it is with connotations which are derived from the sense limitations of human personality, to the absolute. But these difficulties are of small moment to the poetic imagination of religion. It uses the symbols derived from human personality to describe the absolute and it finds them morally potent. Moral attitudes always develop most sensitively in person-to-person relationships. That is one reason why more inclusive loyalties, naturally

[1] Quoted by W. E. Hocking, *The Meaning of God in Human Experience,* p. 235.

more abstract than immediate ones, lose some of their power over the human heart; and why a shrewd society attempts to restore that power by making a person the symbol of the community. The exploitation of the symbolic significance of monarchy, after it has lost its essential power, as in British politics for instance, is a significant case in point. The king is a useful symbol for the nation because it is easier for the simple imagination to conceive a sense of loyalty toward him than toward the nation. The nation is an abstraction which cannot be grasped if fitting symbols are not supplied. A living person is the most useful and potent symbol for this purpose. In religion all the higher moral obligations, which are lost in abstractions on the historic level, are felt as obligations toward the supreme person. Thus both the personality and the holiness of God provide the religious man with a reinforcement of his moral will and a restraint upon his will-to-power.

The history of religion is proof of the efficacy of religious insights in making men conscious of the sinfulness of their preoccupation with self. There is nothing, that modern psychologists have discovered about the persistence of ego-centricity in man, which has not been anticipated in the insights of the great mystics of the classical periods of religion. Asceticism, which is at once the great vice and the great virtue of religion, is the proof of its sensitive realisation of the evil of self-will. Schopenhauer quite rightly interprets religious asceticism as the "denial of the will-to-live." "His will turns round, no longer asserts its own nature but denies it. . . . Voluntary and complete chastity is the first step in asceticism or the denial of the will-to-live. It thereby denies the assertion of the will which extends beyond the individual life. . . . Asceticism then shows itself further in voluntary and intentional poverty which is meant as a constant mortification of the will, so that the satisfaction of wishes, the sweet of life, shall not again arouse the will, against which self-knowledge has gained a horror."[2] It is interesting to note that rigorous mystics frequently arrive at estimates of the selfishness of human action, which bear striking similarity to the analysis of human motives made by naturalistic hedonists. "All generosity," declares Fenelon in a letter to Madame Maintenon, "all natural affection is only self-love of a specially subtle, delusive and diabolical quality. We must wholly die to all friendship."[3] This judgment might be compared with the words of De Mandeville, "The humblest man alive must confess that the reward of a virtuous action, which is the satisfaction that ensues upon it, consists in a certain pleasure he procures to himself by the contemplation of his own worth; which pleasure, together with the occasion of it, are certain signs of pride, as looking pale and trembling at any imminent danger are symptoms of fear."[4] It cannot be denied that mysticism and asceticism involve themselves in every kind of absurdity in their attempt to root out the selfishness of which their mystical contemplation has made them conscious. The mystic involves himself not only in the practical absurdity of becoming obsessed with self, in the very fever of the effort to eliminate it, but in the rational ab-

[2] Schopenhauer, *The World as Will and Idea*, Bk. IV, para. 68.
[3] Hastings, *Encyclopedia of Religion and Ethics*, X, p. 534.
[4] Bernard De Mandeville, "An Enquiry into the Origin of Moral Virtue," in his *The Fable of the Bees*.

[55]

surdity of passing judgment upon even the most unselfish desires as being selfish because they are desires. "We must suppress our desires, even the desire for the joys of paradise," declares Madame Guyon.[5] Bousset, who traces down these morbid efforts of the mystics to achieve absolutely consistent disinterestedness, paraphrases their dominant sentiment in the words, "The desire for God is not God, therefore we close the door upon that as well."[6] The mystics who attempted to satisfy their longing for absolute perfection in ascetic practice were involved in an even more difficult and irrational procedure. They destroyed life and society in the process of refining it. Both Christian and Buddhist ascetics, unable to disassociate selfish desire from the will-to-live, have stopped short only of complete physical annihilation in their effort to destroy desire. In the paradox of Christ, "Whoso seeketh to find his life shall lose it and he that loseth his life for my sake shall find it,"[7] the religious tension which drives toward asceticism is resolved by condemning self-seeking as a goal of life, but allowing self-realisation as a by-product of self-abnegation. This paradox has saved Christianity from the pessimistic denials of life which characterise Hinduism and Buddhism, more particularly the latter. Yet the difference between Western and Eastern religion is only one of degree. Asceticism remains a permanent characteristic of all religious life. It may degenerate into morbid moralities of various kinds, but its complete absence is a proof of a lack of vitality in religion. A sun warm enough to ripen the fruits of the garden must make some fruits overripe.

[5] Quoted by K. E. Kirk, *The Vision of God*, p. 454.
[6] Kirk, *Ibid.*, p. 454.　　　　　　[7] Matt. 10:39.

Criticism of the ascetic note in religion, which regards it merely as an excrescence and not as an inevitable by-product of the religious yearning for the absolute, proceeds from a lack of understanding of the true nature of religion.[8]

On the social limitations of ascetic sensitivity we shall have occasion to say more later. It would be well to consider first another moral resource of religion, which tends to qualify and to destroy the subjectivism into which mysticism and asceticism easily fall. This is the religious emphasis upon love as the highest virtue. A rational ethic aims at justice, and a religious ethic makes love the ideal. A rational ethic seeks to bring the needs of others into equal consideration with those of the self. The religious ethic, (the Christian ethic more particularly, though not solely) insists that the needs of the neighbor shall be met, without a careful computation of relative needs. This emphasis upon love is another fruit of the religious sense of the absolute. On the one hand religion absolutises the sentiment of benevolence and makes it the norm and ideal of the moral life. On the other hand it gives transcendent and absolute worth to the life of the neighbor and thus encourages sympathy toward him. Love meets the needs of the neighbor, without carefully weighing and comparing his needs with those of the self. It is therefore ethically purer than the justice which is prompted by reason. (Since it is more difficult to apply to a complex society it need not for that reason be socially more valuable than the rational principle of justice.) In part the

---

[8] W. P. Montague's criticism of religious asceticism in his *Belief Unbound*, Chap. II, clearly reveals this lack of understanding.

religious ideal of love is fed and supported by viewing the soul of the fellowman from the absolute and transcendent perspective. Your neighbor is a son of God, and God may be served by serving him. "What ye have done unto one of the least of these my brethren, ye have done unto me," said Jesus. "I have come to the stage of realisation in which I see that God is walking in every human form and manifesting himself alike in the sage and in the sinner,"[9] said the Indian saint Ramakrishna. It is this religious insight, flowing from the capacity of the religious imagination to view the immediate and the imperfect from the perspective of the absolute and the transcendent, which prompted St. Francis to kiss the leper and to trust the robber; which persuaded Paul that "in Christ there is neither Jew nor Greek, neither bond nor free"; which inspired an old Indian saint to greet the soldier, who, in the time of the Indian mutiny, was about to put the cold steel of his bayonet into the body of the saint, with the words, "And thou too art divine."[10] Nor does the religious appreciation of human personality reveal itself only in highly mystical natures. Unlike the spirit of asceticism, it manifests itself in more rationalised forms of religion. The Stoic doctrine of brotherhood was rooted in Stoic pantheism. Kant's maxim that human beings must always be treated as ends and never as means, is not the axiom of rational ethics that he supposes. It cannot be, in fact, consistently applied in any rational ethical scheme. It is rather, a religious ideal inherited from Kant's pietistic religious worldview. Religious reverence for human life is the mainspring of the idealism of as

[9] Quoted by James B. Pratt, *India and Its Faiths*, p. 149. [10] *Ibid.*, p. 156.

rationalistic a Christian as William Ellery Channing. He writes: "I have felt and continually insisted that a new reverence for man was essential to the cause of social reform. There can be no spirit of brotherhood, nor true peace, any farther than men come to understand their affinity with and relation to God and the infinite purposes for which he gave them life. . . . None of us can conceive the change of manners, the new courtesy and sweetness, the mutual kindness, deference and sympathy, the life and efforts for social melioration, which are to spring up in proportion as man shall penetrate beneath the body to the spirit, and shall learn what the lowest human being is."[11] This logic impelled Channing to espouse the anti-slavery cause, just as a more mystical Christian, the Quaker, John Woolman, found slavery incompatible with his religious estimate of human personality as a facet of the divine. While, as Troeltsch properly maintains, religious idealism never arrives at equalitarian political ideals without the aid of rationalistic political thought, the doctrine of the transcendent worth of all human personality does tend to become transmuted into the idea of the equal worth of all personalities. This idea may achieve real ethico-political significance; though it must be confessed that its political possibilities are usually vitiated by the suggestion of religion, that equality before God need not imply equality in historic social relations. The religious sense of the absolute may, in this and in other instances, overreach itself and end by destroying the ethical possibilities which it has created.

The introspective character of religion, which results

11 William Ellery Channing, *Works*, Introduction to Vol. VI.

in the spirit of contrition also contributes to its spirit of
love. Egoistic impulses are discovered and analysed in the
profounder types of religious introversion. They are con-
demned with the greater severity because the critical eye
of the self becomes the accusing eye of God in the mystical religious experience. This experience condemns selfishness more readily than it encourages love. It results in
an ideal of disinterestedness rather than an ideal of benevolence. But it may offer strong support to the spirit
of love by its critical attitude toward all egoism. A man's
actions may be regarded as more benevolent than they
really are from an external perspective, from which the
hidden motives cannot be recognised. Even when they are
known to be selfish they may gain approval from a social
perspective. From the inner perspective neither this confusion nor this approval is possible. The alloy of egoism
which corrupts all benevolence is isolated, and sometimes
purged, from it by a rigorous internal analysis. Furthermore the social justification of egoism has no weight in
this analysis. The actions and attitudes of the soul are
judged in the light of an absolute moral ideal, and are
found to fall short in comparison with it. Religious introspection may involve the soul in hopeless obsession
with self, if escape from self is attempted without social
reference. But the check which it places upon egoism is a
potential support for the spirit of love.

If religion be particularly occupied with the absolute
from the perspective of the individual, it is nevertheless
capable of conceiving an absolute society in which the ideal
of love and justice will be fully realised. There is a millennial hope in every vital religion. The religious imagination

is as impatient with the compromises, relativities and imperfections of historic society as with the imperfections of
individual life. The prophet Isaiah dreamed of the day
when the lion and the lamb would lie down together,
when, in other words, the law of nature which prompts
the strong to devour the weak would be abrogated. The
religious idealists of both Egypt and Babylon had their
visions of an ideal reign. Sometimes the contrast between
the real and the ideal is drawn so sharply that the religious man despairs of the achievement of the ideal in
mundane history. He transfers his hopes to another world.
This is particularly true of religion influenced by Pla-
tonic idealism, in which the ideal world is always above
and not at the end of human history. It was the peculiar
genius of Jewish religious thought, that it conceived the
millennium in this-worldly terms. The gospel conception
of the kingdom of God represents a highly spiritualised
version of this Jewish millennial hope, heavily indebted
to the vision of the Second Isaiah. Wherever religion concerns itself with the problems of society, it always gives
birth to some kind of millennial hope, from the perspective of which present social realities are convicted of in-
adequacy, and courage is maintained to continue in the
effort to redeem society of injustice. The courage is needed; for the task of building a just society seems always to
be a hopeless one when only present realities and immediate possibilities are envisaged. The modern communist's dream of a completely equalitarian society is a
secularised, but still essentially religious, version of the
classical religious dream. Its secularisation is partly a reaction to the unrealistic sentimentality into which the

religious social hope degenerated in the middle-class religious community; partly it is the inevitable consequence of the mechanisation of modern life and the destruction of religious imagination. Though it is a secularised version of the religious hope, its religious quality is attested by its emphasis upon catastrophe. It does not see the new society emerging by gradual and inevitable evolutionary process. It is pessimistic about the present trends in society and sees them driving toward disaster; but its hope, as in all religion, grows out of its despair, and it sees the new society emerging from catastrophe. Evolutionary millennialism is always the hope of comfortable and privileged classes, who imagine themselves too rational to accept the idea of the sudden emergence of the absolute in history. For them the ideal is in history, working its way to ultimate triumph. They identify God and nature, the real and the ideal, not because the more dualistic conceptions of classical religion are too irrational for them (though they are irrational); but because they do not suffer as much as the disinherited from the brutalities of contemporary society, and therefore do not take as catastrophic a view of contemporary history. The more privileged proletarians turn catastrophic Marxism into evolutionary socialism for the same reason. Religion is always a citadel of hope, which is built on the edge of despair. Men are inclined to view both individual and social moral facts with complacency, until they view them from some absolute perspective. But the same absolutism which drives them to despair, rejuvenates their hope. In the imagination of the truly religious man the God, who condemns history, will yet redeem history.

The undoubted moral resources of religion seem to justify the religious moralists in their hope for the redemption of society through the increase of religio-moral resources. In their most unqualified form, these hopes are vain. There are constitutional limitations in the genius of religion which will always make it more fruitful in purifying individual life, and adding wholesomeness to the more intimate social relations, such as the family, than in the problems of the more complex and political relations of modern society. The disrepute in which modern religion is held by large numbers of ethically sensitive individuals, springs much more from its difficulties in dealing with these complex problems than from its tardiness in adjusting itself to the spirit of modern culture. A society which is harassed with the urgent political and economic problems, which confront our contemporary world, is inclined to be scornful of any life-expression, which is not immediately relevant to its most urgent tasks. In that attitude it may be no more justified than are the religious sentimentalists, who insist that they have a panacea for every ill to which the human flesh is heir.

The religious sense of the absolute qualifies the will-to-live and the will-to-power by bringing them under subjection to an absolute will, and by imparting transcendent value to other human beings, whose life and needs thus achieve a higher claim upon the self. That is a moral gain. But religion results also in the absolutising of the self. It is a sublimation of the will-to-live. Though God is majestic and transcendent he is nevertheless related to man by both his qualities and his interest in man. His qualities are human virtues, raised to the nth degree. His interest in man remains even when, as in modern Barthian theology, he is described as the "wholly other." In religion man interprets the universe in terms relevant to his life and aspirations. Religion is at one and the same time, humility before the absolute and self-assertion in terms of the absolute. Naturalists, who accuse religion of either too much pride or of too abject self-depreciation, fail to understand this paradox of the religious life. Naturally the two elements are not always equally powerful. F. Heiler divides religions into the "mystical" and the "prophetic," the former emphasising humility before God and the latter expressing "an irresistible will to live, an uncontrollable impulse toward the expression, mastery and exaltation of the sense of living." The mystical prayer is "directed toward God, the exclusive object, the one Reality, the highest value." The object of prophetic prayer, on the other hand, is "man's own joy and sorrow, his troubles and fears, his plans and confidences.[12] Heiler erroneously identifies the former with Catholic and the latter with Protestant piety. The most trenchant exposition of religion as a sublimation of the will to live, with particular emphasis upon the basic character of the religious hope of immortality, has been made by a contemporary Catholic philosopher of religion, Unamuno.[13] The two emphases exist side by side in varying degrees in almost every expression of the religious life. Whether the religious sublimation of the will-to-live mitigates the sharpness of the conflict between the will-to-power of individuals on the historic level, by lifting the energy of life to a higher level

[12] F. Heiler, *Das Gebet*, p. 359.
[13] Miguel de Unamuno, *The Tragic Sense of Life*.

and beguiling the soul to seek ultimate satisfactions in a transhistorical and supramundane world, is a difficult question to answer. In some respects this is the effect of the religious life. The modern radical, who regards religion as an opiate, justifies his indictment in terms of this characteristic of religion. On the other hand, the religious sanctification of the individual life and will, may make it a more resolute force in the historic situation. The power, by which the middle commercial classes defeated the landed aristocracy in the political and economic battles of the past three centuries, was partially derived from the puritan sense of the religious worth of personality and of the spiritual character of secular pursuits. Speaking of the Spanish conquistador, Waldo Frank finds both his courage and his cruelty based on his religious faith. "Without the mystic guidance of the church, he must have sunk in the first jungle and gone no farther. Only a man who believes can do what he did. He has seen cheap wine turn to the blood of Christ; now he can understand how his own bestialities are transfigured into acts which build the Church of Rome. Within his cruelties is the intuition of his destiny as an agent of the divine. His mystic rôle makes his impossible adventure bearable, and makes him bearable to himself."[14] The fact seems to be that the religious sublimation of the will-to-live is also, or may be, an extension of that will in historic and social terms. The prizes of another world may prompt the weak man to resignation, but they will encourage the strong man to deeds of superhuman heroism.

The danger to social life of this impartation of absolute

[14] Waldo Frank, *America Hispana*, p. 49.

value to human life is most apparent when it expresses itself in the life of national and other groups rather than in individuals. There is a moral and social imagination in religion which invests the life of other nations with a significance as great as that which is claimed for one's own nation. But it is not as powerful and not as frequently expressed as the imagination which makes one's own nation the peculiar instrument of transcendent and divine purposes. The prophet Amos could cry in the name of the Lord, "Are ye not as the children of the Ethiopians unto me, saith the Lord?" But his was a voice in the wilderness among the many who regarded Israel as the special servant of God among the nations of the world. It is not only religion which gives a special dignity and worth to the life of the nation to which one belongs. Patriotism is a form of piety which exists partly through the limitation of the imagination, and that limitation may be expressed by savants as well as by saints. The wise men of the nations were just as sedulous in proving, during the late World War, that their particular nation had a peculiar mission to "culture" and to "civilisation" as were the religious leaders in asserting that the will of God was being fulfilled in the policy of their state. But since the claims of religion are more absolute than those of any secular culture the danger of sharpening the self-will of nations through religion is correspondingly greater.

Even when the religious sense of the absolute expresses itself, not in the sublimation of the will, but in the subjection of the individual will to the divine will, and in the judgment upon the will from the divine perspective, it may still offer perils to the highest social and moral life, even though it will produce some choice fruits of morality. One interesting aspect of the religious yearning after the absolute is that, in the contrast between the divine and the human, all lesser contrasts between good and evil on the human and historic level are obscured. Sin finally becomes disobedience to God and nothing else. Only rebellion against God, and only the impertinence of self-will in the sight of God, are regarded as sinful. One may see this logic of religion very clearly in the thought of Jonathan Edwards. "A crime is more or less heinous," he declares, "according as we are under greater or less obligation to the contrary. Our obligation to love, honor and obey any being is in proportion to its loveliness, honorableness and authority. But God is a being infinitely lovely because he has infinite excellence and beauty. So that sin against God, being a violation of infinite obligations, must be a crime infinitely heinous and so deserving of infinite punishment.[15] The sin which the religious man feels himself committing against God is indeed the sin of self-will; but his recognition of that fact may, but need not, have special social significance. So strong is the emphasis upon the God-and-man relationship in the religious conception of sin, that Rudolf Otto is able to interpret it entirely as a feeling of profanity before the sacred.[16] This is probably an overstatement of the fact; for "the holy" achieves a connotation of the morally perfect in the development of religion and sin is correspondingly defined in moral terms. Nevertheless the tendency to lose moral distinctions in the emphasis upon the religious aspect of sin remains a per-

[15] Jonathan Edwards, *Works*, Vol. IV, p. 226.
[16] Rudolf Otto, *Idea of the Holy*.

manent characteristic of vital religious life. In the modern Barthian revival of Lutheran orthodoxy the religious experience is practically exhausted in the sense of contrition. The emphasis upon the difference between the holiness of God and the sinfulness of man is so absolute that man is convicted, not of any particular breaches against the life of the humanity community, but of being human and not divine. Thus, to all intents and purposes, creation and the fall are practically identified and, everything in human history being identified with evil, the "nicely calculated less and more" of social morality lose all significance. It is interesting that Schleiermacher, the *bête noir* of the modern Barthians, interprets the relation of morality and religion in terms which explicitly confess what is implicit in the Barthian position but not as freely admitted. He writes: "The contemplation of the pious is the immediate consciousness of the universal existence of all finite things in and through the eternal. . . . Where this is found religion is satisfied. . . . Ethics on the other hand seeks to distinguish precisely each part of human doing and producing, and at the same time to combine them into a whole of natural relationships. But the pious man confesses that, as pious, he knows nothing about it. He does indeed contemplate human action but it is not the kind of contemplation from which an ethical system can take its rise."[17] The implicit pantheism of Schleiermacher's position is diametrically opposed to Barthian conceptions of divine transcendence and it results in making reverence rather than contrition the dominant religious feeling.

[17] F. Schleiermacher, *On Religion, Speeches to Its Cultural Despisers*, pp. 36, 37.

But both result in an identical separation of religion and morality.

Augustine, writing about the two cities in his *De civitate Dei,* contrasts the religious and the secular in a similar vein; and moral differences are thereby obscured or effaced: "Two loves therefore have given origin to these two cities, self-love in contempt of God unto the earthly; love of God in contempt of one's self to the heavenly. The first seeketh the glory of man, and the latter desires God only, as the testimony of the conscience, the greatest glory. . . . In the earthly city the wise men follow either the goods of the body or mind or both, living according to the flesh . . . but in the other, this heavenly city, there is no wisdom of man but only the piety that serveth the true God and expecteth a reward in the society of the holy angels and men, that God may be all in all."[18] There is a form of religious piety in which religious sensitivity heightens the sense of sin, without destroying its moral connotation; in which the affront to God is the final, but not the only, crime of selfishness, and in which the worship of God is the crown, but not the only, manifestation of the self-conquered life. Such a relation between religion and ethics is found in the thought of Thomas Aquinas for instance. Nevertheless the tendency of religion to obscure the shades and shadows of moral life, by painting only the contrast between the white radiance of divine holiness and the darkness of the world, remains a permanent characteristic of the religious life.

This tendency has more than one dubious effect. It

[18] Augustine, *City of God,* Bk. 4, Chap. 28.

certainly tends very readily to a moral, social and political indifferentism. The individual, and more particularly society, are regarded as too involved in the sins of the earth to be capable of salvation in any moral sense. Usually the individual is saved by the grace of God, while society is consigned to the devil; that is, the social problem is declared to be insoluble on any ethical basis. Thus Augustine concludes that the city of this world is "compact of injustice," that its ruler is the devil, that it was built by Cain and that its peace is secured by strife. That is a very realistic interpretation of the realities of social life. It would stand in wholesome contrast to the sentimentalities and superficial analyses, current in modern religion, were it not marred by a note of defeatism. That note creeps easily into all rigorous religion, with its drift toward dualism. The injustices of society are placed into such sharp contrast with the absolute moral ideal, conceived by the individual conscience, that the religiously sensitised soul is tempted to despair of society. Religion thus degenerates into an asocial quest for the absolute. The soul seeks the perfection of God in either quietistic absorption or ascetic withdrawal from the world; and in each case perfection is defined and experienced in purely individualistic terms. Another possible alternative is to regard the absolute and the perfect as unattainable and to despair of achieving any virtue which would have significance in the sight of God. In that case the religious man is comforted by the experience of grace, an experience in which the religious life accepts the mercy and forgiveness of God as consolation for its failure, and turns defeat into victory by enjoying an anticipatory attainment of what is regarded as unattainable. In all these various forms religion heightens the tensions of life and then relaxes them. The moral tension of life is invariably imperilled in this process of religious relaxation. Religion draws the bow of life so taut that it either snaps the string (defeatism) or overshoots the mark (fanaticism and asceticism). The belief that the moral weaknesses of religion may be eliminated simply by increasing religious vitality is too simple to be true. The greater the vitality of religion, the more it may either support or endanger morality. It may create moral sensitivity and destroy moral vigor by the force of the same vitality.

Both the resources and the limitations of religion in dealing with the social problem, are revealed even more clearly in its spirit of love than in its sense of contrition. Religion encourages love and benevolence, as we have seen, by absolutising the moral principle of life until it achieves the purity of absolute disinterestedness and by imparting transcendent worth to the life of others. This represents a permanent contribution to the moral life which, despite limitations revealed in the more intricate and complex social relations, must be gratefully accepted as an extension and enlargement of the moral attitudes, usually expressed only in the more intimate relations. "If ye love them that love you, what reward have ye?" declared Jesus; and in the logic of those words the whole social genius of the Christian religion is revealed. The transcendent perspective of religion makes all men our brothers and nullifies the divisions, by which nature, climate, geography and the accidents of history divide the human family. By this insight many religiously inspired idealists have transcended national, racial and class distinctions.

The great seers and saints of religion have always placed their hope for the redemption of society in the possibility of making the love-universalism, implicit in religious morality, effective in the whole human society. When Celsus accused the early Christians of destroying the integrity of the empire by their moral absolutism, Origen answered: "There is no one who fights better for the king than we. It is true that we do not go with him to battle, but we fight for him by forming an army of our own, an army of piety, through our prayers to the Godhead. Once all men have become Christians then even the barbarians will be inclined to peace."[19] It was a natural and inevitable hope in the early Christian community that the spirit of love, which pervaded the life of its own group, would eventually inform the moral life of the whole human race. That hope has been reborn again and again in the history of the Western world. Thousands of Christians, who keenly felt the World War as an apostasy from the Christian spirit, consoled themselves with the thought that Christianity had not failed, because it had not been tried. The implication of this observation is that it will some day be tried. Not a few Christian historians have intimated that, but for the unhappy conversion of Constantine, which gave Christianity a premature popularity, the love spirit of the early Christian community might have been preserved for future history. All this leaves definite limitations of the human heart and imagination out of

[19] Quoted by Ernst Troeltsch, *Social Teachings of the Christian Churches*, Vol. I, p. 124.

account. These limitations make it inevitable that the religious spirit of love should lose some of its force in proportion to the size of the communities which profess it, the impersonal and indirect character of social relations in which it operates, and the complexity of the situation which it faces. The Christian sects, such as the Quakers and other small religious communities, have preserved it more purely than the churches with their inclusive membership. It has characterised the lives of individual saints more than that of any religious communities, even small and intimate ones. All of which means that religion may increase the power and enlarge the breadth of the generous social attitudes, which nature prompts in the intimate circle; but that there are definite limits to its power and extension. All men cannot be expected to become spiritual any more than they can be expected to become rational. Those who achieve either excellence will always be a leavening influence in social life; but the political structure of society cannot be built upon their achievement. Religion may consolidate benevolent sentiments and lodge their force in the will, thus giving the whole character a consistent benevolence, more stable than the force of tender sentiments. Nevertheless even this goodwill depends for its encouragement and excitement upon personal contacts, and the revelation of need in vivid terms. We express our love most generously to those who have natural claims upon us, and to those who have no claims at all. The beggar, the completely disinherited, the needy at the ends of the earth, the lepers to whom Father Damien went and the children of the primeval forest, who are being served by Albert Schweitzer, these and our own kin are the inciters and prompters of the spirit of love; love is most active when the vividness or nearness of the need prompts those whose imagination is weak, and the remoteness of the claim challenges those whose imagination is sensitive. Love, which depends upon emotion, whether it expresses itself in transient sentiment or constant goodwill, is baffled by the more intricate social relations in which the highest ethical attitudes are achieved only by careful calculation. If it cannot find an immediate object it has difficulties in expressing itself. The same intellectual analysis which the complex situation requires may actually destroy the force of the benevolent impulse.

Furthermore there is always the possibility that the perfectionism, which prompts religious generosity, is more interested in the perfect motive than in ideal consequences. Preoccupation with motive is an unvarying characteristic of the religious life, which has its own virtues, but is also perilous to the interests of society. It is responsible for the many absurdities which have been committed in the name of religious philanthropy; absurdities which are inevitable when the benevolent spirit disregards the social consequences of generous action. The *Didache*, written in the second century, admonishes Christians to be uneasy until a beneficiary of their almsgiving appears. "Let thine alms sweat in thine hand until thou know to whom to give them," it declares.[20]

The weaknesses of the spirit of love in solving larger and more complex problems become increasingly apparent as one proceeds from ordinary relations between individuals to the life of social groups. If nations and other

[20] Quoted by Kirk, *The Vision of God*, p. 131.

social groups find it difficult to approximate the principles of justice, as we have previously noted, they are naturally even less capable of achieving the principle of love, which demands more than justice. The demand of religious moralists that nations subject themselves to "the law of Christ" is an unrealistic demand, and the hope that they will do so is a sentimental one. Even a nation composed of individuals who possessed the highest degree of religious goodwill would be less than loving in its relation to other nations. It would fail, if for no other reason, because the individuals could not possibly think themselves into the position of the individuals of another nation in a degree sufficient to insure pure benevolence. Furthermore such goodwill as they did possess would be sluiced into loyalty to their own nation and tend to increase that nation's selfishness. This ethical paradox of patriotism will be examined more fully in another chapter. It must suffice at this point to insist upon the rather obvious fact, that no nation in history has ever been known to be purely unselfish in its actions. The same may be said of class groups with equal certainty. Religious idealism may qualify national policies, as much as rational idealism, but this qualification can never completely eliminate the selfish, brutal and antisocial elements, which express themselves in all inter-group life.

The religious idealist, confronted with these stubborn obstacles to the realisation of his ideals, is tempted either to leave the world of political and economic relations to take the course which natural impulse prompts, or to assume that his principles are influencing political life more profoundly than they really are. He is tempted, in other words, either to defeatism or to sentimentality. We have previously considered the social indifferentism which results from a too purely religious interpretation of sin. Very closely akin to this indifferentism is the defeatism which results not from a purely religious conception of good and evil but from a definition of the ideal in such pure moral terms (*i.e.*, absolute love) that the more complex political and economic relations are clearly outside of the pale of the religio-moral ideal. Religion, in short, may be indifferent toward or despair of the politico-moral problem not only when it makes an unequivocal contrast between the divine and the human but when, remaining on the human and moral level, it adopts a rigorous perfectionism in stating its moral ideal. The early church was defeatist in its attitude toward the "world," regarding the world as doomed and expressing its optimism in its millennial hopes. When these began to wane and the church was forced to assume responsibility for political and economic life, there was little disposition to challenge the basic social customs and relationships in the name of the Christian ideal. Slavery, injustice, inequality of wealth, war, these all were accepted as ordained by the "natural law" which God had devised for man's sinful state. Occasionally there was considerable confusion, whether such social arrangements, as slavery for instance, should be regarded as the fruit of man's sinful condition or as the instrument which God uses to hold sin in check. At any rate the prevailing institutions were accepted, even though the church was quite conscious of the conflict between them and its own ideal. Its natural determinism, its faith that nothing in nature or history could exist without the explicit will of God, gave additional support to this tendency. The natural law might be of a lower order than the law of the gospel, but its institutions of state and property, of war and inequality were nevertheless ordained of God. It was left to the monastics, and in Protestant times, to the sects, to incarnate the higher law. For the church, both Catholic and Protestant, the law of love was interpreted religiously rather than socially. It guaranteed equality before God, and therefore in the religious community; but this did not imply that the church would strive to realise an ideal of social justice in society. Luther in fact turned on the peasants of his day in holy horror when they attempted to transmute the "spiritual" kingdom into an "earthly" one by suggesting that the principles of the gospel had social significance.[21]

The fact that slaves had rights of equality in the early church did not aid them in improving their civil status. The church left the institution of slavery undisturbed until economic forces transmuted it into the serfdom of the Middle Ages. The fact that individual Christians manumitted their slaves proves that the principles of the gospel could inspire individuals more readily than they could prompt social and political policies. To this day religious communities and churches pride themselves on their ability to transcend economic and social inequalities within

[21] Luther incidentally managed to combine defeatism and sentimentality in his treatment of the social problem. Sometimes he suggested that all social issues would be solved if only every one would follow the golden rule. At other times he gave the world up as lost. "It is indeed true that Christians, so far as they themselves are concerned, are subject to neither law nor sword, and need neither; but just take heed to fill the world with real Christians before ruling it in a Christian and evangelical manner. This you will never accomplish for the world and the masses are and always will be unchristian." Martin Luther, *Works*, Vol. III, p. 237

the pale of their organisation; but it does not follow that
they will move vigorously against the social injustices in
the larger society which they know to be in conflict with
their religious and moral ideal.[22]

This defeatism of religion is derived from a too consistent God-world, spirit-body dualism, in which the fact,
that natural impulses in the economic and political life
move under less restraint of reason and conscience than in
the private conduct of individuals, persuades the religious
man to despair of bringing any ethical values into them
whatsoever. There is a certain realism in this defeatism,
and it has its own virtues, when compared with the sentimentality derived from a too consistent monism, in which
God and the world, the ideal and the real are identified.
If defeatism is the besetting sin of both Catholic and Protestant orthodoxy, sentimentality is the peculiar vice of
liberal Protestantism. By adjusting its faith to the spirit
of modern culture it imbibed the evolutionary optimism
and the romantic overestimates of human virtue, which
characterised the thought of the Enlightenment and of
the Romantic Movement. The vices are therefore not the
peculiar vices of religion. But religion frequently adds a
sentimental bathos to the illusions under which natural-

[22] In a letter addressed by the Bishop of London in 1727 to the masters
and mistresses of the southern colonies he allays their fears, that the conversion
of Negroes might alter their civil status, in words which are quite true to the
Christian tradition: "Christianity and the embracing of the gospel does not
make the least alteration in Civil property or in any of the duties which belong
to civil relations; but in all these respects it continues Persons just in the
same State as it found them. The Freedom which Christianity gives is freedom
from the Bondage of Sin and Satan and from the Dominion of Men's Lusts
and Passions and inordinate Desires; but as to their outward condition, whatever that was before, whether bond or free, their being baptized and becoming Christians, makes no manner of change in them." Quoted by H. Richard
Niebuhr, *Social Sources of Denominationalism*, p. 249.

istic monists live. "Ye are Gods, you are crystalline, your faces are radiant,"[23] cried Henry Ward Beecher to his congregation, illustrating how the Christian ethos may accommodate itself to naturalistic romanticism. His contemporary Walt Whitman, standing squarely in the romantic tradition, had the same estimate of the moral and spiritual worth of man: "I exist as I am: that is enough. Divine am I inside and out, and I make holy whatever I touch and am touched from."

The evolutionary optimism of the eighteenth and nineteenth century, and the sentimentalisation of the moral and social problem in romanticism, have affected religious idealism with particular force in America, because they suited the mood of a youthful and vigorous people, youth usually being oblivious of the brutality which is the inevitable concomitant of vitality. Furthermore the expanding economy of America obscured the cruelties of the class struggle in our economic life, and the comparative isolation of a continent made the brutalities of international conflict less obvious. Thus we developed a type of religious idealism, which is saturated with sentimentality. In spite of the disillusionment of the World War, the average liberal Protestant Christian is still convinced that the kingdom of God is gradually approaching, that the League of Nations is its partial fulfillment and the Kellogg Pact its covenant, that the wealthy will be persuaded by the church to dedicate their power and privilege to the common good and that they are doing so in increasing numbers, that the conversion of individuals is the only safe method of solving the social problem, and that

[23] Quoted by Constance Mayfield, *Trumpets of Jubilee*, p. 172.

such ethical weaknesses as religion still betrays are due to its theological obscurantism which will be sloughed off by the progress of enlightenment.

It might be added that when the cruelties of economic and political life are thus obscured, and when the inertia, which every effort toward social justice must meet in any society, however religious or enlightened, remains unrecognised, there is always a note of hypocrisy, as well as sentimentality, in the total view. Those who benefit from social injustice are naturally less capable of understanding its real character than those who suffer from it. They will attribute ethical qualities to social life, if only the slightest gesture of philanthropy hides social injustice. If the disinherited treat these gestures with cynicism and interpret unconscious sentimentality as conscious hypocrisy, the privileged will be properly outraged and offended by the moral perversity of the recipients of their beneficences. Since liberal Protestantism is, on the whole, the religion of the privileged classes of Western civilisation, it is not surprising that its espousal of the ideal of love, in a civilisation reeking with social injustice, should be cynically judged and convicted of hypocrisy by those in whom bitter social experiences destroy the sentimentalities and illusions of the comfortable.

Religion, in short, faces many perils to the right and to the left in becoming an instrument and inspiration of social justice. Every genuine passion for social justice will always contain a religious element within it. Religion will always leaven the idea of justice with the ideal of love. It will prevent the idea of justice, which is a politico-ethical ideal, from becoming a purely political one, with the ethical element washed out. The ethical ideal which threatens to become too purely religious must save the ethical ideal which is in peril of becoming too political. Furthermore there must always be a religious element in the hope of a just society. Without the ultrarational hopes and passions of religion no society will ever have the courage to conquer despair and attempt the impossible; for the vision of a just society is an impossible one, which can be approximated only by those who do not regard it as impossible. The truest visions of religion are illusions, which may be partially realised by being resolutely believed. For what religion believes to be true is not wholly true but ought to be true; and may become true if its truth is not doubted.

Yet the full force of religious faith will never be available for the building of a just society, because its highest visions are those which proceed from the insights of a sensitive individual conscience. If they are realised at all, they will be realised in intimate religious communities, in which individual ideals achieve social realisation but do not conquer society. To the sensitive spirit, society must always remain something of the jungle, which indeed it is, something of the world of nature, which might be brought a little nearer the kingdom of God, if only the sensitive spirit could learn, how to use the forces of nature to defeat nature, how to use force in order to establish justice. Knowing the peril of corruption in this strategy, the religious spirit recoils. If that fear can be overcome religious ideals may yet achieve social and political significance.

Meanwhile it must be admitted that no society will ever

be so just, that some method of escape from its cruelties and injustices will not be sought by the pure heart. The devotion of Christianity to the cross is an unconscious glorification of the individual moral ideal. The cross is the symbol of love triumphant in its own integrity, but not triumphant in the world and society. Society, in fact, conspired the cross. Both the state and the church were involved in it, and probably will be so to the end. The man on the cross turned defeat into victory and prophesied the day when love would be triumphant in the world. But the triumph would have to come through the intervention of God. The moral resources of men would not be sufficient to guarantee it. A sentimental generation has destroyed this apocalyptic note in the vision of the Christ. It thinks the kingdom of God is around the corner, while he regarded it as impossible of realisation, except by God's grace.

A day which confronts immediate problems of social reconstruction will have little understanding for this aspect of the religious life, this soaring of the soul beyond the possibilities of history. That appreciation can come only when the new and just society has been built, and it is discovered that it is not just. Men must strive to realise their individual ideals in their common life but they will learn in the end that society remains man's great fulfillment and his great frustration.

CHAPTER FOUR

THE MORALITY OF NATIONS

THE difference between the attitudes of individuals and those of groups has been frequently alluded to, the thesis being that group relations can never be as ethical as those which characterise individual relations. In dealing with the problem of social justice, it may be found that the relation of economic classes within a state is more important than international relations. But from the standpoint of analysing the ethics of group behavior, it is feasible to study the ethical attitudes of nations first; because the modern nation is the human group of strongest social cohesion, of most undisputed central authority and of most clearly defined membership. The church may have challenged its pre-eminence in the Middle Ages, and the economic class may compete with it for the loyalty of men in our own day; yet it remains, as it has been since the seventeenth century, the most absolute of all human associations.

Nations are territorial societies, the cohesive power of which is supplied by the sentiment of nationality and the authority of the state. The fact that state and nation are not synonymous and that states frequently incorporate several nationalities, indicates that the authority of government is the ultimate force of national cohesion. The fact that state and nation are roughly synonymous proves that, without the sentiment of nationality with its common language and traditions, the authority of government is usually unable to maintain national unity. The unity of Scotland and England within a single British state and the failure to maintain the same unity between England and Ireland, suggest both the possibilities and the limitations of transcending nationality in the formation of states. For our purposes we may think of state and nation as interchangeable terms, since our interest is in the moral attitudes of nations which have the apparatus of a state at their disposal, and through it are able to consolidate their social power and define their political attitudes and policies.

The selfishness of nations is proverbial. It was a dictum of George Washington that nations were not to be trusted beyond their own interest. "No state," declares a German author, "has ever entered a treaty for any other reason than self interest," and adds: "A statesman who has any other motive would deserve to be hung."[1] "In every part of the world," said Professor Edward Dicey, "where British interests are at stake, I am in favor of advancing these interests even at the cost of war. The only qualification I admit is that the country we desire to annex or take under our protection should be calculated to confer a tangible advantage upon the British Empire."[2] National ambitions are not always avowed as honestly as this, as we shall see later, but that is a fair statement of the actual facts, which need hardly to be elaborated for any student of history.

What is the basis and reason for the selfishness of na-

[1] Johannes Haller, *The Aera Buelow.*
[2] Quoted by Kirby Page, *National Defense,* p. 67.

tions? If we begin with what is least important or least distinctive of national attitudes, it must be noted that nations do not have direct contact with other national communities, with which they must form some kind of international community. They know the problems of other peoples only indirectly and at second hand. Since both sympathy and justice depend to a large degree upon the perception of need, which makes sympathy flow, and upon the understanding of competing interests, which must be resolved, it is obvious that human communities have greater difficulty than individuals in achieving ethical relationships. While rapid means of communication have increased the breadth of knowledge about world affairs among citizens of various nations, and the general advance of education has ostensibly promoted the capacity to think rationally and justly upon the inevitable conflicts of interest between nations, there is nevertheless little hope of arriving at a perceptible increase of international morality through the growth of intelligence and the perfection of means of communication. The development of international commerce, the increased economic interdependence among the nations, and the whole apparatus of a technological civilisation, increase the problems and issues between nations much more rapidly than the intelligence to solve them can be created. The silk trade between America and Japan did not give American citizens an appreciation of the real feelings of the Japanese toward the American Exclusion Act. Co-operation between America and the Allies during the war did not help American citizens to recognise, and deal sympathetically with, the issues of inter-allied debts and reparations; nor were the Allies able to do justice to either themselves or their fallen foe in settling the problem of reparations. Such is the social ignorance of peoples, that, far from doing justice to a foe or neighbor, they are as yet unable to conserve their own interests wisely. Since their ultimate interests are always protected best, by at least a measure of fairness toward their neighbors, the desire to gain an immediate selfish advantage always imperils their ultimate interests.[3] If they recognise this fact, they usually recognise it too late. Thus France, after years of intransigence, has finally accepted a sensible reparations settlement. Significantly and tragically, the settlement is almost synchronous with the victory of an extreme nationalism in Germany, which her unrelenting policies begot. America pursued a selfish and foolhardy tariff policy until it, together with other imbecilities in international life, contributed to the ruin of prosperity in the whole world. Britain, though her people are politically more intelligent than those of any modern nation, did not yield in Ireland in time to prevent the formation of a virus which is still poisoning Anglo-Irish relations. And while the American Civil War taught her a lesson, which she applied in preserving her colonial empire, there is as yet no proof that she will be wise enough

[3] Sometimes even the most realistic statesmen overestimate the nation's ability, wisely to prefer ultimate to immediate interests. Thus, Dr. Carl Melchior, German diplomat, thought it advisable in 1921 to accept an impossible reparations burden because "We can get through the first two or three years with the aid of foreign loans. By the end of that time foreign nations will have realised that these large payments can only be made by huge German exports and these exports will ruin the trade in England and America so that creditors themselves will come to us to request modification." Quoted by Lord D'Abernon, *An Ambassador of Peace*, Vol. I, p. 194. It required eleven years rather than two or three for the nations to realise what Dr. Melchior predicted, and even then, they did not act voluntarily.

to admit India into partnership, before the vehemence of Indian reaction to British imperialism will make partnership upon even a minimum basis impossible. So runs the sad story of the social ignorance of nations.

There is always, in every nation, a body of citizens more intelligent than the average, who see the issues between their own and other nations more clearly than the ignorant patriot, and more disinterestedly than the dominant classes who seek special advantages in international relations. The size of this group varies in different nations. Although it may at times place a check upon the more extreme types of national self-seeking, it is usually not powerful enough to affect national attitudes in a crisis. The British liberals could not prevent the Boer War; American economists have recently inveighed against a suicidal tariff policy in vain, and German liberals were unable to check the aggressive policy of imperial Germany. Sometimes the humanitarian impulses and the sentiment of justice, developed in these groups, serve the policy of official governments and seem to affect their actions. Thus the agitation of E. D. Morel against the atrocities in the Belgian Congo was supported by the British Government as long as it desired, for other reasons, to bring political pressure upon the Belgian King. Once this purpose was satisfied the British Cabinet dropped Mr. Morel's campaign as quickly as it had espoused it.[4] It is of course possible that the rational interest in international justice may become, on occasion, so widespread and influential that it will affect the diplomacy of states. But this is not usual. In other words the mind, which places

4 See Wilhelm Dibelius, *England*, p. 106.

a restraint upon impulses in individual life, exists only in
a very inchoate form in the nation. It is moreover, much
more remote from the will of the nation than in private
individuals; for the government expresses the national
will, and that will is moved by the emotions of the populace and the prudential self-interest of dominant economic
classes. Theoretically it is possible to have a national elec-
torate so intelligent, that the popular impulses and the
ulterior interests of special groups are brought under the
control of a national mind. But practically the rational
understanding of political issues remains such a minimum
force that national unity of action can be achieved only
upon such projects as are either initiated by the self-
interest of the dominant groups, in control of the government, or supported by the popular emotions and hysterias
which from time to time run through a nation. In other
words the nation is a corporate unity, held together much
more by force and emotion, than by mind. Since there
can be no ethical action without self-criticism, and no
self-criticism without the rational capacity of self-transcendence, it is natural that national attitudes can hardly
approximate the ethical. Even those tendencies toward
self-criticism in a nation which do express themselves
are usually thwarted by the governing classes and by a
certain instinct for unity in society itself. For self-criticism
is a kind of inner disunity, which the feeble mind of a
nation finds difficulty in distinguishing from dangerous
forms of inner conflict. So nations crucify their moral
rebels with their criminals upon the same Golgotha, not
being able to distinguish between the moral idealism
which surpasses, and the anti-social conduct which falls

below that moral mediocrity, on the level of which every society unifies its life. While critical loyalty toward a community is not impossible, it is not easily achieved. It is therefore probably inevitable that every society should regard criticism as a proof of a want of loyalty. This lack of criticism, as Tyrrell the Catholic modernist observed, makes the social will more egotistic than the individual will. "So far as society has a self," he wrote, "it must be self-assertive, proud, self-complacent and egotistical."[5]

The necessity of using force in the establishment of unity in a national community, and the inevitable selfish exploitation of the instruments of coercion by the groups who wield them, adds to the selfishness of nations. This factor in national life has been previously discussed and may need no further elaboration. It may be well to add that it ought not to be impossible to reduce this source of national selfishness. When governing groups are deprived of their special economic privileges, their interests will be more nearly in harmony with the interests of the total national society. At present the economic overlords of a nation have special interests in the profits of international trade, in the exploitation of weaker peoples and in the acquisition of raw materials and markets, all of which are only remotely relevant to the welfare of the whole people. They are relevant at all only because, under the present organisation of society, the economic life of a whole nation is bound up with the private enterprises of individuals. Furthermore the unequal distribution of wealth under the present economic system concentrates wealth which cannot be invested, and produces goods which can-

[5] Quoted by Harold Laski, *Authority in the Modern State*, p. 274.

not be absorbed, in the nation itself. The whole nation is therefore called upon to protect the investments and the markets which the economic overlords are forced to seek in other nations. If a socialist commonwealth should succeed in divorcing privilege from power, it would thereby materially reduce the selfishness of nations, though it is probably romantic to hope, as most socialists do, that all causes of international friction would be abolished. Wars were waged before the modern capitalistic social order existed, and they may continue af.er it is abolished. The greed of the capitalistic classes has sharpened, but not created, the imperialism of nations. If, as Bertrand Russell prophesies,[6] some form of oligarchy, whether capitalistic or communistic, be inevitable in a technological age, because of the inability of the general public to maintain social control over the experts who are in charge of the intricate processes of economics and politics, the communistic oligarch would seem to be preferable in the long run to the capitalistic one. His power would be purely political, and no special economic interests would tempt him to pursue economic policies at variance with the national interest. He might nevertheless have private ambitions and dreams of grandeur which would tempt him to sacrifice a nation to them. Since he would control the organs of propaganda, as do the capitalistic overlords, he might very well manufacture the popular emotion, required for the support of his enterprise.

The social ignorance of the private citizen of the nation has thus far been assumed. It may be reasonable to hope that the general level of intelligence will greatly increase

6 See Bertrand Russell, *The Scientific Outlook*, Chap. XI.

in the next decades and centuries and that growing social intelligence will modify national attitudes. It is doubtful whether it will ever increase sufficiently to eliminate all the moral hazards of international relations. There is an ethical paradox in patriotism which defies every but the most astute and sophisticated analysis. The paradox is that patriotism transmutes individual unselfishness into national egoism. Loyalty to the nation is a high form of altruism when compared with lesser loyalties and more parochial interests. It therefore becomes the vehicle of all the altruistic impulses and expresses itself, on occasion, with such fervor that the critical attitude of the individual toward the nation and its enterprises is almost completely destroyed. The unqualified character of this devotion is the very basis of the nation's power and of the freedom to use the power without moral restraint. Thus the un-selfishness of individuals makes for the selfishness of nations. That is why the hope of solving the larger social problems of mankind, merely by extending the social sympathies of individuals, is so vain. Altruistic passion is sluiced into the reservoirs of nationalism with great ease, and is made to flow beyond them with great difficulty. What lies beyond the nation, the community of mankind, is too vague to inspire devotion. The lesser communities within the nation, religious, economic, racial and cultural, have equal difficulty in competing with the nation for the loyalty of its citizens. The church was able to do so when it had the prestige of a universality it no longer possesses. Future developments may make the class rather than the nation the community of primary loyalty. But for the present the nation is still supreme. It not only possesses a police power, which other communities lack, but it is able to avail itself of the most potent and vivid symbols to impress its claims upon the consciousness of the individual. Since it is impossible to become conscious of a large social group without adequate symbolism this factor is extremely important. The nation possesses in its organs of government, in the panoply and ritual of the state, in the impressive display of its fighting services, and, very frequently, in the splendors of a royal house, the symbols of unity and greatness, which inspire awe and reverence in the citizen. Furthermore the love and pious attachment of a man to his countryside, to familiar scenes, sights, and experiences, around which the memories of youth have cast a halo of sanctity, all this flows into the sentiment of patriotism; for a simple imagination transmutes the universal beneficences of nature into symbols of the peculiar blessings which a benevolent nation bestows upon its citizens. Thus the sentiment of patriotism achieves a potency in the modern soul, so unqualified, that the nation is given *carte blanche* to use the power, compounded of the devotion of individuals, for any purpose it desires. Thus, to choose an example among hundreds, Mr. Lloyd George during the famous Agadir Crisis in 1911 in which a European war became imminent, because marauding nations would not allow a new robber to touch their spoils in Africa, could declare in his Mansion House speech: "If a situation were to be forced upon us in which peace could only be preserved by the surrender of the great and beneficent position Britain has won by centuries of heroism and achievement, by allowing Britain to be treated, when her interests were vitally affected, as if she were of no account in the cabinet of nations, then I say emphatically that peace at that price would be a humiliation intolerable for a great country like ours to endure."[7] The very sensitive "honor" of nations can always be appeased by the blood of its citizens and no national ambition seems too base or petty to claim and to receive the support of a majority of its patriots.

Unquestionably there is an alloy of projected self-interest in patriotic altruism. The man in the street, with his lust for power and prestige thwarted by his own limitations and the necessities of social life, projects his *ego* upon his nation and indulges his anarchic lusts vicariously. So the nation is at one and the same time a check upon, and a final vent for, the expression of individual egoism. Sometimes it is economic interest, and sometimes mere vanity, which thus expresses itself in the individual patriot. Writing of his friend, Winston Churchill, Wilfrid Scawen Blunt said: "Like most of them, it is the vanity of empire that affects him more than the supposed profits or the necessities of trade, which he repudiates."[8] The cultural imperialism which disavows economic advantages, but gains a selfish satisfaction in the aggrandisement of a national culture through imperialistic power, may reveal itself in the most refined and generous souls. Men like Ruskin and Tennyson were not free from it, and it is not absent even from religious missionary enterprises. Paul Pfeffer reports that some Russians hope not only to bestow their form of government upon the whole world but expect that Russian will become the universal

[7] Quoted by G. Lowes Dickinson, *International Anarchy*, p. 34.
[8] Quoted by Kirby Page, *National Defense*, p. 28.

language.[9] While economic advantages of national aggression usually accrue to privileged economic groups rather than to a total population, there are nevertheless possibilities of gain in imperialism for the average citizen; and he does not fail to count upon them. A modern British writer on India declares: "It has been computed that every fifth man in Great Britain is dependent, either directly or indirectly, on our Indian connection for livelihood. That being so it passes comprehension of most thinking people why so little account has been taken of the dangerous forces which are every day gathering in India to destroy our trade and commerce."[10] Such a frank statement admits the motive of national egoism which is usually obscured by English, as by other imperialists, with the pious insistence that nothing but concern for peace and order in India prompts Englishmen to bear their arduous burdens there.

A combination of unselfishness and vicarious selfishness in the individual thus gives a tremendous force to national egoism, which neither religious nor rational idealism can ever completely check. The idealists, whose patriotism has been qualified by more universal loyalties, must always remain a minority group. In the past they have not been strong enough to affect the actions of nations and have had to content themselves with a policy of disassociation from the nation in times of crisis, when national ambitions were in sharpest conflict with their moral ideals. Whether conscientious pacifism on the part of two per cent of a national population could actually

[9] *Cf.* Paul Pfeffer, *Seven Years in Soviet Russia.*
[10] Geoffrey Tyson, *Danger in India.*

prevent future wars, as Professor Einstein maintains, is a question which cannot be answered affirmatively with any great degree of certainty. It is much more likely that the power of modern nationalism will remain essentially unchecked, until class loyalty offers it effective competition.

Perhaps the most significant moral characteristic of a nation is its hypocrisy. We have noted that self-deception and hypocrisy is an unvarying element in the moral life of all human beings. It is the tribute which morality pays to immorality; or rather the device by which the lesser self gains the consent of the larger self to indulge in impulses and ventures which the rational self can approve only when they are disguised. One can never be quite certain whether the disguise is meant only for the eye of the external observer or whether, as may be usually the case, it deceives the self. Naturally this defect in individuals becomes more apparent in the less moral life of nations. Yet it might be supposed that nations, of whom so much less is expected, would not be under the necessity of making moral pretensions for their actions. There was probably a time when they were under no such necessity. Their hypocrisy is both a tribute to the growing rationality of man and a proof of the ease with which rational demands may be circumvented.

The dishonesty of nations is a necessity of political policy if the nation is to gain the full benefit of its double claim upon the loyalty and devotion of the individual, as his own special and unique community and as a community which embodies universal values and ideals. The two claims, the one touching the individual's emotions and the other appealing to his mind, are incompatible with each other, and can be resolved only through dishonesty. This is particularly evident in war-time. Nations do not really arrive at full self-consciousness until they stand in vivid, usually bellicose, juxtaposition to other nations. The social reality, comprehended in the existence of a nation, is too large to make a vivid impression upon the imagination of the citizen. He vaguely identifies it with his own little community and fireside and usually accepts the mythos which attributes personality to his national group. But the impression is not so vivid as to arouse him to any particular fervor of devotion. This fervor is the unique product of the times of crisis, when his nation is in conflict with other nations. It springs from the new vividness with which the reality and the unity of his nation's discreet existence is comprehended. In other words, it is just in the moments when the nation is engaged in aggression or defense (and it is always able to interpret the former in terms of the latter) that the reality of the nation's existence becomes so sharply outlined as to arouse the citizen to the most passionate and uncritical devotion toward it. But at such a time the nation's claim to uniqueness also comes in sharpest conflict with the generally accepted impression that the nation is the incarnation of universal values. This conflict can be resolved only by deception. In the imagination of the simple patriot the nation is not a society but Society. Though its values are relative they appear, from his naïve perspective, to be absolute. The religious instinct for the absolute is no less potent in patriotic religion than in any other. The nation is always endowed with an aura of the sacred, which is one reason

why religions, which claim universality, are so easily cap-
tured and tamed by national sentiment, religion and patriotism merging in the process. The spirit of the nationally
established churches and the cult of "Christentum und
Deutschtum" of pre-war Germany are interesting examples. The best means of harmonising the claim to universality with the unique and relative life of the nation,
as revealed in moments of crisis, is to claim general and
universally valid objectives for the nation. It is alleged to
be fighting for civilisation and for culture; and the whole
enterprise of humanity is supposedly involved in its struggles. In the life of the simple citizen this hypocrisy exists
as a naïve and unstudied self-deception. The politician
practices it consciously (though he may become the victim of his own arts), in order to secure the highest devotion
from the citizen for his enterprises. The men of culture
give themselves to it with less conscious design than the
statesmen because their own inner necessities demand the
deceptions, even more than do those of the simple citizens.
The religious or the rational culture to which they are
devoted helps them to realise that moral values must be
universal, if they are to be real; and they cannot therefore give themselves to national aspirations, unless they
clothe them in the attributes of universality. A few of
them recognise the impossibility of such a procedure.
Among most, the force of reason operates only to give
the hysterias of war and the imbecilities of national politics
more plausible excuses than an average man is capable
of inventing. So they become the worst liars of war-time.
"England," declared Professor Adolf Harnack, most eminent of German war-period theologians, "cuts the dyke

which has preserved western Europe and its civilisation from the encroaching desert of Russia and Pan-Slavism. We must hold out for we must defend the work of fifteen hundred years for Europe and for England itself."[11] The great philosopher Rudolf Eucken was even more unequivocal in identifying his nation's cause with ultimate values. "In this sense," he said, "we have a right to say that we form the soul of humanity and that the destruction of German nature would rob world history of its deepest meaning."[12] M. Paul Sabatier could declare, "No doubt we are fighting for ourselves but we are fighting, too, for all peoples. The France of today is fighting religiously. . . . We all feel that our sorrows continue and fulfill those of the innocent victim of Calvary."[13] The literature of the war period teems with similar examples of the self-deception of intellectuals. There is always the possibility that some of it was prompted by dishonest truckling to the hysteria of the populace and the pressure of governments. But most of it was not as dishonest as that.

Hardly any war of history has been the occasion of more hypocrisy and sentimentality than the Spanish-American War. Yet as intelligent a man as Walter Hines Page could extract the following pious moral from it: "May there not come such a chance in Mexico—to clean out the bandits, yellow fever, malaria, hookworm—all to make the country healthful, safe for life and investment and for orderly self-government, at last? What we did in Cuba might thus be made the beginning of a new epoch

11 Quoted by Kirby Page, *National Defense*, p. 148.
12 *Ibid.*, p. 149.
13 *Ibid.*, p. 152. Mr. Page has gathered innumerable similar examples in Chapter IX of his book.

in history, conquest for the sole benefit of the conquered, worked out by a sanitary reformation. The new sanitation will reclaim all tropical lands; but the work must first be done by military power—probably from the outside. May not the existing military power of Europe conceivably be diverted to this use? . . . And the tropics cry out for sanitation."[14] Perhaps it is rather significant that the American idea of a universal value should express itself in terms of sanitation.

The Spanish-American War offers some of the most striking illustrations of the hypocrisy of governments as well as of the self-deception of intellectuals. The hypocrisy was probably excessive, because a youthful and politically immature nation tried to harmonise the anti-imperialistic innocency of its childhood with the imperial impulses of its awkward youth. It was just beginning to feel and to test its strength and was both proud and ashamed of what it felt. President McKinley's various state papers and addresses are a perfect mine for the cynic. In a message to Congress before the outbreak of hostilities, he declared: "If it shall hereafter appear to be a duty imposed by our obligations to ourselves, to civilisation and humanity to intervene with force it shall be done without fault on our part and only because the necessity for such action will be so clear as to command the support and the approval of the civilised world." He added: "I speak not of forcible annexation for that cannot be thought of. That by our code of morals would be criminal aggression."[15] When the amiable President was finally pushed into the war by

[14] Quoted by Parker Moon, *Imperialism and World Politics*, p. 422.
[15] Quoted by Walter Millis, *The Martial Spirit*, p. 90.

our passionate patriots, though Spain yielded to all of our demands, he answered a "pressing appeal to the feelings of humanity and moderation in the President and people of the United States" from the powers of Europe which sought to avert war by conciliation, by expressing the hope "that equal appreciation will be shown for our own earnest efforts and unselfish endeavors to fulfill a duty to humanity by ending a situation, the indefinite prolongation of which has become insufferable."[16] The war was launched on a wave of patriotic sentimentality in which both the religious idealists and the humanitarians went into ecstasies over our heroic defense of the Cuban people, forgetting that many American statesmen, beginning with the anti-imperialist Thomas Jefferson, had regarded the Spanish hold upon so proximate an island as Cuba as ultimately untenable. The actual annexation of Cuba was prevented only by the fact that the Teller Amendment, disavowing such an aim, was slipped unobserved into the Senate resolution which authorised hostilities.[17]

Since no promises were made in regard to the Philippines, the hypocrisy of a nation could express itself most unrestrainedly in the policies dealing with them. Though the little junta, of which Theodore Roosevelt and Senator Lodge were the leaders, had carefully planned the campaign of war so that the Philippines would become ours, the fiction that the fortunes of war had made us the unwilling recipients and custodians of the Philippine Islands was quickly fabricated and exists to this day. We decided to keep the Philippines against their will at the conclusion of a war ostensibly begun to free the Cubans,

16 *Ibid.*, p. 136.　　　　　　　17 *Ibid.*, p. 143.

The President charged the peace commission which was to negotiate the peace treaty with Spain that it "should be as scrupulous and magnanimous in the concluding settlement as the nation had been just and humane in the original action." Since we constantly increased our demands during the session of the peace conference, the Spaniards must have gained a curious impression of the meaning of magnanimity. In regard to the Philippines the President charged the commissioners: "The march of events rules and overrules human action. We cannot be unmindful that without any design on our part the war has brought us new responsibilities and duties which we must meet and discharge as becomes a great nation on whose growth and career from the beginning the Ruler of Nations has plainly written the high command and pledge of civilisation."[18] When after a great deal of negotiation among the commissioners and much debate between imperialists and anti-imperialists in America it was finally decided to ask for all of the Philippines, Secretary Hay wrote to the commissioners: "You are instructed to insist on the cession of the whole of the Philippines. . . . The questions of duty and humanity appeal to the President so strongly that he can find no appropriate answer but the one he has marked out."[19] There were American citizens, of course, who saw through all of this hypocrisy. "Why," declared Mr. Moorfield Storey, one of the great liberal spirits of that day, "should Cuba with 1,600,000 people have a right to freedom and self-government and the 8,000,000 people who dwell in the Philippines be denied the same right?"[20] But these crit-

[18] *Ibid.*, p. 374.   [19] *Ibid.*, p. 387.   [20] *Ibid.*, p. 254.

ics were not strong enough to prevail against the will-to-power of a vigorous young nation. The instructions to the army, after Spain finally ceded the islands and the peace treaty was signed, complete the chapter in hypocrisy with an almost perfect touch of dishonesty: "It will be the duty of the commander of the forces of occupation to announce and proclaim in the most public manner possible that we have come not as invaders or as conquerors but as friends."[21]

Later Mr. McKinley explained to a group of clergymen just how he arrived at his decision on American policy: "I walked the floor of the White House night after night until midnight; and I am not ashamed to tell you gentlemen that I went on my knees and prayed to Almighty God for light and guidance more than one night. And one night it came to me this way—that there was nothing left for us to do but to take them all, and to educate the Filipinos, and uplift and civilise and Christianise them, and by God's grace do the very best we could by them, as our fellowmen for whom Christ also died. And then I went to bed and went to sleep and slept soundly."[22]

America has not been altogether disobedient to Mr. McKinley's heavenly vision, for it has done a rather creditable job of education and sanitation in the islands. Nevertheless a modern observer of western imperialism in the orient, Nathaniel Peffer, gives a truer estimate than Mr. McKinley of the real motives of imperialism when he observes cynically: "Much might be said of their fitness for self-government, but why? What does it mat-

[21] *Ibid.*, p. 396.   [22] *Ibid.*, p. 384.

ter? The Filipinos will seize the government and proclaim themselves independent tomorrow if they had the
power, And if and when they have the power, they will,
whether fit for self-government or not. And were they
as politically wise as Solons, the American Government
would not give them their independence now, nor a hundred years from now, if American interests were to lose
thereby."[23] Mr. Peffer's observations have received very
recent verification by the fact that a new sentiment in
favor of Philippine independence is prompted by the desire of American sugar interests to place Philippine sugar
outside of the American tariff wall.

Mr. McKinley's hypocrisies were a little more than
usually naïve. But they could be fairly well matched in
the history of other statesmen and nations. Mr. Gladstone was as pious and upright a statesman as Mr. Mc-
Kinley, and probably more intelligent. He was, as Mc-
Kinley, anti-imperialist by conviction. When the occupation of Egypt was forced upon him, he was anxious to
preserve the guise, and perhaps even the reality, of his
anti-imperial policy. He declared "Of all things in the
world, that (permanent occupation) is the thing we are
not going to do." The army was to be withdrawn "as
soon as the state of the country and the organisation of
the proper means for the maintenance of the khedive's
authority will admit of it." This pledge, said Gladstone,
was a sacred pledge. It had "earned for us the confidence
of Europe during the course of this difficult and delicate
operation, and which, if one pledge can be more sacred
than another, special sacredness in this case binds us to

[23] Nathaniel Peffer, *The White Man's Dilemma,* p. 228.

fulfill."[24] Nevertheless Gladstone did not fulfill it, and it has not been fulfilled since. The failure to do so is now proudly exhibited by Englishmen as an example of the British genius for "muddling through." At an earlier date when Kitchener was conquering the Sudan and came into conflict with the French General Marchand at Fashoda, Lord Rosebery declared in an address "I hope that this incident will be pacifically settled but it must be understood that there can be no compromise of the rights of Egypt."[25] The height of national hypocrisy was probably reached in the Preamble of the Treaty of the Holy Alliance in which the reactionary intentions of Russia, Prussia and Austria in forming the alliance are introduced in words reeking with dishonest religious unction: "Their Majesties solemnly declare . . . their unshakable resolution . . . to take as their sole rule the precepts of holy Religion, precepts of righteousness, Christian love and peace. . . . Consequently their Majesties have agreed, conformable to the words of Holy Writ which command all men to regard one another as brethren, to remain united by the bonds of a true and indissoluble brotherhood, and to help one another like fellow countrymen in all conditions and all cases. Towards their peoples and their armies they will behave as fathers to their families and they will guide them in the same spirit of brotherliness as that which inspires themselves. . . . The three allied sovereigns feel themselves but the plenipotentiaries of Providence for the government of the three branches of the same family. . . . All powers that solemnly subscribe to these principles will be received into

[24] Parker Moon, *Imperialism and World Politics*, p. 228. [25] *Ibid.*, p. 153.

this Holy Alliance." This document is particularly interesting because its sentiments betray the hand of that mystic sentimentalist, Czar Alexander of Russia, but the man
who engineered the political deals which it is supposed
to sanctify was the cynic and realist, Metternich. Somewhat in the same fashion the realities of the Treaty of
Versailles were dictated by Clemenceau, while Wilson
supplied the garnish of sentiment and idealism. No
nation has ever made a frank avowal of its real imperial motives. It always claims to be primarily concerned
with the peace and prosperity of the people whom it
subjugates. In the Treaty of 1907 in which Russia and
England partitioned Persia, the two nations promised
to "respect the integrity and independence of Persia"
and claimed to be "sincerely desiring the preservation
of order throughout the country."[26] When Spain and
France divided Morocco they joined in a statement in
which they professed themselves "firmly attached to the
integrity of the Moorish Empire under the sovereignty
of the Sultan."[27] Most of the treaties by which the European nations have divided the spoils of empire are text-
books in hypocrisy. One can never be sure how much
they are meant to fool the outside world, how much they
are meant for the deception of their own deluded na-
tionals, and how much they are meant to heal a moral
breach in the inner life of statesmen, who find themselves torn between the necessities of statecraft and the
sometimes sensitive promptings of an individual conscience. In men like McKinley, Gladstone, Woodrow
Wilson, Herbert Asquith and Sir Edward Grey and

[26] *Ibid.*, p. 279.   [27] *Ibid.*, p. 201.

Bethmann-Hollweg the latter element is quite important.

Our imperialistic policy in Latin-America and the Caribbean, which, as every historian knows, differs from the imperialism of European nations only in that it is slightly less military and more obviously commercial (though of course we are always ready to use our naval power when the occasion warrants), was given the halo of moral sanctity by Secretary Hughes in an address in 1924: "We are aiming not to exploit but to aid; not to subvert, but to help in laying the foundations for a sound, stable and independent government. Our interest does not lie in controlling foreign peoples. . . . Our interest is in having prosperous, peaceful and law abiding neighbors."[28] Such sentiments have been repeated innumerable times by American statesmen, in spite of the fact that every impartial history clearly records the economic motives which prompt our policies in our relation to our southern neighbors. The various messages of President Coolidge in which he dealt with the difficult problems of post-war readjustment were, almost without exception, marvellous examples of sanctimonious hypocrisy. Europe was constantly assured, for instance, that our only interest in post-war debt settlements was to preserve the sanctity of covenants and to prevent European nations from falling into slovenly business habits.

Moralists who have observed and animadverted upon the hypocrisy of nations have usually assumed that a more perfect social intelligence, which could penetrate and analyse these evasions and deceptions, would make them ultimately impossible. But here again they are

[28] *Ibid.*, p. 407.

counting on moral and rational resources which will never be available. What was not possible in 1914–1918, when the world was submerged in dishonesties and hypocrisies (the Treaty of Versailles, with its pledge of disarmament and the self-righteous moral conviction of the vanquished by the victors, being the crowning example), will hardly become possible in a decade or in a century, or in many centuries. Nations will always find it more difficult than individuals to behold the beam that is in their own eye while they observe the mote that is in their brother's eye; and individuals find it difficult enough. A perennial weakness of the moral life in individuals is simply raised to the nth degree in national life. Let a nation be accused of hypocrisy and it shrinks back in pious horror at the charge. When President Wilson addressed a peace communication to the belligerent powers in 1916 and with delicate irony, "took the liberty of calling attention to the fact that the objects which the statesmen of the belligerents on both sides have in mind in this war are virtually the same as stated to their own people and to the world," Lord Northcliffe reported that everybody in England was "mad as hell," that Lord Robert Cecil was "deeply hurt," and that the King actually broke down in pain over the suggestion.[29] In 1927 Senator Hiram Johnson, stung by European strictures of American hypocrisy and greed, declared "In all their long sordid international careers of blood and conquest, these nations that call America Shylock and swine, that sneer at our pretensions and deride our acts, have never done an idealistic, altruistic or unselfish international deed. Ever their

[29] Charles and Mary Beard, *Rise of American Civilization*, Bk. II, p. 629.

cry has been for more land and new peoples and . . . where sinister diplomacy has failed blood and iron have subdued the weak and helpless. . . . Whatever our faults, and they are mostly internal, the United States is the only nation on earth that in its international relations has ever displayed either idealism or altruism. . . . The United States has written an international policy in deeds of generosity and mercy and written indelibly thus the answer to Europe's gibes and jeers."[30] It would be interesting to add that the author of these remarks was particularly active in passing the Japanese Exclusion Act.

Perhaps the best that can be expected of nations is that they should justify their hypocrisies by a slight measure of real international achievement, and learn how to do justice to wider interests than their own, while they pursue their own. England, which has frequently been accused by continental nations of mastering the arts of national self-righteousness with particular skill, may have accomplished this, partly because there is actually a measure of genuine humanitarian interest in British policy. The Italian statesman, Count Sforza, has recently paid a witty and deserved tribute to the British art in politics. They have, he declares, "a precious gift bestowed by divine grace upon the British people: the simultaneous action in those islands, when a great British interest is at stake, of statesmen and diplomats coolly working to obtain some concrete political advantage and on the other side, and without previous base secret understanding, clergymen and writers eloquently busy showing the highest moral reasons for supporting the diplomatic ac-

[30] Quoted by Kirby Page, *National Defense*, p. 196.

tion which is going on in Downing Street. Such was the
case in the Belgian Congo. Belgian rule had been in force
there for years; but at a certain moment gold was discovered in the Katanga, the Congolese province nearest
to the British South African possessions; and the bishops
and other pious persons started at once a violent press
campaign to stigmatise the Belgian atrocities against the
Negroes. What is astonishing and really imperial is that
those bishops and other pious persons were inspired by
the most perfect Christian good faith, and that nobody
was pulling the wires behind them."[31] Another foreign
critic and observer of English life, Wilhelm Dibelius, believes that there is justification for the moral pretensions
of Britain: "England," he declares, "is the solitary power
with a national programme, which while egotistic through
and through, at the same time promises to the world as
a whole, something which the world passionately desires, order, progress and eternal peace. . . . None of
them (the other powers) have as yet succeeded in setting up, against the British ideal, an ideal of their own,
national and international at the same time, as the British."[32] What Britain has achieved, if we are to take Doctor Dibelius' word for it, is probably the best that can be
expected of any nation. It is questionable whether her
achievement is great enough to make the attainment of
international justice, without conflict, possible. Of that
India is an example. In spite of the solid achievement of
Britain in India, her imperialism there has been covered
with the cant and hypocrisy which all nations affect;

[31] Count Carlo Sforza, *European Dictatorship*, p. 178.
[32] Wilhelm Dibelius, *England*, p. 109.

and it is obvious that India will gain a full partnership in the British Empire only as she is able to exert some kind of force against British imperialism.

If it is true that the nations are too selfish and morally too obtuse and self-righteous to make the attainment of international justice without the use of force possible, the question arises whether there is a possibility of escape from the endless round of force avenging ancient wrongs and creating new ones, of victorious Germany creating a vindictive France and victorious France poisoning Germany with a sense of outraged justice. The morality of nations is such that, if there be a way out, it is not as easy as the moralists of both the pre-war and post-war period have assumed.

Obviously one method of making force morally redemptive is to place it in the hands of a community, which transcends the conflicts of interest between individual nations and has an impartial perspective upon them. That method resolves many conflicts within national communities, and the organisation of the League of Nations is ostensibly the extension of that principle to international life. But if powerful classes in national societies corrupt the impartiality of national courts, it may be taken for granted that a community of nations, in which very powerful and very weak nations are bound together, has even less hope of achieving impartiality. Furthermore the prestige of the international community is not great enough, and it does not sufficiently qualify the will-to-power of individual nations, to achieve a communal spirit sufficiently unified, to discipline recalcitrant nations. Thus Japan was able to violate her covenants in her conquest of Manchuria, because she shrewdly assumed that the seeming solidarity of the League of Nations was not real, and that it only thinly veiled without restraining the peculiar policies of various great powers, which she would be able to tempt and exploit. Her assumption proved correct, and she was able to win the quasi-support of France and to weaken the British support of League policies. Her success in breaking her covenants with impunity has thrown the weakness of our inchoate society of nations into vivid light. This weakness, also revealed in the failure of the recent Disarmament Conference and the abortive character of all efforts to resolve the anarchy of national tariffs, justifies the pessimistic conclusion that there is not yet a political force capable of bringing effective social restraint upon the self-will of nations, at least not upon the powerful nations. Even if it should be possible to maintain peace on the basis of the international *status quo,* there is no evidence that an unjust peace can be adjusted by pacific means. A society of nations has not really proved itself until it is able to grant justice to those who have been worsted in battle without requiring them to engage in new wars to redress their wrongs.

Since the class character of national governments is a primary, though not the only cause of their greed, present international anarchy may continue until the fear of catastrophe amends, or catastrophe itself destroys, the present social system and builds more co-operative national societies. There may not be enough intelligence in modern society to prevent catastrophe. There is certainly not enough intelligence to prompt our generation to a voluntary reorganisation of society, unless the fear of imminent catastrophe quickens the tempo of social change.

The sharpening of class antagonisms within each modern industrial nation is increasingly destroying national unity and imperilling international comity as well. It may be that the constant growth of economic inequality and social injustice in our industrial civilisation will force the nations into a final conflict, which is bound to end in their destruction. The disintegration of national loyalties through class antagonisms has proceeded so far in the more advanced nations, that they can hardly dare to permit the logic inherent in the present situation to take its course. Conditions in these nations, particularly in Germany where the forces and factors which operate in modern civilisation may be seen in clearest outline, reveal what desperate devices are necessary for the preservation of even a semblance of national unity and how these very devices seem to make for an international conflict in which the last semblance of that unity will be destroyed. If the possibilities and perils of the contemporary situation are to be fully understood it will be necessary to study the class antagonism within the nations carefully and estimate their importance for the future of civilisation.

CHAPTER FIVE

THE ETHICAL ATTITUDES OF PRIVILEGED CLASSES

ECONOMIC and social classes within a state do not possess, or have not possessed, the authority, inner cohesion and sharply defined reality of the nation. It is therefore more difficult and less accurate to speak of the attitudes and actions of classes. The significant actions of classes in the past have been determined by the attitudes of individuals who were actuated, not so much by a sense of loyalty to the class, as by individual interests which were identical with the individual interests of others who possessed or lacked the same social privileges, and who could therefore make common cause in defense of their common interests. Classes may be formed on the basis of common functions in society, but they do not become sharply distinguished until function is translated into privilege. Thus professional classes may be distinguished by certain psychological characteristics from other middle-class groups; but these psychological distinctions will be ultimately insignificant in comparison with the common political attitudes which professional groups will have with other middle-class groups on the basis of their similar social and economic privileges. "The diversities in the faculties of men," declared James Madison, "from which the rights of property originate, are . . . an insuperable obstacle to uniformity of interests. The protection of these faculties is the first object of government. From the protection of different and unequal faculties of acquiring property, the possession of different degrees and kinds of property immediately results; and from the influence of these on the sentiments and views of the respective proprietors ensues a division of society into different interests and parties."[1] This is a correct analysis of the economic basis of political attitudes, except that too great a significance is attached to inequality of faculty as the basis of inequality of privilege. Differences in faculty and function do indeed help to originate inequality of privilege but they never justify the degree of inequality created, and they are frequently not even relevant to the type of inequality perpetuated in a social system.

What is important for our consideration is that inequalities of social privilege develop in every society, and that these inequalities become the basis of class divisions and class solidarity. We have previously seen that inequalities of privilege are due chiefly to disproportions of power, and that the power which creates privilege need not be economic but usually is. In modern Japan there is still a class of militarists with social and political prestige greater than that of the economically powerful groups. Their power and prestige rest upon feudal traditions in which martial strength and glory outweighs purely economic power. In modern Russia a class may be developing which depends for its power not upon economic strength but upon its ability to manipulate the processes of the state. In modern capitalistic society the significant social power is the power which inheres in the ownership of the means of production; and it is that power which is able to arrogate special social privilege to itself.

[1] Charles Beard, *The Economic Basis of Politics*, p. 31–32.

Varying political convictions and social attitudes depend upon the degree of social power and economic privilege possessed by varying classes. Naturally the chief difference will be between those who own property and those who do not. There will be minor distinctions, however, within these two groups which tend to obscure the major division when viewed from certain perspectives. Thus landholders may have interests which diverge from, and social policies which conflict with, those of the owners of industrial capital until the moment of crisis when all property is under attack or until the two types of property and ownership merge. Industrial workers may find their proletarian class bifurcated and the more privileged skilled workers may not on all occasions make common cause with the unskilled. The insistence of those who strive for proletarian class unity, that there ought not be such a division among industrial workers, will not necessarily establish complete unity. Such unity would be an ethical achievement, attained in defiance of the immediate interests of the more privileged proletarian group, though it might be compatible with their ultimate interests. The class standing between the owners and the workers, composed of professional people, clerks, small retailers and bureaucrats, is ambiguous in membership and social outlook. Whether its position is ultimately untenable and where, in the event of its dissolution, it will cast its lot, whether with the owners or with the workers, are questions which still arouse a great deal of speculation. The answer to them may contain the clue to the riddle of the future of western civilisation. But about that more shall be said later. Modern economic classes are, at the same time, more self-conscious and less sharply defined than the social classes of the Middle Ages. The forces of a technological civilisation, which give classes organs of cohesion and self-expression, also tend to confuse the economic circumstances which create class distinctions, with an endless variety of differentiated function and corresponding differences of privilege.

Whatever may be the degree of the self-consciousness of classes, the social and ethical outlook of members of given classes is invariably colored, if not determined, by the unique economic circumstances which each class has as a common possession. This fact, regarded as axiomatic by economists, still fails to impress most moral theorists and ethical idealists. The latter, with their too unqualified confidence in the capacity of religious or rational idealism, persist in hoping that some force of reason and conscience can be created, powerful enough to negate or to transcend the economic interests which are basic to class divisions. The whole history of humanity is proof of the futility of this hope. The development of rational and moral resources may indeed qualify the social and ethical outlook, but it cannot destroy the selfishness of classes. Moral idealism must express itself within the limits of the imagination by which men recognise the true character of their own motives and the validity of interests which compete with their own. The imagination of very few men is acute enough to accomplish this so thoroughly that the selfish motive is adequately discounted and the interests of others are fully understood. So-called idealism therefore tends to confuse political and social issues more frequently than it clarifies them. For when tender moral sentiments express themselves within the limits of a social organisation, which violates the highest ethical principles, it adds to the moral confusion of peoples.

The moral attitudes of dominant and privileged groups are characterised by universal self-deception and hypocrisy. The unconscious and conscious identification of their special interests with general interests and universal values, which we have noted in analysing national attitudes, is equally obvious in the attitude of classes. The reason why privileged classes are more hypocritical than underprivileged ones is that special privilege can be defended in terms of the rational ideal of equal justice only, by proving that it contributes something to the good of the whole. Since inequalities of privilege are greater than could possibly be defended rationally, the intelligence of privileged groups is usually applied to the task of inventing specious proofs for the theory that universal values spring from, and that general interests are served by, the special privileges which they hold.

The most common form of hypocrisy among the privileged classes is to assume that their privileges are the just payments with which society rewards specially useful or meritorious functions. As long as society regards special rewards for important services as ethically just and socially necessary (and the reversion of equalitarian Russia to this principle of unequal rewards suggests that it will not be easily abrogated), it is always possible for social privilege to justify itself, at least in its own eyes, in terms of the social function which it renders. If the argument is to be plausible, when used by privileged classes who possess hereditary advantages, it must be proved or assumed that the underprivileged classes would not have the capacity of rendering the same service if given the same opportunity. This assumption is invariably made by privileged classes. The educational advantages which privilege buys, and the opportunities for the exercise of authority which come with privileged social position, develop capacities which are easily attributed to innate endowment. The presence of able men among the privileged is allowed to obscure the number of instances in which hereditary privilege is associated with knavery and incompetence. On the other hand it has always been the habit of privileged groups to deny the oppressed classes every opportunity for the cultivation of innate capacities and then to accuse them of lacking what they have been denied the right to acquire. The struggle for universal education in the nineteenth century prompted the same kind of arguments from the privileged in every country. The poor were incapable of enjoying the benefits of education, and if they secured it they would make too good use of it by resisting the exactions of their oppressors more successfully. When the bill which provided for supported schools was before the English Parliament in 1807, a Mr. Giddy, afterward President of the Royal Society, raised objections which could be matched in every country: "However specious in theory the project might be of giving education to the laboring classes of the poor, it would be prejudicial to their morals and happiness; it would teach them to despise their lot in life instead of making them good servants in agriculture and other laborious employments; instead of teaching them subordination it would render them fractious and refractory as was evident in the manufacturing counties; it would enable them to read seditious pamphlets, vicious books and publications against Christianity; it would render them insolent to their superiors and in a few years the legislature would find it necessary to direct the strong arm of power against them."[2]

Southern whites in America usually justify their opposition to equal suffrage for the Negro on the ground of his illiteracy. Yet no Southern State gives equal facility for Negro and white education; and the educated, self-reliant Negro is hated more than the docile, uneducated one. Mr. Watson of the Virginia Convention of 1901–2 opposed educational suffrage tests on the ground that they would discriminate in favor of the educated Negro against the servile, old-time Negro: "Now, sir, the old-time Negro is assassinated by this suffrage plan. This new issue, your reader, your writer, your loafer, your voter, your ginger-cake school graduate, with a diploma of side-whiskers and beaver-hat, pocket pistols, brass knucks and bicycle, he, sir, is the distinguished citizen whom our statesmen would crown at once with the highest dignities of an ancient and respectable commonwealth."[3]

Sometimes a dominant group feels itself strong enough to deny the fitness of a subject group to share in its privileges without offering any evidence of a lack of qualification. The fact is asserted dogmatically without effort to

[2] Quoted by G. M. Trevelyan, *British History of the Nineteenth Century,* p. 162.
[3] Quoted by Paul Lewinson, *Race, Class and Party,* p. 85.

prove it. So Senator Vardaman of Mississippi declared himself "opposed to Negro voting; it matters not what his advertised mental and moral qualifications may be. I am just as much opposed to Booker Washington as a voter, with all his Anglo-Saxon reinforcements, as I am to a cocoanut-headed, chocolate-colored typical little coon, Andy Dotson, who blacks my shoes every morning. Neither is fit to perform the supreme function of citizenship."[4] The Southern whites, as every dominant group, are unwilling to grant equal privileges to a subject class, which happens in this case also to be a subject race, on any terms. They will state that fact unashamedly in circles where their prejudices are shared and the social inequalities of their system are accepted. Where either is challenged, they resort to the hypocrisy of attributing innate and congenital defects to the subject people.

The movements for universal education and general suffrage in the nineteenth century offer perfect illustration of both the limits and the potentialities of growing rationality and moral idealism in the equalisation of privilege and power. The principle of universal education was a product of the democratic movement, initiated by middle-class idealists. While this movement in general was exploited and appropriated by the middle classes, without giving the industrial classes the full share of it, which democratic principles demanded, the idea of universal education redounded, nevertheless, to the benefit of all classes and gave the industrial classes the self-reliance and intelligence by which they could resist the middle-class effort to exploit the democratic movement

4 Lewinson, *op. cit.,* p. 84.

for class purposes. While genuine idealism contributed to the extension of educational privileges to all classes, it must be noted that it was easier to establish universal education than universal suffrage, because the former represents only privilege and the latter both privilege and power. Dominant classes are always slowest to yield power because it is the source of privilege. As long as they hold it, they may dispense and share privilege, enjoying the moral pleasure of giving what does not belong to them and the practical advantage of withholding enough to preserve their eminence and superiority in society. While education is potential power, because it enables the disinherited to protect their own interests by organised and effective methods, the dominant classes have suppressed their fears of this effect of education by the thought that education could be used as a means for inculcating submissiveness. Something of that hope, probably unconscious, is to be found in Adam Smith's defense of universal education: "An instructed and intelligent people are always more decent and orderly than a stupid one. They feel themselves each individually more respectable and more likely to gain the respect of their lawful superiors. . . . They are disposed to examine and are more capable of seeing through the interested complaints of faction and sedition, and they are upon that account less apt to be misled into any wanton or unnecessary opposition to the measures of government."[5] A similar argument for the education of slaves was used by a West Indies missionary: "as they learned chiefly through the violent speeches of their own masters and overseers what was

[5] Adam Smith, *Wealth of Nations*, Bk. V, c i.

going on in their favor . . . it was missionary influence that moderated their passions, kept them steady in the course of duty, and prevented them from sinning against God by offending against the laws of man."[6] Since education is to this day both a tool of propaganda in the hands of dominant groups, and a means of emancipation for subject classes, it is easy to understand both the hopes and the fears of the privileged classes when they first began to yield the privilege of education.

The issue of universal suffrage was more stubbornly fought, for reasons suggested. In England the Reform Bill of 1832, which could not have been enacted but for the agitation of the industrial classes, excluded these classes from all its benefits. In this case, as in Russia during the first revolution, the middle classes won their freedom by the help of labor and then excluded their allies from the benefits of their victory. A half century of agitation and political manœuvring was required in England, from 1832 to 1888, before universal suffrage was fully established; and the privileged classes contested every step of the advance toward full suffrage of the industrial classes with the old argument of all privileged classes: that those who lacked the privilege of suffrage were not fit to exercise it.[7] It must be added that the

[6] Quoted by H. Richard Niebuhr, *Social Sources of Denominationalism*, p. 251.

[7] Macaulay expressed the pride of the British aristocrats and their mistrust of the fitness for government of the lower classes in words of classic arrogance and self-righteousness: "Even in this island where the multitude have long been better informed than in any other part of Europe, the rights of the many have been generally asserted against themselves by the patriotism of the few. . . . The People are governed for their own good; and that they may be governed for their own good they must not be governed by their own ignorance." Quoted by Carless Davis, *The Age of Grey and Peel*, p. 281.

final victory of universal suffrage was not final, because women were excluded from the privilege. They had to gain the right against the same charge of unfitness; and, in England at least, militancy had to be added to the force of moral and rational suasion before the victory for equality of rights was won.

Dominant groups indulge in other hypocrisies beside the claim of their special intellectual fitness for the powers which they exercise and the privileges which they enjoy. Frequently they justify their advantages by the claim of moral rather than intellectual superiority. Thus the rising middle classes of the eighteenth and nineteenth centuries regarded their superior advantages over the world of labor as the just rewards of a diligent and righteous life. The individualism of nineteenth century political economy and the sanctification of the prudential virtues in Puritan Protestantism were used by the middle classes to give themselves a sense of moral superiority over both the leisured classes and the industrial workers. This individualism, and the emphasis upon the virtues of thrift and diligence, allowed them to believe that the poverty of the workers was due to their laziness and their improvidence. Timothy Dwight, President of Yale, leader of New England conservatism and champion of the mercantile interests against the politics of the frontiersmen, described the latter as "too idle, too talkative, too passionate, too prodigal and too shiftless to acquire either property or character. They are usually possessed in their own view of uncommon wisdom, understand medical science, politics and religion better than those who have studied them all their life; and although they manage their own concerns worse than other men, feel perfectly satisfied that they could manage those of the nation far better than the agents to whom they are entrusted by the public."[8] Timothy Dwight was not the only protagonist of middle-class respectability who spoke of "property and character" in the same breath. The middle classes were proud that their property, unlike that of the inheritances of the leisured classes, sprang from character, industry, continence and thrift; and they were therefore quite certain that any one endowed with similar virtues could equal the competence which they enjoyed. Failure to achieve such a competence was in itself proof of a lack of virtue. This middle-class creed sprang so naturally from the circumstances of middle-class life that it ought perhaps, to be regarded as an illusion rather than a pretension. But when it is maintained in defiance of all the facts of an industrial civilisation, which reveal how insignificant are the factors of virtuous thrift and industry beside the factor of the disproportion in economic power in the creation of economic inequality, the element of honest illusion is transmuted into dishonest pretension. When a man like John Hay regarded the labor riots of 1877, which arose from the injustices of a buccaneer capitalism, as evidences of the venality of labor, and took occasion to reaffirm his individualistic creed, the judgment can hardly be regarded as an honest one. "He held," declares his biographer, "as did many of his contemporaries, that the assaults upon property were inspired by demagogues, who used as their tools the loafers, the criminal and the vicious, society's dregs who have been ready at all

8 Quoted by H. Richard Niebuhr, *op. cit.*, p. 153.

times to rise against laws and government. That you
have property is proof of industry and foresight on your
part or your father's; that you have nothing is a judgment
on your laziness and vices or on your improvidence. The
world is a moral world; which it would not be if virtue
and vice received the same rewards."[9]

The idea that the profits of capital are really the rewards of a just society for the foresight and thrift of
those who sacrificed the immediate pleasures of spending
in order that society might have productive capital, had
a certain validity in the early days of capitalism, when
productive enterprise was frequently initiated through
capital saved out of modest incomes. The idea, as a
moral justification of present inequalities of privilege, has
become more and more dishonest, since the increased centralisation of privilege and power makes it possible for
those who make the largest investments in industry to do
so without any diminution of even the most luxurious living standards. Since we are living in a world in which
there is too much capital for production and too little for
consumption, the argument that economic inequality is
necessary for the accumulation of capital resources has
lost even its economic validity. Yet it is still used by privileged classes to establish a specious connection between
virtue or social function and privilege.

The moral excellencies which privileged classes claim
and by which they justify their special advantages in society are not always of the utilitarian type. The middle
classes may emphasize the social usefulness of thrift and

9 William Roscoe Thayer, *Life and Letters of John Hay* (Boston: Houghton
Mifflin Company), Vol. I, pp. 6–7.

industry and may claim to possess these virtues in an extraordinary degree; but the landed aristocrats have always based their claims to eminence upon quite different grounds. They claimed moral superiority because they lacked rather than possessed utilitarian virtues. They affected to despise not only the industry of the worker but that of the trader and of any person who was under the necessity of earning his living.[10] They exalted the amenities of a leisured life and placed manners in the category of morals. There is, in the moral attitudes of the aristocracy, a curious confusion of manners and morals which expresses itself in interesting ambiguities in every language. "Gentlemen" and "noblemen" in English and "adel" and "edel" in German are significant examples of words to be found in all languages, which have the connotation of well-born and well-mannered on the one hand, and virtuous and considerate on the other. They illustrate how those who could cultivate the manners of a leisured life arrogated the prestige of moral virtue for their achievements. The double connotation of "villain" and "Kerl" proves that they were not slow to ascribe lack of moral worth to the poor. The English word "gentle" springs from a Latin root which had the same ambiguity, meaning both well-born and morally tender. The Greek word εὐγενής seems originally to have meant only "well-

10 Otho Freisinger, historian of Frederick Barbarossa, expressed the contempt of the mediæval landed aristocrat for the trader and artisan perfectly when he complained of the high position which the latter were accorded in the Italian city-states. "They did not disdain," he declared, "to admit to the honor of knighthood and other dignities, the workers at even the contemptible mechanical arts, whom other nations exclude as one would the pestilence from the more honorable free callings." Hegel, *Geschichte der Staatsverfassung in Italien*, Vol. II, p. 167.

born," but in the Greek tragedies it is used to describe nobility without reference to birth. Similar evidences of the aristocratic confusion of manners and morals seem to exist in every tongue.

The English word "generous" springs from a Latin root (generosus), which reveals that generosity was also regarded as a unique aristocratic virtue. That was natural enough, since only the wealthy had the time and the pecuniary strength to engage in conspicuous helpfulness to their fellows. Mr. Thorstein Veblen cynically interprets the generosities of the privileged as efforts to incite the envy of their fellowmen by a display of their resources.[11] That is probably as near to the truth as the moral estimate which the wealthy and leisured classes make of their own philanthropies. We have previously suggested that philanthropy combines genuine pity with the display of power and that the latter element explains why the powerful are more inclined to be generous than to grant social justice.

The devotion of the aristocracy to art and culture offers it another occasion for moral justification of its privileges. This devotion may be a refined form of conspicuous waste or it may be prompted by the ennui of men who are not under the necessity of earning their livelihood. Nevertheless social inequality has been so basic to the history of culture that Mr. Clive Bell is able to regard the aristocratic organization of society as a prerequisite of high culture.[12] Both the arts and the sciences had their inception in the leisure of Sumerian and Egyp-

11 Thorstein Veblen, *Theory of the Leisure Class*, Chap. 13.
12 Clive Bell, *Civilization*.

tian priests, who, being priests, could maintain their privileged positions in society with less effort than the soldier, and were consequently free to devote their leisure to arts and speculations which had no immediate utilitarian advantage. The fact that culture requires leisure is, however, hardly a sufficient justification for the maintenance of a leisured class. For every artist which the aristocracy has produced, and for every two patrons of art, it has supported a thousand wastrels. An intelligent society will know how to subsidise those who possess peculiar gifts in the arts and the sciences and free them of the necessity of engaging in immediately useful toil. It will bestow leisure upon those who have the capacity to exploit it, and will not permit a leisured class to justify itself by producing an occasional creative genius among a multitude of incompetents who waste their leisure in vulgarities and inanities. No complex society will be able to dispense with certain inequalities of privilege. Some of them are necessary for the proper performance of certain social functions; and others (though this is not so certain) may be needed to prompt energy and diligence in the performance of important functions. But rational privilege must be related to function and to the capacity to perform it. If such a principle is incompatible with complete equalitarianism, it is equally incompatible with the preservation of class privileges. Privileged classes are maintained by the inheritance of privileges without regard to individual capacities for exploiting them for the common good. Furthermore, the degree of privilege inherited has no relevance to what is necessary for the performance of function. A rational justification of hereditary class privileges is therefore impossible, and every effort in this direction must result in the dishonesties which have characterised the self-defense of privileged classes.

Privileged groups have other persistent methods of justifying their special interests in terms of general interest. The assumption that they possess unique intellectual gifts and moral excellencies which redound to the general good, is only one of them. Perhaps a more favorite method is to identify the particular organisation of society, of which they are the beneficiaries, with the peace and order of society in general and to appoint themselves the apostles of law and order. Since every society has an instinctive desire for harmony and avoidance of strife, this is a very potent instrument of maintaining the unjust *status quo*. No society has ever achieved peace without incorporating injustice into its harmony. Those who would eliminate the injustice are therefore always placed at the moral disadvantage of imperilling its peace. The privileged groups will place them under that moral disadvantage even if the efforts toward justice are made in the most pacific terms. They will claim that it is dangerous to disturb a precarious equilibrium and will feign to fear anarchy as the consequence of the effort. This passion for peace need not always be consciously dishonest. Since those who hold special privileges in society are naturally inclined to regard their privileges as their rights and to be unmindful of the effects of inequality upon the underprivileged, they will have a natural complacence toward injustice. Every effort to disturb the peace, which incorporates the injustice, will therefore seem to them to spring from unjustified malcontent. They will furthermore be only partly conscious of the violence and coercion by which their privileges are preserved and will therefore be particularly censorious of the use of force or the threat of violence by those who oppose them. The force they use is either the covert force of economic power or it is the police power of the state, seemingly sanctified by the supposedly impartial objectives of the government which wields it, but nevertheless amenable to their interests. They are thus able in perfect good faith to express abhorrence of the violence of a strike by workers and to call upon the state in the same breath to use violence in putting down the strike. The unvarying reaction of capitalist newspapers to outbreaks of violence in labor disputes is to express pious abhorrence of the use of violent methods and then to call upon the state to use the militia in suppressing the exasperated workers. Perhaps it is a little too generous to attribute good faith to such reasoning, particularly since the privileged classes are not averse to the policy of augmenting the police power of the state with their own instruments of defense and aggression. The use of company police in labor disputes has resulted in more than one scandal of cruel oppression in the United States. English history in the nineteenth century abounds in similar instances of the use of violence by the privileged classes in alleged support of the police services of the state for the suppression of revolt. Nine years after the Hampshire Riots of 1830, caused by the intolerable poverty of the workers and a wretched system of poor relief, the Duke of Wellington naïvely reported how he had proceeded to augment the state police power: "I induced the magistrates to put themselves on horseback, each at the head of his own servants and retainers, grooms, huntsmen, gamekeepers, armed with horsewhips, pistols, fowling pieces and what they could get, and to attack in concert, if necessary, or singly these mobs, disperse them, destroy them and take and put in confinement those who could not escape. This was done in a spirited manner, in many instances, and it is astonishing how soon the country was tranquilised, and in the best way, by the activity and spirit of the gentlemen."

A particularly "modern" touch is given to the Duke's justification of his extra-legal defense of the peace of the state by his insinuation that the reform agitators, who seemed to him to imperil its peace, were paid agents of some Jacobin club in France. Since the immediate object of the reform agitation of those years was the elimination of the rotten boroughs and a more equitable division of suffrage power, it is interesting that the Duke was honest enough to confess the real motives which inspired his hatred and fear of the reform agitators:

"I see in thirty members for the rotten boroughs, thirty men who would preserve the state of property as it is—the dominion of the country over its foreign colonies, the national honor abroad and its good faith with the King's subjects at home."[13]

America, where class distinctions have been less pronounced than in other nations and where class antagonisms have been less desperately fought than in older industrial nations, offers a particularly interesting field for the analysis of the passion of privileged groups for law and order. In the very beginning of the nation's history

[13] Quoted by Carless Davis, *The Age of Grey and Peel*, pp. 224–226.

the acrimonious controversy between the Hamiltonian commercial interests and the Jeffersonian farmers and frontiersmen culminated in the enactment by the former of stringent alien and sedition laws, passed in 1798, to destroy the citizenship rights of Irish and French immigrant adherents of Jefferson's party and to prevent the expression of Jeffersonian sympathy for the French cause. Despite the obvious bias of these laws the administration organ in New York declared: "When a man is heard to inveigh against the Sedition Law, put him down as one who would submit to no restraint calculated for the peace of society. He deserves to be suspected."[14] At the same time a bishop of the Hamiltonian party preached piously on a text which has been used in every nation and every age to inculcate submissiveness to authority: "Let every soul be subject to the higher powers. The powers that be are ordained of God."

Even before the American Revolution class interest expressed itself in American politics, and the privileged class resisted revolutionary sentiment by appeals to law and order. Speaking of the American Tories, Parrington declares: "Compressed in a sentence it (Tory philosophy) was the expression of the will to power. Its motive was economic class interest and its object the exploitation of society through the instrumentality of the state. Stated thus, the philosophy does not appear to advantage; it lays itself open to unpleasant criticism by those who are not its beneficiaries. In consequence much ingenuity in tailoring was necessary to provide it with garments to cover its nakedness. Embroidered with patriotism, loyalty, law

14 Quoted by Claude Bowers, *Jefferson and Hamilton*, p. 385.

and order, it made a very respectable appearance and when it put on the stately robes of the British constitution it was enormously impressive."[15] Jonathan Boucher, one of the most prominent of the Tories, priest of the Anglican church, presents us with a veritable mine of Tory hypocrisy in his various writings. "Obedience to government is every man's duty as it is every man's interest; but it is particularly incumbent upon Christians because it is enjoined by the positive commands of God." Or again, "To respect the laws is to respect liberty in the only rational sense in which the term can be used; for liberty consists in subservience to law." In speaking of the workers he added to the dishonesty of ascribing their discontent to their lack of virtue, to the hypocrisy of identifying law and liberty: "and the laboring classes, instead of regarding the rich as their guardians, patrons and benefactors, now look upon them as so many overgrown colossuses whom it is no demerit in them to wrong. A still more general topic of complaint is that the lower classes, instead of being industrious, frugal and orderly (virtues so peculiarly becoming to their station in life), are becoming idle, improvident and dissolute."[16]

If we turn to a later period of American history, the period in which the farmers of the west revolted against the exploitation of the government by the eastern commercial classes, finding their creed in populism and their champion in Bryan, we discover as intelligent and as liberal an observer of political life as Godkin, founder and editor of *The Nation,* turning vehemently against the

[15] Vernon Louis Parrington, *Main Currents in American Thought:* Vol. I, *The Colonial Mind* (New York: Harcourt, Brace and Company), p. 197.
[16] Quoted by Parrington, *op. cit.,* pp. 216–17.

disaffected agrarians and accusing them of anarchy. His critical attitude toward the nefarious political practices of the apostles of the gilded age did not help him to understand the revolt of the farmers as a legitimate protest against injustice. When the farmers' protest became militant, he declared "Such an unexpected outbreak as this of the last two or three years shows at least that it is not only in the cities where the foreign born swarm that demagogues may thrive and the doctrine of revolution be preached."[17] The fact that the proposal for the free coinage of silver in Bryan's platform was regarded as "the bold and wicked scheme of repudiation" proves that even as liberal a man as Godkin prefers the injustices of a standardised monetary system, which a depression always aggravates by forcing debtors to repay their debts in depreciated currency, to the possible chaos of an inflationary effort. Here Godkin betrays the typical timidity of the middle-class intellectual. Writing on the Democratic Convention of 1896, he declared: "The country has watched their mad proceedings with disgust and shuddering, only impatient for the coming of November to stamp out them and their incendiary doctrines." Perhaps the most revealing stricture of Godkin against the Democratic party was that which was concerned with the Democratic protest against the abuse of injunctions by the federal courts. Godkin declared: "This blow at the courts shows how true are the instincts of the revolutionary. They know their most formidable enemies. Judicial decisions have again and again drawn the fangs of revolu-

---

[17] Quoted by Parrington, *Main Currents in American Thought:* Vol. III, *The Beginnings of Critical Realism in America,* p. 164.

tionary legislation. . . ."[18] We can realise to what degree class interest colors political opinion if as wise an observer as Godkin could not realise how frequently the courts, because of the very prestige of their supposed impartiality, may be used as the instruments of class domination. "Politics," declares Brooks Adams,[19] "is the struggle for the ascendancy of a class and majority. The Constitution . . . is expounded by judges and this function, which, in essence, is political, has brought precisely that quality of pressure on the bench, which it has been the labor of hundreds of generations to remove. . . . From the outset, the American bench, because it deals with the most fiercely contested of political issues, has been an instrument necessary for political success. . . . The bench has always had an avowed partisan bias." Mr. Adams errs only in assuming that the bias of a judiciary is a unique American characteristic.

The striking fact about Godkin's campaign against Mr. Bryan and the Democratic party is that so fair a man as he should have feared the peril of anarchy and revolution in political policies comparatively so innocent and pacific as those which Mr. Bryan avowed. It is a clear revelation of the power of class bias and of the tendency of the classes which have arrived, to place the advancing classes under the opprobrium of anarchy and revolution. On the morning after Mr. Bryan's defeat *The New York Tribune* said: "The wicked rattle-pated boy . . . was only a puppet in the blood-imbrued hands of Altgeld, the anarchist, and Debs, the revolutionist, and other desperadoes of that

[18] Quoted by Parrington, *op. cit.,* p. 166.
[19] Brooks Adams, *The Theory of Social Revolution,* p. 45.

stripe. But he was a willing pupil, Bryan was, willing and eager."[20]

The human mind is so weak an instrument, and is so easily enslaved and prostituted by human passions, that one is never certain to what degree the fears of the privileged classes, of anarchy and revolution, are honest fears which may be explained in terms of their imperfect perspective upon social facts; and to what degree they are dishonest attempts to put the advancing classes at a disadvantage. One suspects, for instance, that when Joseph Choate assailed the new income tax law before the Supreme Court in 1894 as "communistic, socialistic and populistic"[21] he hardly could have been honest. On the other hand, when Oliver Wendell Holmes, impatient in his quiet genteel New England world, with the cries for political justice which were arising in the West, declared "We do not want the incendiary's pillar of cloud by day and pillar of fire by night to lead us in the march of civilisation, and we don't want a Moses who will smite the rock, not to bring our water for our thirst, but petroleum to burn us all up with,"[22] he was probably expressing the honest bias of a comfortable old man who detested every kind of change. Since the prejudices of honest men are just as great a hazard to ethical relations in politics as the dishonest appeals of demagogues, it may be that moralists have placed too great an emphasis upon the value of honesty as a method of escape from injustice in political life.

[20] Quoted by Millis, *The Martial Spirit*, p. 58.
[21] See Beard, *Rise of American Civilization*, Vol. I, p. 591.
[22] Quoted by Parrington, *op. cit.*, Vol. II, *The Romantic Revolution in America*, p. 458.

The fear of anarchy of American privileged groups and their self-appointment as the guardians of peace and order is significant only because it is so clearly expressed in a nation in which the classes have not become as distinct as in the older nations. It will be found that the history of other nations abounds in even more striking examples of this trait of privileged classes. After the Manchester massacre of 1819, in which election reform agitators were brutally suppressed by the British Government, the privileged classes of Britain were more fearful of the violence which the agitators might use than repentant of the violence which had been used against them. A most oppressive sedition act was passed to prevent further outbreaks and Lord Redesdale declared: "Every meeting for radical reform was not merely a seditious attempt to undermine the existing constitution by bringing it into hatred and disrepute but it is an overt act of treasonable conspiracy against that constitution."[23] The agitation for suffrage reform in Britain which began in 1789 and did not end until 1888 was stoutly contested by the English Tories, who never tired of insisting and reiterating that each new extension of the franchise would result in anarchy.[24] Incidentally it has been an unvarying tendency among governments, and the ruling classes which manipulate government, when anarchy is actually threatened, to re-establish peace by the use of force rather than by eliminating the causes of disaffection. An English historian, writing on the disturbances which accompanied the reform agitation at the beginning of the nine-

[23] M. R. P. Dorman, *A History of the British Empire in the Nineteenth Century*, Vol. II, p. 259.
[24] G. M. Trevelyan, *British History of the Nineteenth Century*, p. 228.

teenth century in Britain declares: "The grand fault of the government of 1817 was that it simply endeavored to scotch the agitation without inquiring into the causes that had produced it. . . . Among the contributory causes there was the impression that the government had no desire to cut down public expenditure for the relief of the taxpayer in general, or to shift part of the poor man's burden of taxation to the shoulders of the property owner."[25] That judgment upon the British Government of 1817 is applicable with almost equal validity to all governments of all ages.[26]

Even when no anarchy is threatened and no violence is used by the classes which seek a more equal share in the processes of government and in the privileges of society, it is always possible for the privileged groups to predict anarchy on the score that the ambitious and advancing classes are unfit for the exercise of the rights which they desire. A learned Englishman, writing on India, makes such a prediction, in perfect analogy with similar dire forebodings of privileged groups in every age: "We cannot foresee the time in which cessation of our rule would not be the signal for universal anarchy and ruin, and it is clear that the only hope for India is the long continuance of the benevolent but strong government of Eng-

[25] Carless Davis, *The Age of Grey and Peel,* p. 190.
[26] As these lines are written the American Government is using troops to disperse the "bonus army" from Washington. Since the bonus army is merely a symptom of the unrest caused by the failure of the government to provide adequate relief for the unemployed, President Hoover's defense of the use of troops against the unemployed presents another perfect example of the superficiality of governments. "A challenge to the authority of the United States has been met swiftly and firmly," the President declared. "After months of patient indulgence the Government met overt lawlessness as it always must be met if the cherished processes of self-government are to be preserved."

lishmen. . . . Mr. J. S. Mill declared his belief that the British Government in India 'was not only one of the purest in intention but one of the most beneficent in act ever known among mankind.' I do not doubt that this is still true now."[27] This judgment combines the pride of a ruling nation with the arrogance of a ruling class. Whatever justification it has (in this case the solid achievements of the British Empire in India give it considerable justification) is vitiated by the unwillingness of the ruling classes to share the experience which is the basis of whatever superior attainments in government they may possess.

So persistent is the cry of peace among the ruling classes and so strong the seeming abhorrence of every form of violence and anarchy that one might imagine them actuated by the purest pacifist principles, were it not for the fact that they betray no pacifist scruples when they consider international affairs. Most insistent upon peace within the nation, they are most easily provoked to join issue in martial combat with other nations. Sometimes specific economic interests prompt their bellicose ardor; at other times they find it convenient to strengthen their rule at home by permitting the fever of war and the resultant hysteria of patriotism to confuse their interests with the general welfare more perfectly than would be possible in a sober nation. More than one ruling caste has saved itself by an opportune war. The inept Russian aristocracy tried to beguile the Russian public from consideration of the misery into which it had been thrown

[27] Sir John Strachey, *India; its Administration and Progress*, pp. 496 and 502.

by the venality and incompetence of its rulers during the World War, by fanning the flames of jingoism to a white heat. The effort proved futile only because the decomposition of Russian society had progressed too far.[28]

The prejudices, hypocrisies and dishonesties of privileged and ruling classes are less determined by class loyalty than similar national attitudes are the consequence of loyalty to the nation. Members of privileged classes are not incapable of loyalty to their class and of concerted action when their common privileges are imperilled. But the attitudes of their several members are under less group pressure than in either the nation or the proletarian class. They merely represent the uniform consequence of a given set of circumstances and the unvarying effect of interest upon attitude and conviction. The group egoism of a privileged class is therefore more precisely the sum and aggregate of individual egoisms than is the case in national selfishness, which is sometimes compounded of the unselfish loyalties of individuals. This may mean that the unethical character of class prejudices may, being less complex, be more easily dissolved by reason than similar national attitudes. Nevertheless the task is not as easy as it seems to rational moralists, who are themselves too much the product of comfortable cimcumstances to understand the desperate problem of social justice. While some of the pretensions of privileged classes are consciously dishonest, most of them arise from the fact that the criteria of reason, religion and culture, to which the class appeals in defense of its position in society are themselves the product of, or at least colored by, the partial

[28] See *inter alia*, Hans von Eckardt, *Russia*, p. 317.

experience and perspective of the class. When the intelligent member of a class appeals to the court of reason and justice the biased judgments of the court are all the more dangerous for having the prestige of impartiality. A higher degree of intelligence and a more acute rational perception might conceivably destroy class bias to some degree. It can certainly increase the number of individuals who are able to penetrate through the moral illusions which confuse the mind and conscience of a majority of the class. It might even qualify the certainty with which most of the members of the class hold to their illusions, and thereby insinuate a rational element into the inevitable struggle between the classes. But it cannot abolish the egoism of a class. David Hume declared that the maxim that egoism is, though not the exclusive, yet the predominant inclination of human nature, might not be true in fact, but that it was true in politics.[29] He held it to be true in politics since group action is determined by majority opinion and it would always be true that the majority would be actuated by the egotistic motive. It is difficult to read the history of mankind and arrive at any other conclusion. It must be taken for granted therefore that the injustices in society, which arise from class privileges, will not be abolished purely by moral suasion. That is a conviction at which the proletarian class, which suffers most from social injustice, has finally arrived after centuries of disappointed hopes.

[29] David Hume, *Essays*, Part I, Essay VI.

CHAPTER SIX

THE ETHICAL ATTITUDES OF THE PROLETARIAN CLASS

ALL societies of the past perpetrated and perpetuated social injustice without meeting significant resistance from those who were victimised by the social system. There were indeed slave revolts in antiquity and peasant rebellions in the Middle Ages; but they were sporadic and usually ineffectual. They represented the rebellious vehemence of hungry men who lacked a social philosophy to give dignity and sustained force to their efforts, and a political strategy adequate to the problem which they faced. Occasional revolts, when hunger and privation exhausted the patience of the serfs, did not materially alter the attitude of submissiveness which generally characterised the lower classes of ancient and medieval ages. The moral cynicism, the equalitarian idealism, the rebellious heroism, the anti-nationalism and internationalism, and the exaltation of their class as the community of significant loyalty, all these characteristic moral attitudes of the modern working classes are the products of the industrial era. To some degree they are the result of the democratic movement, which, while excluding the workers from its chief benefits, did grant them minimum opportunities for education and thus gave them a perspective upon political and economic facts, which the landless and propertyless classes of other ages lacked. But they are chiefly the result of modern capitalism and industrialism.

The medieval social organisation was a personal one. The relations between squire and serf, between master and artisan, were direct, and sometimes intimate. The personal quality mitigated and obscured the social injustice and inequality of the relationship. The sense of personal responsibility on the part of the lord or master actually qualified the unethical character of the relationship; and the sentimental charities of the traditional "lady bountiful" added confusion to this measure of moral achievement. The rise of a technological civilisation increased the centralisation of ownership and power; it destroyed the sense of responsibility of the owner, lost the individual laborer in the mass, and obscured the human factors in industrial relations by the mechanism of stock ownership and the technique of mass production. By making human relations mechanical it increased, and more clearly revealed, the economic motive of human activity. It made Adam Smith's abstraction of the economic man a living reality. Its methods of production and its means of communication provided, moreover, for a higher intensity of social cohesion and a more centralised control within both the owning and the working classes. It therefore intensified the conflict and antagonism between the classes, by drawing individuals of a given economic status more definitely into a self-conscious social and political group and by giving them organs for the expression of a common group interest.[1]

[1] Robert Briffault's *Breakdown* strikingly emphasises the similarities rather than differences between ancient and modern forms of social injustice and class privileges.

The effect of this development of an industrial civilisation is vividly revealed in the social and political attitudes of the modern proletarian class. These attitudes have achieved their authoritative expression and definition in Marxian political philosophy. Critics may contend that Marxism is not so much the natural political philosophy of proletarians, as it is a disease with which they have become infected. They may claim, for instance, that the idea of the class struggle is a dogma which creates, rather than is created by, the conflict experience of the worker. While such criticisms may have a measure of validity, or at least of plausibility, it is a fact that Marxian socialism is a true enough interpretation of what the industrial worker feels about society and history, to have become the accepted social and political philosophy of all self-conscious and politically intelligent industrial workers. Varying political and economic circumstances may qualify socialistic theory in different nations and in different epochs; but it would be impossible to deny that socialism, more or less Marxian, is the political creed of the industrial worker of Western civilisation. If the American worker seems for the moment to be an exception, that fact can be explained in terms which will justify the confident prediction, that the full maturity of American capitalism will inevitably be followed by the emergence of the American Marxian proletarian.

If we analyse the attitudes of the politically self-conscious worker in ethical terms, their most striking characteristic is probably the combination of moral cynicism and unqualified equalitarian social idealism which they betray. The industrial worker has little confidence in the morality of men; but this does not deter him from projecting a rigorous ethical ideal for society.

The moral cynicism expresses itself philosophically in terms of the Marxian materialistic and deterministic interpretation of history. In Marx's preface to his *Critique of Political Economy* he states his economic determinism in succinct terms: "In the social production which men carry on they enter into definite relations that are indispensable and independent of their will; these relations of production correspond to a definite stage of development of their material powers of production. The sum total of these relations of production constitutes the economic structure of society, the real foundation on which rise the legal and political superstructures and to which correspond definite forms of social consciousness. The mode of production in material life determines the general character of the social, political and spiritual processes of life."[2] This determinism was not quite as absolute with Marx and Engels as with some of their disciples. Engels declared, "The economic condition is the basis, but the various elements of the superstructure . . . the political forms of the class contest, and their results, the constitution. . . . the legal forms . . . the political, legal, philosophical theories, the religious views . . . all these exert an influence on historical struggles and in many instances determine their form."[3] Stated in this reasonable form, few economists or historians would dissent from such an interpretation of history. What gives the Marxian determinism uniqueness, is the complete moral cynicism which is derived

[2] Karl Marx, *A Critique of Political Economy*, p. 11.
[3] Quoted by E. R. A. Seligman, *Economic Interpretation of History*, p. 351.

from it. The relation of social classes in society is conceived of wholly in terms of the conflict of power with power. Since all cultural, moral and religious forces are "ideologies," which rationalise, but do not seriously alter, the economic behavior of various classes, it is assumed that the power which inheres in the ownership of the means of production and which makes for social injustice will not be abated, qualified or destroyed by any other means but the use of force against it. "The first condition of salvation," declares Trotsky, "is to tear the weapons of domination out of the hands of the bourgeoisie. It is hopeless to think of a peaceful arrival to power while the bourgeoisie retains in its hands all the apparatus of power. Three times over hopeless is the idea of coming to power —by the path of parliamentary democracy."[4] If this destruction of power seems an impossible task, the Marxian proletarian is consoled and encouraged by the hope that the increased centralisation of power in the capitalist economy, which he regards as inevitable, will make the defense of the owning classes more vulnerable by reducing their numbers, while the increasing misery of the workers will create the vehement energy out of which the revolutionary force is built. While capitalism thus produces both the possibility and the means of its own destruction, the true Marxian does not believe that the process will be automatic. He does not expect to gain control of either the means of production or the apparatus of the state without a revolutionary struggle.

If it should be maintained that this social philosophy and prophecy is the creed of Marx, Lenin and Trotsky,

[4] Leon Trotsky, *Dictatorship or Revolution*, p. 42.

rather than the faith and the hope of the proletarian worker, it need only be pointed out that, wherever social injustice rests heaviest upon the worker, wherever he is most completely disinherited, wherever the slight benefits, which political pressure has forced from the owning classes, have failed to materialise for him, he expresses himself in the creed of the unadulterated and unrevised Marx. The difference between Marx and those who have revised his creed in the direction of a greater optimism is not an academic one. It is literally the difference between the less favored and the more favored workers, between those from whose perspective modern capitalism is really hopeless, and those whose slightly more favorable experiences encourage a more hopeful view. Whether the crises of capitalism and the consequent insecurity of the workers will finally reduce all industrial workers to the status of the former, is a question which history alone can answer. Meanwhile it is rather interesting that economic determinists should be so prone to accuse melioristic and parliamentary socialists, whose convictions obviously grow out of their economic experiences, of moral turpitude. They know that revolutionary sentiment can develop only in economic misery, but they find it difficult to square their moral judgments with their deterministic convictions. The individual proletarian leader, whose philosophy of society grows not out of his own experience but out of an imaginative understanding of the experiences and necessities of the working class, is of course justified, from his own point of view, in criticising those whose theories spring from the experiences of the more favored rather than the less favored workers. Since he *is*

imaginatively identified with the least favored proletarians, he feels that those who stop short of such an
identification are wanting in either courage or imagination. Interestingly enough Lenin was never sufficiently
consistent in his determinism to claim that orthodox
Marxism was the natural product of working class experience. He believed that the worker was incapable of
elaborating an adequate social philosophy without aid.
"The history of all countries," he writes, "testifies to the
fact that the working class can evolve only a trade union-
ist consciousness, i.e., the conviction that it is necessary to
coalesce into unions in order to fight the employers, to
demand laws in favor of labor, etc. The doctrine of socialism grew up out of the philosophical and historical
theories that were elaborated by educated members of the
propertied classes, by the intelligentsia. Marx and Engels
and the founders of scientific socialism of today belonged
themselves to the bourgeois intelligentsia."[5] The idea that
the superior historical perspective of the educated man
must be added to the actual experience of the worker,
who lacks perspective, before a theory can be evolved
which will do justice to that experience, is an interesting
qualification of pure determinism. It enabled Lenin to
avoid many mistakes into which purer determinists fell.

The moral cynicism of Marxism and proletarianism,
which discounts all ethical pretensions and achievements
in the field of politics, is particularly apparent in its estimate of the democratic state. The true proletarian regards
the democratic state as the instrument of the bourgeoisie
for the oppression of the workers. His complete cynicism

[5] Lenin in *Works,* Vol. V, p. 141.

upon this point stands in striking antithesis to the sentimental overestimates of the achievements of political democracy which are current in the middle-class world. Lenin declared "In their sum, these restrictions (of middle-class democracy) exclude and thrust out the poor from politics and from active share in democracy. Marx splendidly grasped the essence of capitalistic democracy, when, in his analysis of the experience of the commune, he said the oppressed are allowed, once every few years, to decide which particular representatives of the oppressing classes are to represent and repress them in politics."[6] An unbiased analysis of the power of the owning classes in modern democracy, their dictation of legislation, the almost unvarying interpretation of ambiguous law in their favor, and their evasion of the law when it suits their purposes, will not find it easy to answer this charge of communism. The dictum of Lenin: "Freedom in capitalist society always remains more or less the same as it was in the ancient Greek republics, that is, freedom for the slave-owners," can be answered only by qualifying it. The most significant qualification upon this thesis has been made by that part of the proletarian world which hopes to use the instruments of democracy for a pacific transmutation of the present capitalist society. Whatever may be the justification for such hopes, it is important for our immediate consideration to note that they also spring from the economic and political experiences of the more favored and less desperate proletarians. In the more orthodox Marxian view, the state is purely an instrument of oppression; and salvation for the worker requires its an-

[6] Lenin, *The State and Revolution,* p. 89.

nihilation. The orthodox Marxian view of the state is not dissimilar from the conviction of Thomas Paine: "Society is the product of our wants and government of our wickedness."

The cynical estimate of the democratic state carries with it a similar estimate of nationalism and patriotism. The true proletarian is completely bereft of patriotic loyalty. He stands outside of the whole system of sentiments and loyalties which give cohesive power to the nation. Here again, communist theory, or orthodox Marxism, is not merely an academic anti-nationalist theory. It conforms to the experience of the real proletarian, the truly disinherited worker, who is defrauded not only of the physical but of the cultural benefits which the nation bestows upon its more favored citizens. So powerful is the sentiment of patriotism, that if the injustice, from which the worker suffers, is not quite unbearable and if some minimum portion of the national cultural inheritance is bequeathed to him, he will respond to the appeals of the nation, though more reluctantly than the middle classes. The attitude of the parliamentary socialist parties during the World War is instructive on this point. Prior to the war they had been uniformly anti-militaristic and pacifistic. They opposed the rising military budgets which made the war inevitable. But they were finally seduced into the war. Lenin, and other communist critics, might sneer at their apostasy, and attribute it to the ambition and dishonesty of their leaders. But this moral explanation of the facts is not only incompatible with the deterministic presuppositions of the critic, but an inadequate analysis of the underlying factors. Whenever a nation does not completely disinherit its workers, it has been able to count upon their loyalty. The loyalty has been a little more hesitant than that of the middle classes; but it has been, on the whole, more generous than the nation deserved, when the real motives of its martial enterprises are considered. The pretensions of nations, which only the most penetrating intellects among the intellectuals are able to discount, are discounted among the workers only by those who have had the bitterest experiences of national greed and brutality. Lenin's uncompromising anti-patriotism, during the World War, found an echo in the hearts of the Russian proletariat, because there the workers were completely and obviously disinherited; and the machinary of state was so manifestly inept and corrupt that it could not claim the usual reverence which even disillusioned workers give a government which manages to maintain its functions. In Europe, on the other hand, the patriotic fervor of the workers was dampened without being destroyed. Even when the German monarchial system succumbed to the vicissitudes of defeat, the German workers made a distinction between anti-monarchism and anti-patriotism. The nationalist of every nation brought the charge of treason against both socialistic and communistic workers indiscriminately; and the German nationalists still affect to believe that they would have won the war but for the socialist "stab in the back." As far as the socialists are concerned, the charge has less foundation in fact than it ought to have had. The modern worker sacrifices his patriotism in almost exact proportion to the measure of social injustice from which he suffers. He disavows the nation only if it has thrust him out of its system of cultural inheritances and economic benefits in the most obvious terms. It may be taken for granted that all workers will be more sophisticated in a future war than in the past one. Social intelligence may prompt disillusionment without the immediate lesson of complete disinheritance. But the degree of anti-nationalism among workers will always depend somewhat upon the measure of social injustice from which they suffer.

The exaltation of class loyalty as the highest form of altruism is a natural concomitant of the destruction of national loyalty. The proletarian worker in general, whether socialistic or communistic, makes loyalty to the class a primary claim in his scheme of fealties. Whether class loyalty becomes for him the sole loyalty or only the primary one, whether he conceives the class in such absolute terms that he is able to cut through all of the complexities of social life with a vigorous and potent oversimplification, that again depends upon the degree to which society has cast him out. We have previously noted that nations arrive at full self-consciousness only as they stand in juxtaposition to other nations, particularly in the vivid juxtaposition of controversy. The class arrives at self-consciousness in the same manner. The more it feels itself in conflict with other classes the more it achieves a distinct self-consciousness. A fighting proletarian class will tend to depreciate whatever common interests it may possess with other classes in a national structure, and to interpret the conflict of interest between classes in more absolute terms than the facts warrant. This oversimplification is the kind which the passions of conflict, whether national or intra-national, make inevitable. It is also a natural cynical reaction to the sentimental and dishonest efforts of the privileged classes, to obscure the conflict of interest between the classes by a constant emphasis upon those minimum interests which they have in common. This cynical reaction to, what John Stuart Mill described as, a "goody morality" is at least as near to the truth as the romantic and patriotic descriptions of mutuality of interest between all classes within a national community. "It is the interest of both laborers and employers," declares Mill, "that business should prosper and that the returns of labor and capital should be large. But to say that they have the same interest as to the division is to say that it is the same thing to a person's interest whether a sum of money belongs to him or to somebody else." Inevitably the exaltation of the class, as the community of most significant loyalty, is justified by the proletarian by attaching universal values to his class. He does not differ from the privileged classes in attempting this universalisation of his particular values. It is the tribute he pays to the inner rational and moral necessities of the human spirit. His class for the proletarian is not merely a class. It is the class which is destined by history to usher a classless society into existence. "When the proletariat proclaims the dissolution of the existing order of things," declares Karl Marx, "it is merely announcing the secret of its own existence, for it is itself the virtual dissolution of this order of things. When the proletariat desires the negation of private property it is merely elevating, as a general principle of society, what it already involuntarily embodies in itself as the negative product of society."[7] There is something rather

[7] In his Introduction to Hegel's *Philosophy of Law*.

imposing in this doctrine of Marx. It is more than a doctrine. It is a dramatic, and to some degree, a religious interpretation of proletarian destiny. In such insights as this, rather than in his economics, one must discover the real significance of Marx. His economic theory of labor value may be impossible, but this attempt at the transvaluation of values is in the grand style. To make the degradation of the proletarian the cause of his ultimate exaltation, to find in the very disaster of his social defeat the harbinger of his final victory, and to see in his loss of all property the future of a civilisation in which no one will have privileges of property, this is to snatch victory out of defeat in the style of great drama and classical religion. Nietzsche could regard Christianity as the revolt of slaves. He could see in its morality of meekness and forgiveness the revenge which the weak took upon the strong by imposing moral ideals which sanctified the virtues of the lowly and robbed the traditional virtues of the strong of their moral significance. Marxism is another kind of slave revolt. It exalts not the virtues but the estate of the lowly. These modern helots also engage in the transvaluation of values. It is not the meek but the weak who are given the promise of inheriting the earth. If the Christian poor hoped that spiritual forces would ultimately endow meekness with strength, these modern poor believe that historical, "materialistic" forces will automatically rob the strong of their strength and give it to the weak.

The whole tragedy and the whole promise of modern life is in the difference between these hopes. It is a tragic difference inasfar as it represents modern man's loss of confidence in moral forces. It is a helpful one inasfar as it recognises the brutalities of the conflict of power as basic to the collective history of mankind. If there are excesses and extravagances in its amoralism and unqualified determinism, they may be regarded as the poison which the amoral mechanism of a technological civilisation generates. But they must also be appreciated as the antidote which is needed for the toxin of the hypocrisies by which modern society hides its brutalities. An industrial mechanism, which moves by instinct and defies the canons of reason and conscience, makes determinists of those who suffer most from its cruelties. A culture which tries to hide the cruelties by moral pretensions that do not change the facts makes cynics of those who know the facts. History alone will determine whether the proletarian who is both the spiritual victim and the moral savior of such a civilisation will be more the victim or more the savior. Since all history is a conflict between human character and impersonal fate, and since one may never be certain which of the two is more potent in a given instant, there is something of an overstatement in any philosophy of history which reads the future in terms of the complete triumph of one or the other. In the eschatology of the true Christian, virtue will ultimately triumph by the power of its own strength, or by the strength supplied by God's grace. In the eschatology of the true Marxian, justice will be established because weakness will be made strong through economic forces operating with inexorable logic in human history. The Marxian imagines that he has a philosophy or even a science of history. What he has is really an apocalyptic vision. A confident prophecy of the future is never more than that. In him political hopes achieve religious

proportions by overleaping the bounds of rationally verifiable possibilities, just as, in the soul of the true Christian,
moral hopes achieve religious verification. There is something both sublime and ridiculous in expecting either the
meek or the weak to inherit the earth, that is, in expecting
the disinherited to conquer either by virtue of their moral
qualities or by virtue of their very disinheritance. Yet
there is an element of truth in both expectations; for there
are tendencies in history which make for the casting of
the mighty from their seats, both morally and politically.
Since the political defeat of the mighty is more verifiable
in historic terms, and probably more significant socially,
than their moral defeat, the religio-political dreams of the
Marxians have an immediate significance, which the re-
ligio-ethical dreams of the Christians lack. The religious
element is in both of them, because both expect the realisation of the absolute. But since political ideals are more
capable of historic realisation than purely ethical ones, the
Marxian dream is less religious for being more germane
to history. In classical religion the realisation of the pure
ideal in history is indeed expected, but it is really too pure
to have any possibility of complete realisation. The transhistorical element in it therefore gains the ascendency in
the long run.

It is not difficult for the moralist to detect immoral
elements in the Marxian exaltation of class. It is charged
with both egotism and vindictiveness. The egotism is the
more pronounced for being a compensation of frustrated
ego in the contemporary situation. The class which has
its human meaning and significance destroyed in the
immediate situation, declares itself the most significant

class for the future of history. While this may lead to a deification of the class, reaching absurd mystical proportions, it is on the subjective side an understandable reaction to present social inferiority, and, objectively considered, it may be justified by the strategic importance of the proletarian class in the task of rebuilding society. Who is better able to understand the true character of a civilisation than those who suffer most from its limitations? Who is better able to state the social ideal in unqualified terms than those who have experienced the bankruptcy of old social realities in their own lives? Who will have more creative vigor in destroying the old and building the new than those in whose lives hunger, vengeance and holy dreams have compounded a tempestuous passion?

The element of vengeance is of course as dangerous as it is vehement and vital. It may lead to very destructive social consequences. The modern Russians pursue the surviving members of the classes, regarded as their hereditary foes, with relentless vindictiveness. This vengeance, which they justify by the supposed necessity of making a clean sweep of the past, not only outrages the conscience by its cruelties but frequently interferes with the orderly establishment of the new society. Recently Stalin had to call a halt upon the policy of force and fear which was used upon experts and specialists who were suspected of belonging psychologically to the old order. Experience had taught him that there are limits to the policy of "liquidating" the foes of the new order. No community, whether class or nation, can build a society by destroying everything outside itself. It must finally yield to the complexities of society and hope to win its foes to co-operation rather than to destroy them, or to trust that force will coerce a doubtful allegiance.

The patriots and nationalists who condemn the exaltation of class as immoral merely because it is in conflict with national loyalties do not present a serious moral problem. Their condemnations rest upon prejudices and traditional sentiments rather than upon reason. For there is nothing inherently more sacrosanct about a territorial than a functional community; nor are the claims of the nation, that it embodies values which transcend its own interests, any better than those of a class which dreams of an ideal commonwealth. The rational legitimacy of the claims of the proletarian class does not, of course, guarantee the complete vicory over the nation which it expects. Wherever the nation does not totally disinherit its proletarians, they tend to qualify their class loyalty with a measure of national loyalty and to interpret their mission as one of national regeneration. They see themselves as a redemptive community within the nation, rather than as a community standing outside of the nation; and they call upon all those who understand the peril in which the national community stands, to make common cause with them, irrespective of class. This has been the trend particularly in British socialism.[8] Whether this type ot socialism sacrifices too much to the national feeling and sacrifices it too prematurely is a question which we must consider later.

The moral cynicism of the worker, which expresses itself in discounting all moral pretensions of bourgeois cul-

[8] See *inter alia*, J. Ramsay MacDonald, *Parliament and Revolution.*

ture and politics and in disavowing the means of moral suasion, or even political pressure, as adequate for the creation of a new society, is paradoxically relieved by the uncompromising character of his socio-ethical ideal. The proletarian is a rigorous equalitarian. The victory of his class is to usher in a classless society. If his equalitarianism is too absolute to meet the needs of a complex society and the weaknesses of human nature, it has at least the merit of offering a wholesome and necessary antidote to all the specious justifications of inequality, in which the history of human thought abounds, and of projecting a social goal which must always be regarded as the ultimate rational ideal of society. "Equality," declares Hobhouse, "lies at the foundation of justice in the sense that every person and every function capable of harmony must be equally taken into account in framing the plan of harmony. . . . It follows that the good, which one may claim, all may claim, unless there is a grounded difference; and the only ultimate ground of difference is some requirement of the working system of harmony as a whole."[9] The principle of equality, stated in such rationally acceptable terms, might possibly admit some functional inequalities which a consistent Marxian would not allow, but it would certainly exclude most of the inequalities which the present economic system permits. If Marxian equalitarianism is stated in too rigorous terms, that may well be due to the religious overtones which a vigorous ethical idealism always creates. "From each according to his ability, to each according to his needs" is indeed an ideal, which is as impossible of consistent application in the complexities of

[9] L. T. Hobhouse, *The Elements of Social Justice*, p. 172. See also R. H. Tawney, *Equality*.

society as the Christian ideal of love. But it is an ideal toward which a rational society must move, and the religious overtone may be regarded as a guarantee against the dilution of the ideal. Whether the reorganisation of society will reform human nature sufficiently to make an approximation of the ideal possible, is a question which only history can answer, and which sober reason would certainly not answer with as confident an affirmative as the Marxian enthusiast gives.

The fact that the equalitarian ideal does not spring from pure ethical imagination, but is the result of the peculiar circumstances of proletarian life, does not detract from its validity as the ultimate social ideal. It is a question whether the proletarian is so rigorous an equalitarian because he suffers so much from inequality or because he has had equality, within the confines of the proletarian class, forced upon him. Both elements may enter into the formation of the ideal. Social ideals are sometimes the converse of the social realities in which people live. Henrik Ibsen observed that the most passionate lovers of liberty were Russians who suffered from the autocracy of Czardom. So the proletarian, who suffers most from inequality, may naturally arrive at his equalitarianism by way of reaction. An element of envy may enter into his motives as DeMan suggests.[10] Furthermore the equality of living conditions which is forced upon the working class, and the comparative insignificance of differentials in living standards which obtain among the workers, may prompt them to bestow the virtues of this estate upon the whole of society (and, unconsciously, to wish that the

10 See Henry DeMan, *The Psychology of Socialism.*

whole of society would suffer from its disadvantages). Whatever the mixture of motives may be which enters into the compound of proletarian idealism, its social validity remains undisturbed by these considerations. Nor can it be denied that a genuine moral idealism, a passionate desire for a just society, is a significant element in the social outlook of the working class. The disinherited of every age have dreamt of a just society. The modern proletarian distinguishes himself from the underprivileged of other ages only in that his vision is less obviously religious and more definitely political in its orientation.

The ethical quality of this dream must be affirmed even when the Marxian is too involved in moral cynicism to be willing to affirm it. Among the early socialists, William Liebknecht was most unequivocal in disavowing the ethical quality of the socialist goal. "Pity for poverty," he declared, "enthusiasm for equality and freedom, recognition of social injustice and the desire to remove it, is not socialism. Condemnation for wealth and respect for poverty as we find it in Christianity and other religions is not socialism. . . . Modern socialism is the child of capitalist society and its class antagonisms. Without these it could not be." This effort to interpret the class struggle in purely amoral terms is a note, but a minor one, running through socialist thought. It is negated by the promise of a just society, a promise which the proletarian makes and believes with such fervor and religious feeling. The vision of a classless world gives moral dignity to the dream of the victory of his class. By that vision the proletarian escapes the partial and the relative and bestows the value of universality upon his efforts. If there is an element of religious illusion in estimating the contribution which his class is to make to the redeemed world, it is largely an error of overemphasis. There are other redemptive forces in society beside those of proletarian spirituality. There are eyes which see clearly, other than those which have been clarified by his suffering; and there are wills which are resolute beside those which have been fortified by his bitter personal experience. Yet their number is restricted by the limits of the human imagination which permit only a few to see what they do not personally experience. The element of illusion in the proletarian claim to universality is certainly no greater, more probably it is considerably less, than similar claims of nations and privileged classes. Its conscious dishonesties and deceptions are fewer; for the proletarian does not desire advantages for himself which he is not willing to share with others. If the proletarian should have the virtue of this honesty thrust upon him by the fact that he has no special advantages to defend, it may be well to remember that virtue, which is not tempted, is not thereby robbed of its moral quality, though it may not be as pure as the virtue which has overcome temptation. The blessings which Jesus pronounced upon the poor and the warnings he sounded against riches are justified by the recognition that there are temptations of riches which are too great to be overcome. They can only be escaped by voluntary or involuntary poverty. Special privileges make all men dishonest. The purest conscience and the clearest mind is prostituted by the desire to prove them morally justified. Nothing proves the prejudices of the middle-class world more clearly than its unwillingness to recognise the genuine morality of proletarian aspirations. Steeped as it is in petty virtues and major vices, it has no perspective high enough from which it might achieve a real appreciation of the morality of the rebellious worker. Yet the unbiased observer is forced to admit with Laski, "Communism has made its way by its idealism and not by its realism, by its spiritual promise, not its materialistic prospects."[11]

While the idealism is genuine, it is nevertheless in constant commerce with a realism so searching, that it is in danger of discounting moral and rational factors in social life too completely. There have been other dreams of justice and equality. The distinctive feature of the Marxian dream is that the destruction of power is regarded as the prerequisite of its attainment. Equality will be established only through the socialisation of the means of production, that is, through the destruction of private property, wherever private property is social power. If the Marxian should incline at times to too much cynicism, in underestimating the capacity of social reason to destroy power and bring it under control, he is not cynical but only realistic, in maintaining that disproportion of power in society is the real root of social injustice. We have seen how inevitably special privilege is associated with power, and how the ownership of the means of production is the significant power in modern society. The clear recognition of that fact is the greatest ethical contribution which Marxian thought has made to the problem of social life. It may at times not see with sufficient clarity, that a com-

[11] Harold Laski, *Communism*, p. 250. For interesting analyses of spiritual elements in proletarian life see Piechowski, *Proletarischer Glaube*, and Gertrude Hermes, *Geistige Gestalt des Marxistischen Arbeiters*.

plex society will always centralise power, whether political or economic, in a dangerous degree; and that the
coagulation of economic power can be prevented only by
a vigilant and potent state which substitutes political
power for economic power. The chief gain in such a sub-
stitution is that privilege is only a possible, and not an
inevitable, concomitant of political power; and that it is
not as easily transmitted by inheritance as economic
power. The expectation of changing human nature by
the destruction of economic privilege to such a degree
that no one will desire to make selfish use of power, must
probably be placed in the category of romantic illusions.
We shall have more to say about it later. If power remains
in society, mankind will never escape the necessity of en-
dowing those who possess it with the largest measure of
ethical self-control. But that does not obviate the necessity of reducing power to a minimum, of bringing the
remainder under the strongest measure of social control;
and of destroying such types of it as are least amenable
to social control. For there is no ethical force strong
enough to place inner checks upon the use of power if its
quantity is inordinate. "The truth is," declared James
Madison, "that all men having power ought to be dis-
trusted."[12] The history of nations bears testimony to the
truth of that observation, as we have seen; and it is the
perennial error of moralists that they do not recognise its
validity. Thus they dream of justice, but have no political
programme which would establish justice by eliminating
the cause of injustice.

Only the Marxian proletarian has seen this problem

12 *Papers of James Madison* edited by H. D. Gilpin, Vol. II, p. 1073.

with perfect clarity. If he makes mistakes in choosing the means of accomplishing his ends, he has made no mistake either in stating the rational goal toward which society must move, the goal of equal justice, or in understanding the economic foundations of justice. If his cynicism in the choice of means is at times the basis of his undoing, his realism in implementing ethical ideals with political and economic methods is the reason for his social significance.

He is right not only in the projection of his social goal but in his insistence upon the urgency of its attainment. Comfortable classes may continue to dream of an automatic progress in society. They do not suffer enough from social injustice to recognise its peril to the life of society. Only the proletarian sees how the centralisation of power and privilege in modern society proceeds so rapidly that it not only outrages the conscience but destroys the very foundations of society. He sees how inequality within each nation forces the nation to be as unmutual as possible in its relation to other nations, demanding markets without giving them, that it may make profits on producing goods which it will not allow its masses the capacity to consume.[13] He sees how this unmutuality of international

13 A non-Marxian economist has analysed the weakness of capitalism in terms which are a perfect substantiation of the Marxian diagnosis of our difficulties. The German economist, M. J. Bonn, writes: "The capitalist world in which we live has formed the habit of conveying credit, the elasticity of which is exceedingly large, mainly into channels of production. It is still obsessed by the precapitalistic notion that consumption is an evil which represents a more or less unavoidable extravagance. . . . Apart, however, from consumer-financing, which, after all, constitutes only a comparatively small part of total consumption, the fact remains that production is over and over again expanded with the aid of credit derived from or built up on savings, in particular by the construction or expansion of costly plants which can turn out

conduct not only makes wars inevitable but finally fails to serve even its immediate purposes. It results in international depressions in which all nations find themselves glutted with goods, which inequality of distribution prevents their masses from consuming. He sees this more clearly than other classes because he stands in the ranks of the unemployed. And if he is employed, he knows how a surplus of labor makes his labor cheap and imperils his living standards more than ever. Others may see these facts, but no one sees them so clearly as those who experience their consequences in their own lives. Thus it is the proletarian who predicts disaster for modern society (and may actually become the instruments of catastrophe), who is potentially the strongest force of redemption in society. Whether he still hopes to save society from disaster, or whether he has become completely catastrophic and expects redemption only after disaster, will depend in a large measure upon the degree of his suffering. We need not therefore regard either his historical prophecies or his political strategies as authoritative. Though he claims absolute truth for them, they are conditioned by peculiar circumstances, as all convictions are. If comfortable people are too complacent, he may be too desperate to see all the relevant facts. Since he stands more completely outside of modern civilisation than any other group, his perspective

goods as cheaply as estimates proclaim, only if they are fully employed; whereas consumption is left to itself. . . . So it comes about that production is governed mainly by technical considerations, and far outsteps consumption both in time and quantity, since it has secured for itself technical perfection, but no financial success." M. J. Bonn, *The Crisis of Capitalism in America*, pp. 141–142.

The only error in this analysis is the assumption that the disproportion between capital for production and capital for consumption is due to precapitalistic habits rather than to the blind self-interest of power in a world of unequal economic power.

is relatively better than that of any other. But since he stands outside, he may fail to recognise some rational and redemptive forces in society which must be taken into account. If we accept his social vision as society's legitimate goal, we ought nevertheless to scrutinise his means of attaining the goal with critical judgment. Society needs greater equality, not only to advance but to survive; and the basis of inequality is the disproportion of power in society. In the recognition of the goal of equal justice and in the analysis of the roots of present injustice the proletarian sees truly. But whether the means he intends to employ are the only possible means, as he thinks, or whether they are the most efficacious which an intelligent and realistic society could devise, is another question. His own belief that he has, in Marxism, an absolutely authoritative philosophy of history and an equally absolute and valid technique of social change must be placed in the category of religious overbeliefs rather than that of scientific truths. His confidence in the inevitability of revolution and the efficacy of violence may have a measure of truth; but the truth in it may not be as convincing or as unqualified as he imagines. It must be subjected to careful analysis. Such an analysis necessarily involves the consideration of other alternatives. The question which confronts society is, how it can eliminate social injustice by methods which offer some fair opportunity of abolishing what is evil in our present society, without destroying what is worth preserving in it, and without running the risk of substituting new abuses and injustices in the place of those abolished. That question raises two issues which the proletarian is not willing to consider. From his perspective there is nothing good in modern society which deserves preservation. In his mood he is not inclined to worry about the future. Like all desperate men he can afford to be romantic about it.

CHAPTER SEVEN

JUSTICE THROUGH REVOLUTION

THE disillusioning consequences of the World War, the inability of the nations to extricate themselves from the financial and defensive burdens which the war left them as an unholy legacy, the comparative failure of the peace machinery devised to prevent future conflicts, the world depression and the consequent misery and insecurity of millions of workers in every land, and finally the dramatic success of the Russian Revolution, all these factors have made the despised political philosophy of rebellious helots, the great promise and the great peril of the political life of the Western world. It no longer expresses merely the political conviction of advanced proletarians. Intellectuals show covert and overt sympathy toward it, and the business men use it as the bogey man with which to scare the timorous community and prevent it from granting significant concessions to the impatient and sullenly rebellious labor world. The breadth and the depth of the world depression have, moreover, tempted others beside proletarians to express a temper of catastrophism. If they do not share the proletarian hope, that salvation will come out of catastrophe, they are at least inclined to question the possibility of avoiding catastrophe by methods of gradual social change, and await the revolution in the ambivalence of hope and fear.

In spite of the more general consideration and sympathy which the prophecies of revolution receive in the middle-class community, the methods of revolution remain abhorrent to it. Violence and revolution are usually ruled out as permissible instruments of social change on *a priori* grounds. The middle classes and the rational moralists, who have a natural abhorrence of violence, may be right in their general thesis; but they are wrong in their assumption that violence is intrinsically immoral. Nothing is intrinsically immoral except ill-will and nothing intrinsically good except goodwill. We have previously examined proletarian motives and discovered that, while they are not altogether pure, they are as pure as the motives of collective man usually are; and are certainly not less moral than the motives of those who defend special privileges by more covert means of coercion than the proletarians are able to command.

Since it is very difficult to judge human motives, it is natural that, from an external perspective, the social consequences of an action or policy should be regarded as more adequate tests of its morality than the hidden motives. The good motive is judged by its social goal. Does it have the general welfare as its objective? When viewing a historic situation all moralists become pragmatists and utilitarians. Some general good, some *summum bonum,* "the greatest good of the greatest number" or "the most inclusive harmony of all vital capacities" is set up as the criterion of the morality of specific actions and each action is judged with reference to its relation to the ultimate goal. We have previously analysed the ultimate objectives of Marxian politics and have found them to be identical with the most rational possible social goal, that of equal justice.

The choice of instruments and immediate objectives which fall between motive and ultimate objective, raises issues which are pragmatic to such a degree that they may be said to be more political than they are ethical. The realm of politics is a twilight zone where ethical and technical issues meet. A political policy cannot be intrinsically evil if it can be proved to be an efficacious instrument for the achievement of a morally approved end. Neither can it be said to be wholly good merely because it seems to make for ultimately good consequences. Immediate consequences must be weighed against the ultimate consequences. The destruction of a life or the suppression of freedom result in the immediate destruction of moral values. Whether the ultimate good, which is hoped to be accomplished by this immediate destruction, justifies the sacrifice, is a question which depends upon many considerations for its answer. How great is the immediate and less inclusive value which is sacrificed for a more ultimate and more inclusive one? How certain is the attainment of the ultimate value? Is there any certainty that violence can establish equality or that an equality so established can be maintained? These are some of the pragmatic questions which suggest themselves. The questions are important but none of them can be dealt with adequately if it is assumed that any social policy, as violence for instance, is intrinsically immoral. The assumption that violence and revolution are intrinsically immoral rests upon two errors.

The one error is the belief that violence is a natural and

inevitable expression of ill-will, and non-violence of goodwill, and that violence is therefore intrinsically evil and
non-violence intrinsically good. While such a proposition
has a certain measure of validity, or at least of plausibility, it is certainly not universally valid. It is less valid in
inter-group relations than in individual relations, if our
assumption is correct that the achievement of harmony
and justice between groups requires a measure of coercion, which is not necessary in the most intimate and the
most imaginative individual relations. Once we admit the
factor of coercion as ethically justified, though we con-
cede that it is always morally dangerous, we cannot draw
any absolute line of demarcation between violent and non-
violent coercion. We may argue that the immediate consequences of violence are such that they frustrate the ultimate purpose by which it is justified. If that is true, it is
certainly not self-evident; and violence can therefore not
be ruled out on *a priori* grounds. It is all the more difficult to do this if we consider that the immediate consequences of violence cannot be differentiated as sharply
from those of non-violence, as is sometimes supposed.
The difference between them is not an absolute one, even
though there may be important distinctions, which must
be carefully weighed. Gandhi's boycott of British cotton
results in the undernourishment of children in Manchester, and the blockade of the Allies in war-time caused the
death of German children. It is impossible to coerce a
group without damaging both life and property and without imperilling the interests of the innocent with those
of the guilty. Those are factors which are involved in the
intricacies of group relations; and they make it impos-

sible to transfer an ethic of personal relations uncritically to the field of inter-group relations.

The second error by which violence comes to be regarded as unethical in intrinsic terms is due to an uncritical identification of traditionalised instrumental values with intrinsic moral values. Only goodwill is intrinsically good. But as soon as goodwill expresses itself in specific actions, it must be determined whether the right motive has chosen the right instruments for the attainment of its goal and whether the objective is a defensible one. For reason may err in guiding the righteous will in the choice of either means or ends. But there are certain specific actions and attitudes which are generally not judged in terms of their adequacy in achieving an approved social end. Experience has established them; and their traditionalised instrumental value is regarded as an intrinsic one. Respect for the life, the opinions and the interests of another is regarded as intrinsically good and violence to the fellowman's life, opinions and interests is prohibited. It is not only assumed that they will have the right ultimate consequences but that they are the natural and inevitable expression of goodwill. In purely personal relations these assumptions are quite generally justified. The moral will expresses itself unconsciously in terms of consideration for the life, the interests and the rights of others; and the consequences of such consideration may be presumed to be good. It is good to trust the neighbor, for it will prompt him to trustworthy action; it is good to respect his life because this respect helps to establish and preserve that general reverence for life upon which all morality rests; it is good not to coerce the opinions of the other because coercion does not change opinion or because it may give an undue advantage to the wrong opinion; it is good to tell the truth because truth-telling facilitates the sharing of experience which is basic to all social life. Such judgments as these may not be universally accepted, but they are the working capital of personal morality.

It is well to note that even in the comparatively simple problems of individual relationships there is no moral value which may be regarded as absolute. It may, in a given instant, have to be sacrificed to some other value. Every action resolves a certain competition between values, in which one value must be subordinated to another. This is necessary in a specific instance even though there may be an ultimate harmony of all high and legitimate moral values. Thus a physician who believes that the neighbor has a right to the truth as well as a right to his life, and that there is no ultimate conflict between the two rights, may nevertheless deny his patient the truth in a given instant, because in that instant the truth might imperil his life. In the same way, though believing that reverence for life is basic to all morality, he may have to make a choice between types of life, and sacrifice an unborn infant to save the life of a mother. A reflective morality is constantly under the necessity of reanalysing moral values which are regarded as intrinsically good and of judging them in instrumental terms. The more inclusive the ends which are held in view, the more the immediate consequences of an action cease to be the authoritative criteria of moral judgment. Since society must constantly deal with these inclusive ends, it always seems to capitulate to the dangerous principle that the end justifies the means. All morality really accepts that principle, but the fact is obscured by the assumption, frequently though not universally justified, that the character of immediate consequences guarantees the character of the ultimate end. A community may believe, as it usually does, that reverence for life is a basic moral attitude, and yet rob a criminal of his life in order to deter others from taking life. It may be wrong in doing this; but if it is, the error is not in taking the life but in following a policy which does not really deter others from murder. The question cannot be resolved on *a priori* grounds but only by observing the social consequences of various types of punishment. Society may believe that the preservation of freedom of opinion is a social good, not because liberty of thought is an inherent or natural right but because it is a basic condition of social progress. Yet in a given instance the principle of freedom may have to yield to the necessities of social cohesion, requiring a measure of coercion. If the state usually errs in throttling freedom, its error is in using an undue measure of coercion, in applying it prematurely before efforts to achieve solidarity by a mutual accommodation of interests have been exhausted, and in exploiting the resultant social solidarity for morally unapproved ends. On the question of the relative value of freedom and solidarity no final and authoritative answer can be given. Every answer will be relative to the social experience of particular individuals and groups, who have suffered from either anarchy or autocracy and tend to embrace the evils of the one in the effort to escape the perils of the other.

The differences between proletarian and middle-class morality are on the whole differences between men who regard themselves as primarily individuals and those who feel themselves primarily members of a social group. The latter will emphasise liberty, respect for individual life, the rights of property and the moral values of ˙mutual trust and unselfishness. The former will emphasise loyalty to the group and the need of its solidarity, they will subject the rights of property to the total social welfare, will abrogate the values of freedom for the attainment of their most cherished social goal and will believe that conflicts of interest between groups can be resolved, not by accommodation but by struggle. The middle class tries to make the canons of individual morality authoritative for all social relations. It is shocked by the moral cynicism, the tendency toward violence and indifference toward individual freedom of the proletarian. Inasfar as this represents an honest effort to make the ideals of personal morality norms for the conduct of human groups, it is a legitimate moral attitude which must never be completely abandoned. Inasfar as it represents the illusions and deceptions of middle-class people, who never conform their own group conduct to their individual ideals, it deserves the cynical reaction of the proletarian. The illusory element must be admitted to be very large. The middle classes believe in freedom, but deny freedom when its exercise imperils their position in society; they profess a morality of love and unselfishness but do not achieve an unselfish group attitude toward a less privileged group; they claim to abhor violence and yet use it both in international conflict and in the social crises in which their interests are imperilled; they want mutuality of interest between classes rather than a class struggle but the mutuality must not be so complete as to destroy all their special privileges.

The proletarian on the other hand is not enough of an individual, in the attainments of his own cultural life and in the conditions of his social life, to be strongly moved by the canons of individual morality. He is most conscious of the reality of group behavior. He is not only more completely immersed in his own group than the more privileged classes, but he feels the effect of the behavior of other groups upon his life more definitely than do the members of privileged classes. His moral attitudes are determined by the moral behavior of groups rather than by the moral behavior of individuals. He discounts the latter not only because he is himself not an individual, as more privileged persons are, but because he has not found individual morality qualifying the dominant greed and lust to power of privileged groups to any appreciable degree. He has come to the conclusion that the hope of achieving a moral group life results in illusion. The conflict between proletarian and middle-class morality is thus a contest between hypocrisy and brutality, and between sentimentality and cynicism. The limitations of the one tend to accentuate the limitations of the other. The full import of that conflict is revealed in Trotsky's words: "As for us, we were never concerned with the Kantian priestly and vegetarian-Quaker prattle about the 'sacredness of human life.' We were revolutionaries in opposition and remain revolutionaries in power. To make the individual sacred we must destroy the social order which crucifies him and this problem can only be solved by blood and iron."

The communist's reaction to middle-class morality is directed not only against the hypocrisy of the men of power, who profess individual moral ideals but are governed in their group behavior by motives of greed and use the instruments of coercion and violence to gain their ends, but also against middle-class intellectual and religious moralists who hope to insinuate the ideal of personal morality into the behavior of groups. The proletarian is as certain that the hopes of the latter represent a futile sentimentality as he is that the protestations of the former are hypocritical. He is going to build an ideal world, not by trusting in the moral resources of individuals but by remaining on the level of the men of power and using their own instruments against them. Since it is obvious that most middle-class idealists overestimate the available moral resources for radical social change, the proletarian is manifestly not completely mistaken in the moral cynicism which informs his political strategy. But since he is too completely immersed in the social group and too much the victim of group brutalities, he may not have the whole truth about the moral resources of human life. The brutality of his political strategy can be justified only if the moral cynicism which inspires it is true to all the facts. On the other hand the middle-class idealist may, and probably does, live under illusions. He is too completely an individual to be conscious of the most significant behavior of groups. He does not suffer enough, in his comfortable position, from the brutality of collective man, fully to understand his dominant impulses. He may have separated himself from those impulses and detached himself psychologically. But he is not detached economically and therefore does not feel the full force and the real meaning of the impulses of dominant groups. He sees moral forces working efficaciously within the confines of his group, and erroneously imagines that they can be extended until they resolve all group conflict.

The differences in moral outlook between the proletarian and middle-class world can therefore not be judged by any purely *a priori* criteria. The question between them can be solved only by a study of history. And some of the history which must be studied has not yet been made. Wherefore every analysis trenches inevitably to a certain degree into the field of prophecy. Meanwhile it is important to recognise, that revolutionary strategy is not wanting in either the motives or the objectives which give it a solid moral basis. Neither do its motives or objectives guarantee the validity of its methods or means. These must be judged in the light of all the facts and possibilities in regard to collective human behavior.

If a season of violence can establish a just social system and can create the possibilities of its preservation, there is no purely ethical ground upon which violence and revolution can be ruled out. This could be done only upon the basis of purely anarchistic ethical and political presuppositions. Once we have made the fateful concession of ethics to politics, and accepted coercion as a necessary instrument of social cohesion, we can make no absolute distinctions between non-violent and violent types of coercion or between coercion used by governments and that which is used by revolutionaries. If such distinctions are made they must be justified in terms of the consequences in which they result. The real question is: what are the political possibilities of establishing justice through violence?

A certain system of power, based upon the force which inheres in property, and augmented by the political power of the state is set against the demands of the worker. Efforts to destroy the economic power by giving the worker the political power, inherent in the strength of his numbers, are frustrated by the use of the organs of education and propaganda in control of the dominant group, and the ignorance of a portion of the workers. Can the workers overthrow the existing power and come in control of both the apparatus of the state and organs of education so that they can establish an equalitarian world and educate a new generation which will maintain it? The realistic Marxians who have analysed this problem in terms of the comparative resources of power available on each side, do not give themselves to the romantic illusions current among certain classes of intellectuals, who think that a revolution is a fairly easy achievement. They know that the task is not easy, even though they believe the inexorable forces of history are gradually changing the proportion of power and making the ultimate victory of the worker possible. They believe that the increased centralisation of power and privilege will reduce the comparative strength of the privileged groups, that the increased misery of the workers, and of the lower middle classes, will augment their numbers and increase their revolutionary fervor and that international wars, in which capitalism inevitably involves the present social order, will finally reduce the prestige and the power of the national state sufficiently to make a transfer of power possible.

These catastrophic predictions, which in the true proletarian achieve the character of a religious hope and creed, have been neither proved nor disproved in any authoritative fashion by the history of industrial civilisation. There is very strong evidence both for and against the possibility of their realisation. The fact that industrial workers actually shared some of the benefits of modern technology in the past fifty years, so that their living standards were raised, compared to their previous status, even though they did not win a comparatively larger share of the national income, and that their growing political power actually forced the dominant classes to yield concessions to them, seems to cast grave doubts upon the Marxian theory of revolution through the increasing misery of the workers. In Germany it led to a new school of socialist thought which accepted the revisions of Eduard Bernstein on the original Marxian doctrines[1] and changed the expectations of catastrophe into hopes of evolutionary progress toward equal justice. The fact that the concentration of capital did not proceed with the rapidity which Marxian prophesy had envisaged, that a petty bourgeois class, more numerous and more tenacious than anticipated, was developed under capitalism, that the growing political power of labor parties forced the state partially to equalise the inequalities created by the concentration of capital; all these factors seemed to justify the revision of socialism into an evolutionary doctrine. The contention of Bernstein, that the concentration of capital proceeds

[1] Eduard Bernstein, *Evolutionary Socialism*.

more slowly in agriculture than in industry, has been borne out completely by history. Even where the farmer and the peasant becomes dispossessed he does not turn collectivist. His political attitudes remain equivocal. Trotsky is right, "The peasantry always has two faces, one turned toward the proletariat, the other toward the bourgeoisie."[2]

In countries more advanced than Russia, the peasant develops his own political organisations, which fight much more stubbornly against proletarian collectivism than they were able to in Russia. Furthermore the middle class, even when the independent retailer becomes a chain store clerk through the force of capital concentration, does not react to the situation in proletarian terms. The white collar worker may not own any property and may therefore logically belong to the proletariat, but the dictum of Boudin and others that salaried workers "are in reality just as much a part of the proletariat as the merest day laborer"[3] fails to take important psychological factors into consideration. If we may regard Germany, where all the social and political forces of modern civilisation have reached their most advanced form, as a criterion, none of the disinherited middle classes express themselves politically in proletarian terms. On the contrary they turn to fascism, which combines enough radicalism, to give the poorer middle classes some hope of better things to come, with the political strategy of anti-Marxian and nationalism, by which it gains the support of the economic overlords, who are afraid of the

[2] Trotsky, *The History of the Russian Revolution*, p. 317.
[3] L. B. Boudin, *Theoretical System of Karl Marx*, p. 206.

rising tide of labor. That the middle classes can be drawn into a party in which the wealthiest and the poorest ostensibly make common cause, is the measure of their political intelligence. Whatever may be the logic of their position in economic terms, they would rather express their resentments in a nationalistic spirit, and in minimum demands for the elimination of financial abuses, than in thoroughgoing economic changes. They will never be reduced to proletarian terms politically (even though they are reduced to those terms economically) until they have lost their cultural as well as their economic inheritance. Unlike the proletarian, they do not stand outside, but thoroughly inside, the national culture. Whether continued economic pressure will limit the educational advantages of this class sufficiently to reduce it to a proletarian status, is one of the questions which cannot be answered confidently at this time. Nothing is certain now, but that the middle classes have had a more solid economic basis in the modern social structure than Marxism predicted, and that even when the economic basis is destroyed, they are prevented by psychological considerations from becoming proletarians.

The German situation, where the Catholic party has made itself indispensable to the preservation of bourgeois democracy by the solidity and tenacity of its religiously motivated support and by the astuteness of its political leadership, is again roughly typical of another aspect of the social problem in Western civilisation. The cultural opposition to the proletarian negation of the whole historical and traditional cultural life of the bourgeois world, cannot be disposed of in Western civilisation as easily as it was in Russia. There an inept Greek church, completely identified with social reaction and incidentally never really indigenous to Slavic culture, fell an easy prey to proletarian revolt against traditional culture. Ancient cultural and religious inheritances may not always achieve the same living relationship to contemporary politics as is the case in the Catholic party of Germany, but the political power of that party is broadly illustrative of factors in modern society which Marxism has underestimated.

The complexity of modern society, with its multifarious economic and social groups, which refuse to accept the destiny assigned to them by a consistent logic of economics, and which are able to defend their position in society by political, and if need be, by more martial weapons, seems to offer permanent resistance to the revolutionary venture of which Marxians dream. The strength of the peasants, the urban middle classes and the groups which are fortified by vital cultural defenses against the revolt of the proletarians, may seem to justify revolution, because it seems to offer a permanent bar to the gradual attainment of parliamentary majorities by labor parties. But their power may be able to prevent the revolutionary as well as the parliamentary victory of labor. They need only attain a social cohesion, somewhat comparable to that of the proletarians, and they achieve possession of political and military force sufficient to frustate revolutionary efforts.

There is a further complexity to be considered, and that is the division in the proletarian ranks, to which allusion has been made in a previous chapter. Modern technology develops a class of skilled and semi-skilled laborers, who achieve a more privileged social position than the unskilled. Ethical motives ought to prompt them to make common cause with the unskilled and the more completely disinherited. But these ethical motives are not always sufficiently potent; and the theory, that economic motives will create the solidarity, has been proved erroneous. In America this type of worker expresses himself politically in the reactionary policies of the American Federation of Labor, and leaves the unskilled worker in his misery. In the more advanced industrial nations, England and Germany, he defends his cause through the instrumentality of parliamentary socialism. He is more collectivistic than the white collar worker, but in many respects less revolutionary. In Germany he has become, in union with the Catholic party, the chief support of bourgeois democracy against revolutionary efforts from both the right and the left. He proves that as soon as workers have something more to lose than their chains, as soon as they have the slightest stake in the *status quo* (it need not be property, it need be only a fairly secure job or the minimum security of a semi-adequate unemployment dole), they will suffer the slings and arrows of outrageous fortune, rather than fly to evils that they know not of. They will fight the real proletarians, the completely disinherited, almost as vigorously as their reactionary foes. If increased misery forces some of their numbers into the ranks of the communists, as has been the case in Germany, they still outnumber the revolutionists. In the German election of July 31, 1932, they lost roughly ten per cent of their strength to the communists, but still remain, under an economic pressure greater than any proletarian group in any industrial country is likely to suffer for many years, fifty per cent stronger than the communists.

It is interesting to note that their political attitudes have completely wiped out the differences between the revisionism of Bernstein and the more revolutionary parliamentarism of Kautsky. The dictum of Kautsky, "The emancipation of the laboring class is not to be expected from its increasing demoralisation but from its increasing strength,"[4] may be true, but not in the sense that he intended. The envy upon which Henry DeMan enlarges, and the more purely economic motives which Kautsky regards as the basis of revolutionary fervor, will continue to unite industrial workers into political parties which have socialism as their goal. But it will not make revolutionists of them, except in the very qualified sense in which Kautsky uses the term. Here the communists are much more realistic and their analysis is much truer. Trotsky quotes the words of Marat with approval: "A Revolution is accomplished and sustained only by the lowest classes of society, by all the disinherited, whom the shameless rich treat as *canaille* and whom the Romans with their usual cynicism once named proletarians."[5] It may be that workers will not turn revolutionists until their present state of misery can be compared with a previous state of comparative security; but it is equally certain that hunger and not envy or impatience with injustice produces revolution. The communist realism on this point clarifies what middle-class and semi-proletarian thought frequently confuses. They may be wrong in their prediction that inex-

[4] Karl Kautsky, *Social Revolution*, p. 38. [5] Trotsky, *op. cit*, p. 240.

orable forces will produce the prerequisites of revolution but they are very clear in their understanding of what these prerequisites are.

If we want to predict the future of revolution in Western civilisation, we would do much better to make Germany, and possibly England, rather than Russia, the basis of our predictions. The complete ineptness of the Russian aristocratic bureaucracy and its thorough dissolution in the war, the formlessness and lack of prestige of the commercial middle class, the political defenselessness of the peasants and their momentary identity of interest with the workers, created by their desire for land and peace; the medieval ignorance of the church; the revolutionary solidarity of the workers, created by economic disinheritance; and a political cynicism, perfectly justified by the brutal inertia and terror of a moribund state; all these factors produced a basis for the Russian Revolution, and conformed to the formula of Marxism much more perfectly than will probably ever be the case in the industrial civilisation for which the formula was designed.

Even when a modern state is disintegrated by economic and social conflict to the degree which the life of Germany reveals, a vague instinct of self-preservation, a still potent sense of national unity, creates a temper in which a little junta may manipulate the unimpaired police power of the state and use it to frustrate revolutionary efforts from the right and the left. Here again communist realism stands in wholesome contrast to the vague hopes of parlor revolutionists. "No great revolution has happened or can happen," wrote Lenin, "without the disorganisation of the army. . . . The new social class which aspires to power has never been able and is even today unable, to assure and maintain its authority without the complete dislocation of the old army."[6] But a modern state may maintain its police power even when social disintegration has proceeded to a very far degree, simply because a large portion of the population, at variance on every question of economic policy, is united in its common fear of the dislocations of revolution. Thus in Germany where 44 per cent of the voters are more or less revolutionary in the fascist sense and 36 per cent are either socialist or communist, the impossibility of any group establishing itself in power, without facing years of revolutionary opposition from the other group, creates a temper in the nation which allows either a Bruening or a Von Papen government to wield the unimpaired police power of the nation in the interest of national unity. The lack of revolutionary ardor of the socialists and the political power of the Catholic vote creates the specific political support for such a policy. This kind of national unity is manifestly precarious. It could not be maintained indefinitely if Germany remained under the economic pressure of the moment. But it does illustrate perfectly, how tenacious the will to unity in a modern nation is and how it survives even when every economic basis for it has been destroyed.

The fear of the international consequences of a revolution in nations who are inserted into a system of economic interdependence by the forces of a technological civilisation, is an additional cause of this caution. A comparatively self-sufficient agrarian Russia is, again, not a

[6] Quoted by Harold Laski, *Communism*, p. 205.

good example of the probable political reactions of more complex nations. The success of the Marxian revolutionary formula in Russia has, in other words, given rise to confusions and hopes, which could be realised in Western civilisation only through the rarest concatenation of circumstances.

Difficult as the method of revolution is for any Western industrial civilisation, it must not be regarded as impossible. The forces which make for concentration of wealth and power are operative, even though they do not move as unambiguously as the Marxians prophesied. Whatever the errors in the prophesies of Marx, he certainly made no mistake in his prophesies of periodic crises of increasing frequency and extent in the business world. Neither was he wrong in attributing them to the overproduction caused by the lack of consuming power of the worker. The fact that we are in such a world crisis today, proves that the concessions which the workers have won by their political power have not been sufficient to give health to the present economic system. Whether this and other crises will prompt enough fear and create enough intelligence in the privileged classes to allow for a more rapid transmutation of the present social system into a more mutual one is a question which cannot be confidently answered in either the affirmative or negative. Such financial crises as the present are more productive of fascist tendencies than of communist revolutions, as long as the middle classes maintain their present power. In both England and Germany the depression has made labor more radical but also stiffened the conservative opposition against it, and thrown the neutral middle classes into the arms of reaction. Revolutionists easily underestimate the patience of peoples. Thus Engels prophesied in 1844: "By the time of the next following crisis, which, according to the analogy of its predecessors, must break out in 1852 or 1853, the English people will have enough of being plundered by their capitalists and left to starve when the capitalists no longer require their services. If, up to that time, the English bourgeoisie does not stop to reflect, and to all appearances it certainly will not do so, a revolution will follow with which none hitherto known can be compared."[7]

Predictions made at present may have as little validity as this quite plausible prediction of Engels in the middle of the nineteenth century. Meanwhile it is true that each decade adds to the tension created by the increasing inequalities of the economic order. Yet it is hardly conceivable that any modern state will be subjected to greater social tensions than the Germany of today; and we have noted what the consequences have been. If any prediction can be made with a fair degree of certainty, it is that Western civilisation will not be ripe for proletarian revolutions for many decades, and may never be ripe for them, unless one further condition of the Marxian prophecy is fulfilled, and that is, that the inevitable imperialism of the capitalistic nations will involve them in further wars on a large scale. Such a war would not necessarily result in communistic revolutions but it would shatter the authority of some states sufficiently and create enough social chaos to make some kind of revolution possible. Whether the chaos would be re-

[7] Quoted by Harry Laidler, *A History of Socialist Thought*, p. 216.

solved by fascism, as was the case in Italy, or by a bourgeois, semi-socialistic democracy, as was the case in Germany, would depend upon the comparative strength of
the various economic classes at the conclusion of the war.
There is no modern industrial state in which the number
of the completely disinherited is sufficiently large, or has
the possibility of becoming large enough in any imminent
future, to guarantee the success of a communist revolution. But that remains a possibility for the more distant
future. The aftermath of another World War might very
well result in such a general impoverishment. Without
another World War, the possibilities of establishing communism by revolution are extremely slight in the whole
of the Western world. There is a much greater probabil-
ity that communism will gain its victories in the agrarian
orient than in the industrial occident. In the west even
agrarian Spain shows signs of stabilizing its revolution
upon the semi-bourgeois, semi-socialistic pattern, which
Germany has made familiar. The world may become divided between a communistic orient and a semi-socialistic occident, moving slowly toward the socialistic goal, but
always running the danger of moving too slowly to avert
another catastrophe.

So much for the possibilities of establishing an equalitarian world by violence. Before the issue is dismissed, one
further problem ought to be considered. Is it possible to
maintain such a world once it has been established? The
uncompromising equalitarian always has a moral advantage over those who propose slower methods of social
change, by pointing out that these methods invariably beguile society to be satisfied with something less than the

ideal and to retain many forms of ancient and traditional
injustice. If a revolution can destroy social injustice and
preserve equal justice, much might be forgiven it in the
methods which it employs. This is the more obvious if it
is considered that the whole of society is constantly involved in both coercion and violence and that the moral
advantages of the more traditional and more covert forms
of coercion over the less traditional and more overt forms
are not as absolute as moralists usually assume. But it
would be tragic indeed if the immediate consequences of
revolutionary chaos, naturally greater in an industrial civilisation than in an agrarian one, should fail to issue in
the final consequence of a lasting justice.

The fear that they will fail is associated with a sus-
picion that communists, in spite of their realism, become
hopeless romantics when they estimate the social consequences of a new economic society. They seem to believe
that it will be easy to create perfect social mutuality by destroying inequality of power. But can they destroy economic power without creating strong centres of political
power? And how may they be certain that this political
power will be either ethically or socially restrained? We
have seen that it is difficult to prevent the centralisation
of economic power without giving the political state tremendous authority. A powerful state necessitates dangerous concentrations of political power in the hands of a
few individuals and a small group. There is no certainty
that this new power can be brought under either perfect
ethical or social restraint. Ethical restraint is provided,
for the moment, in Russia by the moral idealism of revolutionaries who espoused the cause of revolution before it

offered the rewards of power. Even that idealism is no guarantee against the abuse of power. The abuse of power by communistic bureaucrats is very considerable, and is bound to grow as the purer revolutionary idealists are supplanted by men who have consciously sought for the possession of power. Though the equalitarian traditions of the revolutionary movement prevent them from using their positions for private economic gain, the abuse of power is a fact for which economic equalitarianism only partially compensates. An officious bureaucrat may cause intolerable injustices, even if he eats the same food and wears the same clothes as his victim.[8]

The theory of communism is, that the dictatorship is only a transitory state and that it will become unnecessary as soon as the whole community has accepted the equalitarian ideals of communism and no one challenges the regime. This theory fails to do justice to the facts of human nature, revealed not only in the men of power but in ordinary men. If the Russian oligarchy strips itself of its own power, it will be the first oligarchy of history to do so. It cannot, of course, transmit its power by inheritance; but the inheritance of power is not the only cause of its abuse or basis of its perpetuation. The American business oligarchy is not as hereditary as European landed aristocracies, but is for that reason neither more virtuous

[8] For a realistic analysis of the growth rather than diminution of political terrorism in Russia, see Waldemar Gurian, *Bolshevism: Theory and Practice,* Chap. 2.

The possibilities of petty chicane and capricious tyranny on the part of all-powerful Soviet officials is implicitly acknowledged in a recent decree of the Kremlin in which general rules of "revolutionary legality" are laid down to restrain the officiousness and caprice of officials. See news dispatch, *New York Herald Tribune,* August 21, 1932.

nor less tenacious in clinging to its power and privilege. Since, according to the tenets of communism, the dictatorship is necessary until all the enemies of the proletarian state are "liquidated," and since external enemies will remain for many decades or centuries, even if all internal enemies should be destroyed, the power of dictatorship could be perpetuated indefinitely without any conscious dishonesties.

The hope that the internal enemies will all be destroyed and that the new society will create only men who will be in perfect accord with the collective will of society, and will not seek personal advantage in the social process, is romantic in its interpretation of the possibilities of human nature and in its mystical glorification of the anticipated automatic mutuality in the communist society. The symbol of this romanticism in communist thought is the virtual anarchism which crowns the structure of communist theory. The state will gradually wither away because it is merely the instrument of domination, which will not be needed in a completely mutual society. Lenin, the brutal realist, when dealing with the realities of today, thus turns sentimentalist when envisaging the possibilities of tomorrow: "When people have become accustomed to observe the fundamental principles of social life and their labor is so productive that they will voluntarily work according to their abilities . . . there will be no need of any exact calculation of the quantity of products to be distributed to each of its members; each will take freely 'according to his needs.'" This perfect mutuality is achieved partly by destroying the disproportion of power and privilege, thus equalising the interests of all and establishing an identity of interest. "Theirs (the masses'),” declares William Z. Foster, "will be an individuality growing out of an harmonising with the interests of all."[9] The communist is right in assuming that the initial equalisation of power and privilege enhances the possibilities of mutuality in society. If there is no insecurity to compel, and no power to tempt, men to think of themselves before they think of the total needs of society, it is manifestly possible to reduce individual self-seeking. The hope that it can be destroyed to such a degree as not to become the basis of future inequality in society, unless the iron will of society, operating through a potent state, suppresses such tendencies, is as romantic as Rousseauistic interpretations of human problems. The Rousseauistic element in communist thought is, in fact, very clearly expressed in Bukharin's identification of the individual will and the general will: "In such a society (a fully developed communist one) all relations between men will be obvious to each and the social volition will be the organisation of all their wills. It will not be a resultant, obtained by elemental accident, independent of the will of the individual, but a consciously organised social decision. . . . It will be impossible to observe social phenomena whose effect on the majority of the population will be harmful and ruinous."[10] In all these prophesies pure sentimentality obscures the fact, that there can never be a perfect mutuality of interest between individuals who perform different functions in society. There must, for instance, always be, as there is now in Russia, a certain degree of

9 W. Z. Foster, *Toward Soviet America*, p. 333.
10 N. Bukharin, *Historical Materialism*, p. 41.

tension between the peasant who wants as many manufactured articles as possible for the food which he delivers to urban workers, and these workers, who want more food from the peasant than he is inclined to give them for their manufactured goods. The hope that there will ever be an ideal society, in which every one can take without restraint from the common social process "according to his need," completely disregards the limitations of human nature. Man will always be imaginative enough to enlarge his needs beyond minimum requirements and selfish enough to feel the pressure of his needs more than the needs of others. Every society will have to maintain methods of arbitrating conflicting needs to the end of history; and in that process those who are shrewder will gain some advantage over the simple, even if they should lack special instruments of power. Bukharin's idea, that a social policy harmful or ruinous to the population would be unthinkable in a communist society, is buttressed by the further prediction that the "abolition of the educational monopoly" would equalise intelligence sufficiently to arm every citizen with the power to defend his interests in society. But the idea that intelligence can be equalised by equal educational opportunities, is just as unrealistic as to suppose that present inequalities of intelligence are purely innate and could not be partially eliminated by equal educational advantages for all.

Significantly the communist does not completely trust the automatic identity of interest to establish perfect mutuality. He believes in moral education for the creation of attitudes of mutuality. With Lenin, he wants people to "become accustomed to observe the fundamental principles of social life." And he is right in assuming that a society in which the whole power of social approval is behind the co-operative attitude rather than the motive of self-seeking, will have a tremendous effect upon moral attitudes, as it has today in Russia. And when a co-operative society adds the precept of the school to the potent example set by the practice of society itself, there is no reason why it should not be able to minimise individual self-seeking and maximise social co-operation. But it is sentimental and romantic to assume that any education or any example will ever completely destroy the inclination of human nature to seek special advantages at the expense of, or in indifference to, the needs and interests of others. It is significant that the Russians have been forced to compromise with this force in human nature by establishing wage differentials in both industry and agriculture, in order to augment the socialised motive forces with the motive of seeking personal rewards for labor. They have tried to hide the fact that this is a concession to, and compromise with, an inevitable weakness in human nature by insisting that it is merely a concession to a vestigial remnant of capitalist psychology. They hope that the next generation will be entirely emancipated from it. Waldo Frank reports the following interesting conversation with a communist factory director: " 'Is there then no danger,' I said at last, 'to your communist ideal?' 'From each according to his ability, to each according to his need' has always seemed to me to be the golden rule of socialism. . . . Yet here you are, remunerating inventions with money, paying superior sums of money to the more capable men. Here you are, planning your new hierarchy of merit by the old hated symbol of money. . . . It almost seems to me as if you were fighting the old order by infecting yourselves with the disease which rotted it.' The communist answers him. . . .'To meet the temporary emergency, we must induce the men we have, men brought up in the capitalist world, men still open to capitalist ideas, to speed up production. We must do this by any means that will convince them. . . . But meantime, our children are being brought up on pure communist values.' 'You mean that the standard by which your young people are being taught to live will be stronger than the example they see before them? . . . When has education been according to an ideal superior to the practised way of life? And when has an ideal prevailed against the reality which belied it?' "[11]

Inequality of reward need not of course, even if it represents a permanent concession to the weaknesses of human nature, as is probably the case, result in the old inequalities of power which breed inequalities of privilege, which are either disproportionate or totally irrelevant to the importance of function and the efficiency with which function is performed. It is possible for society to prevent accumulations of unequal rewards from being transmuted into instruments of social power. But it cannot prevent them from becoming symbols of unequal social prestige. In other words, if the desperate means which the communist uses are to be justified by the totally different and more ideal society which he creates, the justification is not as convincing as it seems to the romantic communist. If the new society does not eliminate the weak-

[11] Waldo Frank, *Dawn in Russia*, p. 142.

nesses of human nature, which cause injustice, as completely as he supposes, he has lost the moral advantage of his absolutism. Perhaps a society which gradually approximates the ideal will not be so very inferior morally to one which makes one desperate grasp after the ideal, only to find that the realities of history and nature dissolve it. Absolutism, in both religious and political idealism, is a splendid incentive to heroic action, but a dangerous guide in immediate and concrete situations. In religion it permits absurdities and in politics cruelties, which fail to achieve justifying consequences because the inertia of human nature remains a nemesis to the absolute ideal. Individuals may aspire to the absolute with more justification and less peril than societies. If the price which they must pay is high, the probable futility of their effort involves only their own losses. And the sense of a noble tragedy may compensate for the defeat. But societies risk the welfare of millions when they gamble for the attainment of the absolute. And, since coercion is an invariable instrument of their policy, absolutism transmutes this instrument into unbearable tyrannies and cruelties. The fanaticism which in the individual may appear in the guise of a harmless or pathetic vagary, when expressed in political policy, shuts the gates of mercy on mankind.

CHAPTER EIGHT

JUSTICE THROUGH POLITICAL FORCE

THE division of the working class into a more favored and a less favored group, roughly identical with the skilled and the unskilled workers, has been previously considered. The group, which feels itself defrauded of its just proportion of the common wealth of society, but which has a measure of security and therefore does not feel itself completely disinherited, expresses its political aspirations in a qualified Marxism in which the collectivist goal is shared with the more revolutionary Marxians, but in which parliamentary and evolutionary methods are substituted for revolution as means of achieving the goal.

In all industrial nations, except America, the trade unions are the source of the voting strength of this evolutionary socialism, though its political philosophy has usually been elaborated by middle-class intellectuals. In America the trade unions still adhere to the futile policy of rewarding their friends and punishing their foes in the old parties. Their failure to recognise the futility of this procedure proves how difficult it is to transfer the results of social experience from one nation to another; for the history of European industrial nations has fully discredited this kind of political strategy. Inasfar as it rests upon confidence in the adequacy of the purely economic weapons of the trade union movement it is no less fallacious. The combination of political and economic power which the dominant classes set against the worker in the modern state must be met by a combination of political and economic power. The power of the worker in the economic society (chiefly the weapon of the strike) is not adequate for the defense of his interests. It suffers from several limitations. It is lamed by the state, which under the influence of the dominant classes passes legislation to diminish the power of the strike weapon as much as possible. The use and abuse of federal injunctions in labor disputes, compulsory arbitration, the declaration of martial law and the use of troops against the strikers are a few of the many methods used by the state against the worker. Even without facing the opposition of political power, the worker's economic weapon is weak, and is becoming weaker. It is weak because the worker is never able to match the economic resources of the owner in a dispute of some duration. He can be starved into submission. It is becoming weaker because the very overproduction which imperils his living standards and forces him to resort to the strike weapon also creates a vast reservoir of unemployed and hungry men who can be used to supplant the strikers. Furthermore the tendency of automatic industry is to rob the worker of his skill and place it in the machine. Thus the backbone of modern labor power is semi-skilled rather than skilled, and can be replaced much more quickly than in the past.

The worker is thus under the necessity of adding as much political power as possible to his never adequate and increasingly inadequate power in industrial society.

In developing political power he cannot naturally rely for representation upon individuals whose political life is rooted in economic interests other than his own. The few concessions into which he can scare them by the threat of his potential political strength mean little in comparison to what he might accomplish in an organised movement of his own. The fact that the large body of American workers have not learned this lesson is the mark of their political ignorance. They will have to learn it, though it require years of disillusioning experience, which might have been saved them had they been able to profit by the experience of European workers. Though the skilled and semi-skilled worker is bound to become disillusioned in the efficacy of his purely economic weapons (trade union organisation and strike action), and to organise his political power, he distinguishes himself from the more completely disinherited by preserving a qualified confidence in the potentialities of his newly acquired instruments of political power.

The unconscious basis of the relative optimism of this type of worker is his comparative security. He suffers from social injustice and fails to gain his rightful share of the benefits of modern industry; but as long as the unequal distribution of wealth does not reduce him to complete penury, he eschews violence and revolution and trusts in political methods to establish a gradual equality of privileges in society. The conscious philosophy by which he rationalises his political conduct is expressed by a qualified trust in the instruments of democracy. Unlike the middle classes, he does not regard democratic forms as the proof of equality of privilege. He suffers too much from economic inequality to give himself to the illusion that political equality is real or important as long as economic injustice prevails. But he believes that the democratic state can be used to establish justice. Jaurés, the French social democratic leader, expressed this faith in democracy at a party congress in 1903 in terms which are typical of both the reservations and affirmations which such a faith usually contains: "In a democracy," he said, "in a republic where there is universal suffrage, the state is to the proletarian not a hard, refractory, absolutely impermeable and impenetrable block. Penetration has begun already. In the municipalities, in the central government, there has begun the penetration of proletarian and socialistic influence; and really it is a strange conception of human affairs which can imagine any institution whatever, any political or social form whatever, capable of being closed to the influence, the penetration of one of the great social forces. To say that the state is the same— the same closed, impenetrable rigid state, brazenly bourgeois—under an oligarchic regime, which refuses proletarians universal suffrage and under a regime of universal suffrage, which, after all, lets the workers transmit their will to the government by delegates with the same powers and rights of the delegates of the bourgeoisie itself, is to contradict the laws of nature."[1]

Translated into practical politics, this faith has meant a faithful participation in the democratic process, even if the victory of the proletariat must be postponed until it can be gained by the democratic method of winning a

[1] Quoted by Charles W. Pipkin, *Social Politics and Modern Democracies,* Vol. II, p. 228.

clear majority of all parliamentary votes. The participation of the German socialists in the Revolution of 1918 is not really an exception to this policy. That revolution was due to a complete breakdown of the German monarchy under the stress of war. The socialists did not engineer it. Since they were the strongest party they might well have exploited it, and used the occasion of the resulting political and social chaos to establish a dictatorship. What they did was to help in the establishment of a democratic republic in which they were the most powerful but not a majority party, and were therefore under the necessity of collaborating with non-proletarian parties in the maintenance of government. For years they co-operated with their arch foes in domestic policies, the industrialists, in order to maintain the international policy of conciliation under Stresemann.

It is interesting to note that differences in shades of political philosophy between continental and English socialists, and between German socialists of the school of Bernstein and those of the school of Kautsky, have finally made little difference in the political strategy of the various parliamentary socialists. The Germans and French always had a stronger Marxian influence in their thought than the British socialists. Fabianism, which gave British socialism its philosophy, had little use for the class conflict. It was an ethical socialism, in which the nation as such was called upon to extend the principles of justice which had been previously accepted in the more radical type of liberalism. The spiritual history of British socialism, as an extension and logical consequence of radical liberalism, is rather well symbolised in the development of the thought of John Stuart Mill, who turned in his later years from individualistic to collectivistic political ideas. "In view of the fact," declared Sidney Webb, "that the socialist movement has been hitherto inspired, instructed and led by members of the middle class or bourgeoisie, the Fabian society protests against the absurdity of socialists, denouncing the very class from which socialism has sprung, as especially hostile to it."[2] This judgment is, interestingly enough, a good example of the natural confusion into which ethically motivated middle-class leaders, who have identified themselves with the working class, fall, when they imagine that their own attitudes and convictions offer a significant clue to the dominant attitudes of their class. The middle class, though it has furnished leadership for the labor movement, has remained hostile to the labor cause, for all of Mr. Webb's assurances. The less bellicose attitude of British labor and its softer emphasis upon the class conflict may be a result of the long history of British parliamentarism and the solid achievements of British liberalism in the nineteenth century, which justified, or seemed to justify, confidence in the democratic movement as something more than mere middle-class strategy.

Nevertheless it is significant that the difference between the more Marxian socialism of the continent and the quite indigenous socialism of England has been pretty well wiped out by subsequent history. The parliamentary socialists of the continent have not been more revolutionary than the English, even though they did have a stronger admixture of Marxism in their thought. And the

[2] *Report on Fabian Policy*, p. 7.

British socialists, who seemed for a time to be winning the middle classes to a degree, which the continental socialists found impossible, saw in the election of 1931 how the middle class will inevitably turn against socialism in a crisis when national patriotism is arrayed against the policy of the working class. In both England and Germany the socialist party has been at one time or another the largest party in the nation; and in these countries as well as in France, Belgium and the Scandinavian countries, the party has collaborated in government in either a major or minor capacity.

The hope that socialism could be achieved progressively by parliamentary action has been at least partially justified by the history of all these nations. The increasing social control which government has placed upon economic activity and the larger and larger areas of economic action, in which the government has assumed not only control but actual ownership, offer at least some verification of the judgment of Mr. Webb: "The economic history of the century is an almost continuous record of the progress of socialism." Everywhere the state has interfered in the processes of economic society with the purpose of diminishing the privileges and restraining the power of the owners, and adding to the privileges and power of the workers. Old laws which prohibited the right of the worker to organise, and thus increase his power in the industrial society, have been abolished; constantly severer income and inheritance taxes have diminished both the rights and the usufructs of property, and the resulting revenue has been used by the state to enlarge the social services for those who were worsted in the economic process. Unemployment insurance, old age pensions, work-men's liability acts, and other similar legislation repre-sent the effort of political society to mitigate the inequal-ities which are created by the processes of economic so-ciety. Thus the economic system robs the worker of his security, and the state steps in to re-establish a measure of that security. The economic system heaps up profits in the hands of the owners of property, and the state uses the power of taxation to reduce these profits, sometimes to such a degree that those affected complain that the power of taxation has been extended until it has become the power of confiscation. The state may even, as has been the case in Germany recently, place limits upon interest, rents and dividends, and thus completely destroy the autonomy of economic society.

In this whole development we may discover the usual combination of moral and coercive factors which are evident in political change when violence is avoided and pressure is exerted in purely political terms. The various abridgments and diminutions of the social privilege and power of the owners are accomplished partly by the po-litical power which is exerted by the workers; but there is always an element of voluntary acceptance of the new social standard because it appeals to the total community as a logical and inevitable extension of previously ac-cepted political and social principles. The fact that a very considerable amount of social legislation was passed in all modern nations before the labor parties gained their full strength, and sometimes even before they existed, reveals the capacity of the general community to recog-nise minimum social needs. In England the Combination

Act of 1875, the Trade Union Acts of 1871–6, the Arbitration Acts of 1867, the Education Act of 1870, and the Sanitary Code of 1875 were types of legislation, passed before the advent of the labor party, which justified the statement of a liberal statesman, "We are all socialists now." Such legislation is of course never due purely to a growing social insight of a privileged community. For even before the workers are politically organised they exert a measure of political pressure. Before they had even the vote in England, the fear of what they might do in revolutionary terms helped the middle classes to win the right of suffrage from the landed aristocracy. In America the threat of political reprisals on the part of Negroes and workers, neither of them organised in their own political parties, was able to accomplish the defeat in the Senate of a nominee to the Supreme Court who was regarded as inimical to their interests.

Sometimes the privileged classes yield certain advantages because they hope to retard the growth of labor parties or to frustrate more radical demands by labor groups. Bismarck's social legislation, which remained for some time a model of its kind in Europe, was clearly prompted by the hope of taking the wind out of the sails of the growing German Socialist party. On the other hand such actions as that of Herbert Asquith, when he defied conservative opinion and permitted the first labor government to assume office with liberal support, is a rather clear example of a purer moral motive in politics. Asquith believed that the principles of democracy gave labor the right, as the largest party, to assume responsibility for the government. The opposition to his action on the part of many politicians, who had long paid lip service to democratic principles, but who nevertheless regarded Mr. Asquith's policy as "treason" to his class, and, of course, to England, clearly revealed the limits of pure principle in politics, and the inevitable influence of class interests upon even the noblest political ideals. It is impossible for this reason ever to rely altogether on reason or conscience in politics. Pressure must be used. If it is gradually applied and the new standard of justice is gradually approximated, there is always a possibility that those who lose privileges in the process will accept the loss voluntarily. If they should fail to be convinced by its justice, and if only the threat of political power should secure their acquiescence, their children may regard it as an established standard of society. So society may move toward the goal of equal justice by gradual and evolutionary processes, in which coercive and educational factors operate in varying proportions.

Yet there are difficulties and hazards in the programme of evolutionary and parliamentary socialism, which are not recognised as clearly as they ought to be by those who place unqualified confidence in the parliamentary method. It is not at all certain that political society can fully transform industrial society by an increased pressure in the direction of equality. The chief instrument which it uses for this purpose, taxation, seems subject to a law of diminishing returns. Excessive tax burdens destroy the effectiveness of the weakest units in the capitalistic system and arouse the strongest units to resistance. Steeply graduated inheritance taxes finally force the state to take over productive enterprises or lose the tax. If enterprises are thus taken over piecemeal, it is difficult to develop a systematic and coherent scheme of social ownership and there is a possibility that society will be plunged into a chaos in which the vices of both systems of ownership, private and social, are compounded. Furthermore there is as yet no evidence that a privileged class, which yields advantage after advantage peacefully, will finally yield the very basis of its special position in society without conflict. It will not only use such influence as it is still able to exert upon the government, for the purpose of frustrating the development toward equality; but it will be tempted in the moment of crisis to resort to violence to maintain itself. The power of the banks in the British political crisis of 1931 and their ability to dictate terms to a labor-dominated parliament, is a good illustration of the defeat of political power by unreconstructed economic power. The fascist efforts in both Italy and Germany, the one successful and the other still hanging in the balance, are examples of the resort to violence by imperilled privileged classes. The long history of gradual equalisation of political power in parliamentary countries is not an analogy which can be made the basis of as confident prophecies of peaceful economic change as is usually supposed. The analogy is faulty because economic power is more basic than political power, and is able to bend even the forms and principles of political equalitarianism to its own purposes. Willingness to grant privileges which are only quasi- or pseudo-privileges, is therefore no guarantee of peaceful acquiescence to radical economic change.

Parliamentary socialists usually preserve their hope that

these difficulties can be overcome and these hazards surmounted, by the belief that the attainment of a clear parliamentary majority will cut through all such difficulties, and put the power and the prestige of the state into the hands of the proletarian class for the reorganisation of society. In the case of socialist thinkers like Kautsky, the old Marxian prophecy of the concentration of capital and the inevitable numerical increase in the laboring classes, is used to substantiate this hope. The only portion of the prophecy which is rejected is that which predicts the increasing misery of the workers. The difficulty with this hope is that the whole experience of Western industrial nations negates it. The workers alone cannot become the majority party. To win a majority they must gain the support of a very considerable proportion of the middle classes of the city and of the peasants and farmers.

The theory which assumes that the middle classes can be won to the side of parliamentary socialism, though they are affronted by the threat of violence of revolutionary socialism, and permanently alienated from its cause, has a very important bearing upon the question of the relation of moral and coercive factors in politics. In defense of the theory, it may be regarded as true that there is always a considerable class in every community which is chiefly interested in social peace, and will accept any government which is able to establish itself without violence and without interfering too seriously with the even tenor of its ways. It is even possible that a considerable proportion of this class will become rationally and morally committed to the labor ideal of an equalitarian society. That possibility seems to justify the ambition of socially minded educators, to save society by increasing the social and political intelligence of the general community through the agency of the school. One of the most prominent and most imaginative of these leaders in America, Professor Harold Rugg, states the social ideal of education in these words: "The new secondary curriculum will introduce youth frankly and courageously to the difficulties of experimenting with democracy in a country of large territory, of varied climate, of heterogeneous population and increasing urbanisation. It will reveal the tendency of dominant economic classes to control local state and national governments. . . . Correspondingly the creative imagination of our secondary school youth will be released and set at the task of helping to erect a nation-wide planned regime, in which the expert functions of government are performed by trained and experienced specialists in these fields."[3] While this hope of the educators, which in America finds its most telling presentation in the educational philosophy of Professor John Dewey, has some justification, political redemption through education is not as easily achieved as the educators assume. The very terms in which they state the political problem proves that they are themselves bound by middle-class perspectives, which will naturally increase in force and narrowness in proportion to the distance from the ideal of the educator. Thus Professor Rugg, in the very book in which he clearly analyses the economic influences upon culture, gives himself nevertheless to the hope that education can really achieve a significant critical detachment from a contemporary

[3] Harold Rugg, *Culture and Education in America*, p. 355.

culture and its official propagation in the public schools. Furthermore the ideal of a planned society is projected without recognition of the fact that social planning is possible only by the rigid circumscription or total abolition of the rights of property.[4] It is implicitly assumed that modern society fails to plan its economic processes because it lacks the intelligence to do so; and that the schools will furnish this intelligence. The fact is that the interests of the powerful and dominant groups, who profit from the present system of society, are the real hindrance to the establishment of a rational and just society. It would be pleasant to believe that the intelligence of the general community could be raised to such a height that the irrational injustices of society would be eliminated. But unfortunately there is no such general community. There are many classes, all of them partially deriving their perspectives from, or suffering them to be limited by, their economic interest. The failure of modern socially minded educators to realise this fact proves that their very educational theory, which partly transcends the impulses of the dominant economic groups by force of sheer intellectual honesty and penetration, is also partly bound and limited by the environment of their own class, the middle class. For this class, living in comfort and security, is unable to recognise the urgency of the social problem; and, living in a world of individual re-

[4] For a discussion of the incompatibility between the necessities of a planned economy and the rights of private property see *Socialist Planned Economy in the Soviet Union*, by V. Ossinsky and others, being the report by Russian engineers to the International Planned Economy Conference held in Amsterdam in 1931. See also *Can We Have a Planned Economy without a Revolution*, publication of the Foreign Policy Association, April 2, 1932, containing addresses by Louis Fischer, George Soule and Edward A. Filene.

lationships, is unable to appreciate the consistency with which economic groups express themselves in terms of pure selfishness. The conception that what society needs and, if intelligent enough, will be able to secure, is "trained and experienced specialists" to perform the "expert functions" of government, betrays an additional class prejudice, the prejudice of the intellectual, who is so much the rationalist, that he imagines the evils of government can be eliminated by the expert knowledge of specialists. Any kind of government must of course avail itself of the specialised knowledge of experts. But the idea that such expert knowledge can ever guarantee the impartiality and justice of a state is to overestimate the impartiality of reason in general and the reason of experts in particular. Politics are given their general direction by the pressure of interest of the groups which control them; the expert is quite capable of giving any previously determined tendency both rational justification and efficient detailed application. Such is the inclination of the human mind for beginning with assumptions which have been determined by other than rational considerations, and building a superstructure of rationally acceptable judgments upon them, that all this can be done without any conscious dishonesty. If the expert can function under any type of regime, whether conservative or radical, the experience of socialist governments of Britain and Germany proves that the civil servant is more inclined to conservatism than to radicalism and that he sometimes knows how to frustrate and divert the general policy of the government which he serves by the kind of detailed application which he makes of its general line of policy.

A careful study of the history of political and economic life proves conclusively that the educators, as all other middle-class moralists, underestimate the conflict of interest in political and economic relations, and attribute to disinterested ignorance what ought usually to be attributed to interested intelligence. Their very error in this regard is a result of the faulty perspective of their class. There will always be individuals in the more privileged classes who will, by force of rational and moral idealism, identify themselves with the less privileged classes and fight their political battles. But the number of these will probably always remain limited. Whatever social intelligence is created in the total body of any privileged class, can be used to mitigate the conflict between the classes, but it will not be powerful enough to obviate the necessity of such a conflict. If it should be maintained that the past does not yield conclusions which are valid for the future, since no middle-class group has ever been subjected to an educational process which placed it in full possession of all relevant social facts, the answer is that there is no educational process which can place any class in possession of all the facts, or cause it to appreciate all the feelings which actuate another class. Since civilisation constantly increases indirect and mechanical human relations, this will probably be even more true in the future than it is at present. It is a question whether any middle class will ever be intellectually better disciplined and socially more intelligent than that class in England and Germany. In both of these nations the entire middle-class community turned to conservatism rather than radicalism in the moment of crisis; in England in the election of 1931, when it participated in the overwhelming tory defeat of labor, and in Germany, where it expresses itself through the policies of fascism. These very recent examples of middle-class attitudes in politically advanced and socially intelligent nations are a fairly good basis for predicting middle-class political attitudes in the future. No one would care to deny that the degree of social idealism and intelligence which prevails in any class will affect the total quality of a community's life; will increase the wholesomeness and honesty of economic and political relations which develop within any given equilibrium of political and economic power, and will add to the possibility of adjusting conflicts of interest without violence. But it will not guarantee an adjustment of such conflicts in entirely new terms if some new radical force and interest is not introduced into the political situation.

The peasant and farmer offers another problem to parliamentary as well as to revolutionary socialism. His aversion to revolutionary socialism has been previously considered. The question is whether a moderate type of radical political policy could win his allegiance. There is not much evidence that it can. The parliamentary socialist parties have made practically no gains among his ranks. They have won some agricultural laborers in England and in Germany but very few of the poorer farmers. Even in Denmark, where highly developed farmers' co-operatives might be expected to diminish the agrarian's inveterate individualism, the industrial worker and the farmer remain in opposite political camps. In Europe the still powerful medieval traditions of the countryside and the sense of personal fealty to the landholder frequently determine the peasant's conservative political opinions. In America these traditions do not exist and the farmer is under stronger urban influence. He remains nevertheless an individualist. Even when he is poor, he may take refuge in a modest self-sufficing economy and have only a minimum dependence upon the outside world. This self-sufficiency prompts an indifference to the larger and more intricate problems of society which, in times of crisis, is translated into, or exploited by, political conservatism. If the farmer should try to save himself from his present plight in an industrial civilisation by voluntary co-operative enterprises or if he should be reduced to the status of a proletarian by large scale capitalistic farm projects, he may ultimately come to terms with the urban industrial worker. If he attempted escape by way of voluntary co-operatives he would discover that increased efficiency alone would not establish his prosperity, as long as greater economic and political power is used against him in determining state policies detrimental to his interests. The greater efficiency of co-operative farming would not eliminate the handicaps of tariff and money policies which financial and industrial classes force upon the state at the expense of the farmer. Gradual disillusionment, which may require many decades, might in that event force the farmer on the side of his natural ally, the industrial worker. If large scale farming, backed by strong financial interests, should reduce the independent farmer to the position of an agrarian proletarian, the convergence of the political theories of the farmer and the worker might also proceed more rapidly; but in either case such a development is not to be reckoned with in any realistic political prognostication limited to the next decades. The hope of establishing a third party in America on the combined strength of the farmer and the worker, will remain unrealistic for many decades to come.[5] It may never be realized. It may be that the farmer will never be able to espouse collectivist political goals fervently, no matter how much he suffers from a capitalistic system. The necessities of an industrial civilisation may never seem relevant to the needs of an agrarian, who wants his own piece of land more than he wants anything else, and who will never quite understand the industrial worker's passion for common ownership.[6] It is not even certain that Russia, where the industrial worker established complete political supremacy by a momentary convergence of agrarian and proletarian political interests, and then used that supremacy to force the peasant into collectivisation, may not yet witness the revenge of the peasant upon the industrial worker. It may be that the proletarian will be able to use force upon the peasant long enough to change the circumstances of his life so completely, that collectivist social ideals will finally be accepted by the agrarian. But the degree of force which the Russian dictatorship is using is so great, that it would be rather remarkable if it did not create profound psychological and moral reactions. It may, as in the case of suppressed nationalities, generate and increase a vehemence of resentment which will be its ultimate undoing.

[5] See for an exposition of this thesis of farmer-labor co-operation *inter alia* Paul Douglas, *The Coming of a New Party*.
[6] The complete indifference of as honest and intelligent a champion of agrarian interests as Senator George Norris to the radical political philosophies of industrial workers is an interesting case in point.

At any rate it is not safe to count upon the farmer as a political ally of the industrial worker, however much the logic of economic facts might seem to make him a natural ally of the proletarian. If we thus exclude the middle-class urbanite and the farmer as possible adherents of a parliamentary socialist party, we must arrive at the conclusion that the possibility of winning a parliamentary majority for evolutionary socialism is fairly remote and may be entirely out of question. If this should be the case, the same political forces which make the victory of revolutionary socialism doubtful would also cast doubt upon the possibility of a final triumph for melioristic socialism. If these conclusions are valid we would be forced to the further conviction that there is no single political force which can break through and completely reorganise the present unstable equilibrium of forces in modern society. If such a conclusion should be correct (always with the reservation that another war might completely change the picture), it would become necessary to abandon the hope of achieving a rational equalitarian social goal, and be content with the expectation of its gradual approximation. The latter expectation need not be abandoned, because the economically and politically weaker classes of society have not yet, in any nation, developed the full strength which they potentially hold. They can exert more political and economic pressure than they have thus far exerted. Furthermore the social intelligence of the general community, or rather of all classes in the community, can rise higher than its present level, even if there are limits beyond which it cannot rise. If it is the fate of modern society thus to approach a gradual approximation of a rational social ideal by the progressive adjustment and readjustment of power to power, and interest to interest, a non-violent type of political coercion is clearly preferable to a violent one. Parliamentary socialism would, in that case, be justified, even if it were robbed of the hope of a final and complete triumph. It would be justified because no community can live in a permanent state of civil war, which would result from a revolutionary socialism unable to press through to its goal. If violence can be justified at all, its terror must have the tempo of a surgeon's skill and healing must follow quickly upon its wounds.

A parliamentary socialism which presses toward the goal of social ownership by exerting the full force of the worker's political power in the shifting equilibrium of social and political forces, without certainty that the ultimate goal can be reached, and which is forced to use the method of collaboration with other parties, is, however, under some moral and psychological difficulties which have not been fully appreciated by socialists. The abandonment of the eschatological element in socialism means the sacrifice of its religious fervor and the consequent loss of motive power. The effort of evolutionary socialists to interpret this loss as a gain merely proves that they have become too completely rationalistic to understand the roots of human fervor. The goal, said Eduard Bernstein, philosopher of evolutionary socialism, means nothing, the movement everything. "I have at no time had an excessive interest in the future beyond general principles; I have not been able to read to the end any picture of the future. My thoughts and my efforts are concerned with duties of the present and the nearest future, and I only busy myself with the perspectives beyond as far as they give me a line of conduct for suitable action now."[7] If Bernstein could have known how closely that sentiment would approximate the liberal middle-class educational theory of the modern day, he might have taken thought and recognised it as the mark of socialism's descent and degeneration into liberalism. It is much more rational to refrain from defining an ultimate goal and to abandon some degree of certainty in the possibility of its attainment. But moral potency is sacrificed for this higher degree of rationality. The naïve faith of the proletarian is the faith of the man of action. Rationality belongs to the cool observers. There is of course an element of illusion in the faith of the proletarian, as there is in all faith. But it is a necessary illusion, without which some truth is obscured. The inertia of society is so stubborn that no one will move against it, if he cannot believe that it can be more easily overcome than is actually the case. And no one will suffer the perils and pains involved in the process of radical social change, if he cannot believe in the possibility of a purer and fairer society than will ever be established. These illusions are dangerous because they justify fanaticism; but their abandonment is perilous because it inclines to inertia. Henry DeMan, another evolutionary socialist, rather misses the point when he declares: "The idolisation of the ideal which is characteristic of sentimentalists and romanticists, is repugnant to me. Those who promise collective happiness in some remote future seem to me to be naïve when they are honest, and detest-

[7] Eduard Bernstein, *Evolutionary Socialism*, p. 15.

able when they are humbugs."[8] Sentimentality and romanticism is the disease of observers who dream of an ideal goal without seeking its achievement. The true proletarian who nerves himself for heroic action by believing both in the purity of his goal and in the possibility of its achievement is no doubt touched with sentimentality and romanticism, but he is something more than a sentimentalist. He is both more dangerous and more vital than the sentimentalist. He is a fanatic.

We have previously considered the perils of his fanaticism to a complex society. The temptation to inertia and opportunism which the rationalistic radical faces is no less perilous. The history of parliamentary socialism is filled with evidences of it, and Christian history offers interesting analogous instances. There is only one step from a rationally moderated idealism to opportunism, and only another step from opportunism to dishonest capitulation to the *status quo*. The absolutist and fanatic is no doubt dangerous; but he is also necessary. If he does not judge and criticise immediate achievements, which always involve compromise, in the light of his absolute ideal, the radical force in history, whether applied to personal or to social situations, finally sinks into the sands of complete relativism. Once the religious quality of the proletarian creed is abandoned, and the eschatological emphasis in Marxism is disavowed, evolutionary socialism may easily lose the furious energy which alone is capable of moving against the stubborn inertia of society. There is no way of measuring the perils of fanaticism against the perils of opportunism; but it is rather obvious that so-

[8] Henry DeMan, *The Psychology of Socialism*, p. 473.

ciety as a whole is more inclined to inertia than to fool-
ish adventure, and is therefore in greater need of the challenge of the absolutist than the sweet reasonableness of
the rationalist. Communism is bound to become a force
in modern society, as certainly as modern society disin-
herits a portion of its community completely. Perhaps that
fact ought to be welcomed. Perhaps communism will furnish the criticism which will save parliamentary socialism
from complete opportunism and futility.

Parliamentary socialism is imperilled not only by the
loss of the religious absolutism, which characterises un-
spoiled proletarian thought, but by the temptations which
arise from the practical tactics which it must pursue. It
must collaborate with other parties in the administration
of government. In such co-operation it must try to bar-
gain for the realisation of as much of its programme as
the opposition will accept. This bargaining must be done
by leaders, who are increasingly drawn into the high
places of government, who consort with the great and
mighty in the financial and industrial world, and are
subject to all the blandishments with which aristocracies
have learned to confuse their political opponents. If they
are not unusually discerning and intellectually stubborn
they will forget the viewpoint of the toilers, who endowed them with political power, and will unconsciously
absorb the social and political viewpoints of the more
privileged groups. If they are not more than usually honest their ambition will be tempted by the power and prestige which they may win as national rather than as
proletarian leaders. Parliamentary socialism presents a
dismal story of repeated apostasies, too frequent to be re-

garded as exceptional and politically insignificant cases of personal weakness. MacDonald and Snowden in England, Millerand, Viviani and Briand in France; Scheidemann and Noske in Germany, are but a few of the more conspicuous examples. Sometimes the apostasy expresses itself in terms of complete severance from the socialist party; at other times it is seen in the abandonment of socialist principles and in the defense of national policies which are inimical to labor. This phenomenon of perennial apostasy in parliamentary socialism has two aspects. The personal and moral aspect is less significant than the political one, but it is interesting.

No doubt every socialist leader who has succumbed to the temptation of prestige and power had an Achilles heel of personal vanity and ambition, which one would hope not to find in a leader of purer metal. Perhaps MacDonald's foes are right in suggesting that his vanity was his undoing; and that the King, who seems to have played a rather more influential part in the formation of the national government than the constitution assigns to him, may have touched that vanity by suggesting that no one else was as competent as he to lead the coalition government. Perhaps the insinuations, that social ambitions in Snowden's family partly determined his policy, have a measure of justification. Such details are not particularly important, unless they suggest how strong personal character must be to withstand the temptations which face the labor leader in high office. Resolutions which are made before office is assumed seem to be no proof against the peril. In 1920 Ramsay MacDonald wrote: "Our task is vaster than anything that has yet faced a nation. And yet if at the end of this devastating tragedy (the War), feeble futility philanthropy and sham are to be accepted by our people as their portion, if the leaders of labor, with the way open in front of them to citadels which they have long been assaulting, turn away blinded in vision and craven in heart, and come to truces that are surrenders, they will have betrayed their class and by that their nation."[9] In the crisis of 1931 MacDonald accepted the dictation of the financial interests and preferred a cut in the dole to heavier burdens upon investments of British citizens in foreign lands. In 1899 Aristide Briand defended the syndicalist doctrine of the general strike in these words: "You can go to battle with the ballot. I have nothing to object. You can go to battle with spears, pistols and rifles; I shall consider it my duty when the time comes, to take my place in your ranks. . . . But do not discourage the workers when they attempt to unite for an action which is entirely their own, and in the efficacy of which they firmly believe. The general strike presents this attraction to the militant, that it is, after all, but the exercise of an incontestable right."[10] In 1909 Briand as Premier stopped a peaceful strike of railroad workers by arresting the union leaders and pressing the workers into military service.

No one can penetrate into the secret place where the curious mixture of motives, which lie at the basis of every human action, is compounded. Even the author of the action has some difficulty in doing so. Yet it is fair to sus-

[9] J. Ramsay MacDonald, *Socialism after the War*. Quoted in *New Leader* (London), July 29, 1932.
[10] Quoted by Max Nomad, *Rebels and Renegades*, p. 75.

pect that purely personal weaknesses are frequently the cause of such apostasies. There have been and there will be leaders in parliamentary socialism, too honest to capitulate to personal temptation. The fact that much may depend upon them in the future, reveals the importance of personal character in politics, however insignificant it may appear in comparison with the great impersonal forces which go into the making of history. If French parliamentary socialism produced a Millerand, a Viviani and a Briand, it also brought forth a Jaurés, whose murder on the eve of the World War was one of the great tragedies of that war and undoubtedly prevented a demonstration of the ability of a great socialist leader to remain free of nationalist hysteria. The esteem in which he was held by socialists of all nations might have prevented international socialism from committing its fatal war-time blunders.

The questions of the personal morality of socialist leaders are of course secondary to the whole problem of maintaining parliamentary socialism as a critical, radical and detached force within a national community and preventing its absorption in the national ethos. We have previously recognised the tremendous power of the sentiment of nationalism and also the practical impossibility of a national community arising to the heights of effective self-criticism. It is probably not too severe a judgment to declare that no group within a nation will ever criticise the nation as severely as the nation ought to be criticised, if it does not stand partly outside of the nation. That is the strategic and moral significance of the proletarian class. If only those proletarians are completely outside of the national ethos, whom the nation has absolutely disinherited, it ought to be possible, at least for the slightly more privileged proletarians, to stem themselves against the tide of national sentiment which always threatens to engulf them. The apostasy of parliamentary proletarians can never be explained completely in terms of personal weakness. It is partially due to the reabsorption of the whole semi-proletarian movement into the national soul. That will seem a virtue to those who identify the nation with absolute values; but it must appear a weakness to those who recognise the perils of nationalism to all high human values. The nation will always claim a portion of man's loyalties. Since it usually claims too large a portion, it is necessary that other communities compete with it. There is no reason why a class which is fated by its conditions of life to aspire after an equalitarian society should not have a high moral claim upon the loyalty of its members. Both its ultimate aims and the peril in which it stands justify such a loyalty by every rule of reason. If the nation's claims seem to be higher, that is only because traditional sentiments overpower rational considerations.

The tendency of socialist leaders to espouse the cause of the enemies of labor under the guise of preserving the peace of the state, may be actuated by the motives of personal ambition, which we have suggested; but the political milieu in which such a policy is at all possible is created by the semi-nationalism of the whole political movement which they lead. The parliamentary working class movement stands inside of the national ethos and thus creates the opportunities for its leaders to become imbued with the national instinct of self-preservation. This instinct expresses itself in defense against both internal and external foes of the state. Evolutionary socialists are therefore involved in both international wars and the suppression of strikes and other alleged perils to the state's internal peace. When Briand defended himself against the attacks of Jaurés for his suppression of the strike of French railroad workers, he gave a very illuminating example of the triumph of the national spirit over class loyalty in the heart of a labor leader who had become a national official: "I am ready to admit that theoretically they possess the right to strike and that they may use it legally. But there is another right which has not been mentioned in this debate, and which is superior to all other rights. It is society's right to live. There is no liberty, time-honored though it may be, whose exercise can be permitted to endanger the nation's right to live. . . . The right that is above all other rights is the nation's right to live and to maintain its independence and pride."[11] The identification of the nation with society in Briand's statement, and the easy logic which makes the nation's right "to maintain its pride" a part of its right to survival, shows how quickly a nation's impulses of self-preservation may justify coercive policies against disturbers of its internal peace, and imperialistic policies against its external foes, even in the mind of a former socialist radical. During the War the German socialist leader Philip Scheidemann gave qualified support to German imperial ambitions by declaring that "only political infants could believe that frontier posts would not

[11] Max Nomad, *ibid.*, p. 77.

be moved"; and the scholar of German socialism, Heinrich Cunow, thought the German imperialism deserved the support of socialists because it would hasten the coming of international socialism by giving capitalism its expected climax. Middle-class intellectuals failed to invent a justification of participation in the war more ingenious than that.

The impulses of nationalism grip the soul of every statesman whose hands are on the helm of the state. It is probably natural that socialistic statesmen should not be immune to such influences; and it may be equally natural that nationalistic impulses should gain the ascendancy over class loyalties. But if that is altogether inevitable, it is vain to expect parliamentary labor parties to preserve that critical detachment from national prejudices and hysterias which gives the working class its redemptive mission to modern society. A nation's impulses of self-preservation make for a premature internal peace and for unnecessary external war. The social peace, upon which the nation insists, inevitably incorporates social injustice which can only be eliminated by disturbing the peace; and the same injustice makes for international conflict. To capitulate to the nation means therefore to prefer international conflict to the class struggle. Such a preference cannot be rationally justified. The weight of reason is against it; for international conflict grows out of intra-national injustice and the class struggle seeks to abolish such injustice. Any moral judgment which expresses such a preference merely reveals the influence of traditional sentiments upon it. It represents the capitulation of reason to prejudice.

Since the pure force of reason is never powerful enough to achieve a critical detachment from nationalism, if actual experience does not detach the individual from the nation, only the obviously disinherited worker will achieve it completely. But it may not be too much to hope that increasing intelligence will at least extend slightly beyond personal experience, so that a labor movement which is not completely disinherited will have the intelligence to offer more stubborn resistance to the will of the nation and to the all-pervasive sentiment of nationality. Here, as in other instances, the future of society is served best if we accept the limitations of the human imagination, recognise that it cannot be extended too far beyond the actual experiences of an individual or a class; but bend every effort to increase its penetration so that the obvious may be recognised before its bitter consequences lead to a recognition of the truth after it is too late to profit by it.

The contrasting virtues and vices of revolutionary and evolutionary socialism are such that no purely rational moral choice is possible between them. Whatever judgments are made depend partly upon personal inclination; whether one prefers the partial preservation of traditional injustices or the risk of creating new iniquities by the attempt to abolish old ones completely. They depend partly upon the extent to which one suffers from traditional social abuses; and they are partly determined by the degree of crisis in which a society finds itself.

CHAPTER NINE

THE PRESERVATION OF MORAL VALUES IN POLITICS

ANY political philosophy which assumes that natural impulses, that is, greed, the will-to-power and other forms of self-assertion, can never be completely controlled or sublimated by reason, is under the necessity of countenancing political policies which attempt the control of nature in human history by setting the forces of nature against the impulses of nature. If coercion, self-assertion and conflict are regarded as permissible and necessary instruments of social redemption, how are perpetual conflict and perennial tyranny to be avoided? What is to prevent the instruments of today's redemption from becoming the chain of tomorrow's enslavement? A too consistent political realism would seem to consign society to perpetual warfare. If social cohesion is impossible without coercion, and coercion is impossible without the creation of social injustice, and the destruction of injustice is impossible without the use of further coercion, are we not in an endless cycle of social conflict? If self-interest cannot be checked without the assertion of conflicting self-interests how are the counter-claims to be prevented from becoming inordinate? And if power is needed to destroy power, how is this new power to be made ethical? If the mistrust of political realism in the potency of rational and moral factors in society is carried far enough, an uneasy balance of power would seem to become the highest goal to which society could aspire. If such an uneasy equilibrium of conflicting social forces should result in a tentative social peace or armistice it would be fairly certain that some fortuitous dislocation of the proportions of power would ulimately destroy it. Even if such dislocations should not take place, it would probably be destroyed in the long run by the social animosities which a balance of power creates and accentuates.

The last three decades of world history would seem to be a perfect and tragic symbol of the consequences of this kind of realism, with its abortive efforts to resolve conflict by conflict. The peace before the War was an armistice maintained by the balance of power. It was destroyed by the spontaneous combustion of the mutual fears and animosities which it created. The new peace is no less a coerced peace; only the equilibrium of social and political forces is less balanced than it was before the War. The nations which pretended to fight against the principle of militarism have increased their military power, and the momentary peace which their power maintains is certain to be destroyed by the resentments which their power creates.

This unhappy consequence of a too consistent political realism would seem to justify the interposition of the counsels of the moralist. He seeks peace by the extension of reason and conscience. He affirms that the only lasting peace is one which proceeds from a rational and voluntary adjustment of interest to interest and right to right. He believes that such an adjustment is possible only through a rational check upon self-interest and a rational comprehension of the interests of others. He points to the fact that conflict generates animosities which prevent the mutual adjustment of interests, and that coercion can be used as easily to perpetuate injustice as to eliminate it. He believes, therefore, that nothing but an extension of social intelligence and an increase in moral goodwill can offer society a permanent solution for its social problems. Yet the moralist may be as dangerous a guide as the political realist. He usually fails to recognise the elements of injustice and coercion which are present in any contemporary social peace. The coercive elements are covert, because dominant groups are able to avail themselves of the use of economic power, propaganda, the traditional processes of government, and other types of non-violent power. By failing to recognise the real character of these forms of coercion, the moralist places an unjustified moral onus upon advancing groups which use violent methods to disturb a peace maintained by subtler types of coercion. Nor is he likely to understand the desire to break the peace, because he does not fully recognise the injustices which it hides. They are not easily recognised, because they consist in inequalities, which history sanctifies and tradition justifies. Even the most rational moralist underestimates them, if he does not actually suffer from them. A too uncritical glorification of co-operation and mutuality therefore results in the acceptance of traditional injustices and the preference of the subtler types of coercion to the more overt types.

An adequate political morality must do justice to the insights of both moralists and political realists. It will recognise that human society will probably never escape social conflict, even though it extends the areas of social co-operation. It will try to save society from being involved in endless cycles of futile conflict, not by an effort to abolish coercion in the life of collective man, but by reducing it to a minimum, by counselling the use of such types of coercion as are most compatible with the moral and rational factors in human society and by discriminating between the purposes and ends for which coercion is used.

A rational society will probably place a greater emphasis upon the ends and purposes for which coercion is used than upon the elimination of coercion and conflict. It will justify coercion if it is obviously in the service of a rationally acceptable social end, and condemn its use when it is in the service of momentary passions. The conclusion which has been forced upon us again and again in these pages is that equality, or to be a little more qualified, that equal justice is the most rational ultimate objective for society. If this conclusion is correct, a social conflict which aims at greater equality has a moral justification which must be denied to efforts which aim at the perpetuation of privilege. A war for the emancipation of a nation, a race or a class is thus placed in a different moral category from the use of power for the perpetuation of imperial rule or class dominance. The oppressed, whether they be the Indians in the British Empire, or the Negroes in our own country or the industrial workers in every nation, have a higher moral right to challenge their oppressors than these have to maintain their rule by force. Violent conflict may not be the best means to attain freedom or equality, but that is a question which must be deferred for a moment. It is important to insist, first of all, that equality is a higher social goal than peace. It may never be completely attainable, but it is the symbol for the ideal of a just peace, from the perspective of which every contemporary peace means only an armistice within the existing disproportions of power. It stands for the elimination of the inequalities of power and privilege which are frozen into every contemporary peaceful situation. If social conflict in the past has been futile that has not been due altogether to the methods of violence which were used in it. Violence may tend to perpetuate injustice, even when its aim is justice; but it is important to note that the violence of international wars has usually not aimed at the elimination of an unjust economic system. It has dealt with the real or fancied grievances of nations which were uniformly involved in social injustice. A social conflict which aims at the elimination of these injustices is in a different category from one which is carried on without reference to the problem of justice. In this respect Marxian philosophy is more true than pacifism. If it may seem to pacifists that the proletarian is perverse in condemning international conflict and asserting the class struggle, the latter has good reason to insist that the elimination of coercion is a futile ideal but that the rational use of coercion is a possible achievement which may save society. It is of course dangerous to accept the principle, that the end justifies the means which are used in its attainment. The danger arises from the ease with which any social group, engaged in social conflict, may justify itself by professing to be fighting for freedom and equality. Society has no absolutely impartial tribunal which could judge such claims. Nevertheless it is the business of reason, though always involved in prejudice and subject to partial perspectives, to aspire to the impartiality by which such claims and pretensions could be analysed and assessed. Though it will fail in instances where disputes are involved and complex, it is not impossible to discover at least the most obvious cases of social disinheritance. Wherever a social group is obviously defrauded of its rights, it is natural to give the assertion of its rights a special measure of moral approbation. Indeed this is what is invariably and instinctively done by any portion of the human community which has achieved a degree of impartiality. Oppressed nationalities, Armenians fighting against Turkey, Indians against England, Filipinos against America, Cubans against Spain, and Koreans against Japan have always elicited a special measure of sympathy and moral approbation from the neutral communities. Unfortunately the working classes in every nation are denied the same measure of sympathy, because there is no neutral community which is as impartial with reference to their claims as with reference to the claims of oppressed nationalities. In the case of the latter there is always some group in nations, not immediately involved in the struggle, which can achieve and afford the luxury of impartiality. Thus Europeans express their sympathy for our disinherited Negroes and Americans have a special degree of interest in the struggle for the emancipation of India.

In spite of the partiality and prejudice which beclouds practically every social issue, it is probably true that there is a general tendency of increasing social intelligence to withdraw its support from the claims of social privilege and to give it to the disinherited. In this sense reason itself tends to establish a more even balance of power. All social power is partially derived from the actual possession of physical instruments of coercion, economic or martial. But it also depends to a large degree upon its ability to secure unreasoned and unreasonable obedience, respect and reverence. Inasfar as reason tends to destroy this source of its power, it makes for the diminution of the strength of the strong and adds to the power of the weak. The expropriators are expropriated in another sense beside the one which Marx analysed. Reason divests them of some of their moral conceit, as well as of some measure of the social and moral approbation of their fellows. They are not so certain of the approval of either their own conscience or that of the impartial community. Divested of either or both, they are like Samson with his locks shorn. A considerable degree of power has gone from them. The forces of reason in society are not strong enough to guarantee that this development will ever result in a complete equality of power; but it works to that end. The very fact that rational men are inclined increasingly to condemn the futility of international wars and yet to justify the struggles of oppressed nationalities and classes, proves how inevitably reason must make a distinction between the ultimate ends of social policies and how it must regard the end of equal social justice as the most rational one.

We have previously insisted that if the purpose of a social policy is morally and rationally approved, the choice of means in fulfilling the purpose raises pragmatic issues which are more political than they are ethical. This does not mean that the issues lack moral significance or that moral reason must not guard against the abuse of dangerous political instruments, even when they are used for morally approved ends. Conflict and coercion are manifestly such dangerous instruments. They are so fruitful of the very evils from which society must be saved that an intelligent society will not countenance their indiscriminate use. If reason is to make coercion a tool of the moral ideal it must not only enlist it in the service of the highest causes but it must choose those types of coercion which are most compatible with, and least dangerous to, the rational and moral forces of society. Moral reason must learn how to make coercion its ally without running the risk of a Pyrrhic victory in which the ally exploits and negates the triumph.

The most obvious rational check which can be placed upon the use of coercion is to submit it to the control of an impartial tribunal which will not be tempted to use it for selfish ends. Thus society claims the right to use coercion but denies the same right to individuals. The police power of nations is a universally approved function of government. The supposition is that the government is impartial with reference to any disputes arising between citizens, and will therefore be able to use its power for moral ends. When it uses the same power against other nations in international disputes, it lacks the impartial perspective to guarantee its moral use. The same power of coercion may therefore represent the impartiality of society, when used in intra-national disputes, and a threat against the interests of the larger community of mankind when used in international disputes. Thus the effort is made to organise a society of nations with sufficient power to bring the power of individual nations under international control. This distinction between the impartial and the partial use of social and political coercion is a legitimate one, but it has definite limits. The limits are given by the impossibility of achieving the kind of impartiality which the theory assumes. Government is never completely under the control of a total community. There is always some class, whether economic overlords or political bureaucrats, who may use the organs of government for their special advantages. This is true of both nations and the community of nations. Powerful classes dominate the administration of justice in the one, and powerful nations in the other. Even if this were not the case there is in every community as such, an instinctive avoidance of social conflict and such a superficiality in dealing with the roots of social disaffection, that there is always the possibility of the unjust use of the police power of the state against individuals and groups who break its peace, no matter how justified their grievance. A community may be impartial in using coercion against two disputants, whose dispute offers no peril to the life and prestige of the community. But wherever such a dispute affects the order or the prestige of the community, its impartiality evaporates. The prejudice and passion with which a staid, genteel and highly cultured New England community conducted itself in the Sacco-Vanzetti case is a vivid example. For these reasons it is impossible **to draw too** sharp a moral distinction between the use of

[239]

force and coercion under the control of impartial tribunals and its use by individuals and groups who make it a frank instrument of their own interests.

The chief distinction in the problem of coercion, usually made by moralists, is that between violent and non-violent coercion. The impossibility of making this distinction absolute has been previously considered. It is nevertheless important to make a more careful analysis of the issues involved in the choice of methods of coercion in the social process. The distinguishing marks of violent coercion and conflict are usually held to be its intent to destroy either life or property. This distinction is correct if consequences are not confused with intent. Non-violent conflict and coercion may also result in the destruction of life or property and they usually do. The difference is that destruction is not the intended but the inevitable consequence of non-violent coercion. The chief difference between violence and non-violence is not in the degree of destruction which they cause, though the difference is usually considerable, but in the aggressive character of the one and the negative character of the other. Non-violence is essentially non-co-operation. It expresses itself in the refusal to participate in the ordinary processes of society. It may mean the refusal to pay taxes to the government (civil disobedience), or to trade with the social group which is to be coerced (boycott) or to render customary services (strike). While it represents a passive and negative form of resistance, its consequences may be very positive. It certainly places restraints upon the freedom of the objects of its discipline and prevents them from doing what they desire to do. Furthermore it destroys property values, and it may destroy life; though it is not generally as destructive of life as violence. Yet a boycott may rob a whole community of its livelihood and, if maintained long enough, it will certainly destroy life. A strike may destroy the property values inherent in the industrial process which it brings to a halt, and it may imperil the life of a whole community which depends upon some vital service with which the strike interferes. Nor can it be maintained that it isolates the guilty from the innocent more successfully than violent coercion. The innocent are involved with the guilty in conflicts between groups, not because of any particular type of coercion used in the conflict but by the very group character of the conflict. No community can be disciplined without affecting all its members who are dependent upon, even though they are not responsible for, its policies. The cotton spinners of Lancashire are impoverished by Gandhi's boycott of English cotton, though they can hardly be regarded as the authors of British imperialism. If the League of Nations should use economic sanctions against Japan, or any other nation, workmen who have the least to do with Japanese imperialism would be bound to suffer most from such a discipline.

Non-co-operation, in other words, results in social consequences not totally dissimilar from those of violence. The differences are very important; but before considering them it is necessary to emphasise the similarities and to insist that non-violence does coerce and destroy. The more intricate and interdependent a social process in which non-co-operation is used, the more certainly is this the case. This insistence is important because non-re-

sistance is so frequently confused with non-violent resistance. Mr. Gandhi, the greatest modern exponent of non-
violence, has himself contributed to that confusion. He
frequently speaks of his method as the use of "soul-force"
or "truth-force." He regards it as spiritual in distinction
to the physical character of violence. Very early in his
development of the technique of non-violence in South
Africa he declared: "Passive resistance is a misnomer.
. . . The idea is more completely expressed by the term
'soul-force.' Active resistance is better expressed by the
term 'body-force.' "[1] A negative form of resistance does
not achieve spirituality simply because it is negative. As
long as it enters the field of social and physical relations
and places physical restraints upon the desires and activities of others, it is a form of physical coercion. The confusion in Mr. Gandhi's mind is interesting, because it
seems to arise from his unwillingness, or perhaps his inability, to recognise the qualifying influences of his political responsibilities upon the purity of his original ethical
and religious ideals of non-resistance. Beginning with the
idea that social injustice could be resisted by purely
ethical, rational and emotional forces (truth-force and
soul-force in the narrower sense of the term), he came
finally to realise the necessity of some type of physical coercion upon the foes of his people's freedom, as every political leader must. "In my humble opinion," he declared,
"the ordinary methods of agitation by way of petitions,
deputations, and the like is no longer a remedy for moving to repentance a government so hopelessly indifferent

[1] *Speeches and Writings of M. K. Gandhi* (Mardas Edition, 1919), p. 132.

to the welfare of its charge as the Government of India has proved to be,"[2] an indictment and an observation which could probably be made with equal validity against and about any imperial government of history. In spite of his use of various forms of negative physical resistance, civil-disobedience, boycotts and strikes, he seems to persist in giving them a connotation which really belongs to pure non-resistance. "Jesus Christ, Daniel and Socrates represent the purest form of passive resistance or soul-force," he declares in a passage in which he explains the meaning of what is most undeniably non-violent resistance rather than non-resistance. All this is a pardonable confusion in the soul of a man who is trying to harmonise the insights of a saint with the necessities of statecraft, a very difficult achievement. But it is nevertheless a confusion.

In justice to Mr. Gandhi it must be said that while he confuses the moral connotations of non-resistance and non-violent resistance, he never commits himself to pure non-resistance. He is politically too realistic to believe in its efficacy. He justified his support of the British Government during the War: "So long as I live," he said, "under a system of government based upon force and voluntarily partook of the many facilities and privileges it created for me, I was bound to help that government to the extent of my ability when it was engaged in war. . . . My position regarding that government is totally different today and hence I should not voluntarily participate in its wars."[3] Here the important point is that the violent character of government is recognised and the

[2] C. F. Andrews, *Mahatma Gandhi's Ideas*, p. 238.   [3] *Ibid.*, p. 141.

change of policy is explained in terms of a change in national allegiance and not in terms of pacifist principles. His controversy with his friend C. F. Andrews over his policy of permitting the burning of foreign cloth and his debate with the poet Rabindranath Tagore about the moral implication of the first non-violent resistance campaign in 1919–21, prove that in him political realism qualified religious idealism, in a way which naturally bewildered his friends who carried less or no political responsibility.[4] The first non-co-operation campaign was called off by him because it issued in violence. The second campaign also resulted in inevitable by-products of violence, but it was not called off for that reason. Gandhi is not less sincere or morally less admirable because considerations of political efficacy partly determine his policies and qualify the purity of the doctrine of "ahimsa" to which he is committed. The responsible leader of a political community is forced to use coercion to gain his ends. He may, as Mr. Gandhi, make every effort to keep his instrument under the dominion of his spiritual ideal; but he must use it, and it may be necessary at times to sacrifice a degree of moral purity for political effectiveness.

The use of truth-force or soul-force, in the purer and more exact meaning of those words, means an appeal to the reason and goodwill of an opponent in a social struggle. This may be regarded as a type of resistance, but it is not physical coercion. It belongs in the realm of education. It places no external restraints upon the object of its discipline. It may avail itself of a very vivid and dra-

4 *Ibid.*, Chap. 15.

matic method of education. It may dramatise the suffering of the oppressed, as for instance Mr. Gandhi's encouragement to his followers to endure the penalties of their civil disobedience "long enough to appeal to the sympathetic chord in the governors and the lawmakers." But it is still education and not coercion.

It must be recognised, of course, that education may contain coercive elements. It may degenerate into propaganda. Nor can it be denied that there is an element of propaganda in all education. Even the most honest educator tries consciously or unconsciously to impress a particular viewpoint upon his disciples. Whenever the educational process is accompanied by a dishonest suppression of facts and truths, relevant to the point at issue, it becomes pure propaganda. But even without such dishonest intentions there is, in all exchange of ideas, a certain degree of unconscious suppression of facts or inability to see all the facts. That is the very reason the educational process alone cannot be trusted to resolve a social controversy. Since reason is never pure, education is a tool of controversy as well as a method of transcending it. The coercive elements in education do not become moral merely because they operate in the realm of mind and emotion, and apply no physical restraints. They also must be judged in terms of the purposes which they serve. A distinction must be made, and is naturally made, between the propaganda which a privileged group uses to maintain its privileges and the agitation for freedom and equality carried on by a disinherited group. It may be true that there is a difference in degree of coercive power between psychological and physical types of coercion, as there is between violent and non-violent types. But such differences would establish intrinsic moral distinctions, only if it could be assumed that the least coercive type of influence is naturally the best. This would be true only if freedom could be regarded as an absolute value. This is generally believed by modern educators but it betrays the influence of certain social and economic circumstances to a larger measure than they would be willing to admit. Freedom is a high value, because reason cannot function truly if it is under any restraints, physical or psychic. But absolute intellectual freedom is achieved by only a few minds. The average mind, which is molded by a so-called free educational process, merely accepts contemporary assumptions and viewpoints rather than the viewpoints which might be inculcated by an older or a newer political or religious idealism. The very education of the "democratic" educators is filled with assumptions and rationally unverifiable prejudices, taken from a rapidly disintegrating nineteenth-century liberalism. Psychic coercion is dangerous, as all coercion is. Its ultimate value depends upon the social purpose for which it is enlisted.

Mr. Gandhi's designation of non-violence and non-co-operation as "soul-force" is less confusing and more justified when this emphasis upon non-violence of spirit is considered. Non-violence, for him, has really become a term by which he expresses the ideal of love, the spirit of moral goodwill. This involves for him freedom from personal resentments and a moral purpose, free of selfish ambition. It is the temper and spirit in which a political policy is conducted, which he is really designating, rather than a particular political technique. Thus, while justifying his support of England during the War, he declared: "Non-violence works in a most mysterious manner. Often a man's actions defy analysis in terms of nonviolence; equally often his actions may bear the appearance of violence when he is absolutely non-violent in the highest sense of the term, and is subsequently found to be so. All I can claim for my conduct is that I was, in that instance cited, actuated in the interest of non-violence. There was no thought of sordid national or other interests."[5] What Mr. Gandhi is really saying in these words is that even violence is justified if it proceeds from perfect moral goodwill. But he is equally insistent that nonviolence is usually the better method of expressing goodwill. He is probably right on both counts. The advantage of non-violence as a method of expressing moral goodwill lies in the fact, that it protects the agent against the resentments which violent conflict always creates in both parties to a conflict, and that it proves this freedom of resentment and ill-will to the contending party in the dispute by enduring more suffering than it causes. If non-violent resistance causes pain and suffering to the opposition, it mitigates the resentment, which such suffering usually creates, by enduring more pain than it inflicts. Speaking of the non-violent resistance which Gandhi organised in South Africa he declared: "Their resistance consisted of disobedience to the orders of government, even to the extent of suffering death at their hands. Ahimsa requires deliberate self-suffering, not a deliberate injuring of the supposed wrong-doer. In its positive form, Ahimsa means the largest love, the greatest char-

[5] *Ibid.*, p. 142.

ity."[6] Speaking before the judge who was to sentence him to prison during his first civil disobedience campaign in India he said: "Non-violence requires voluntary submission to the penalty for non-co-operation with evil. I am therefore to invite and submit cheerfully to the highest penalty which can be inflicted upon me for what in law is a deliberate crime."[7] The social and moral effects of these very vivid proofs of moral goodwill are tremendous. In every social conflict each party is so obsessed with the wrongs which the other party commits against it, that it is unable to see its own wrongdoing. A non-violent temper reduces these animosities to a minimum and therefore preserves a certain objectivity in analysing the issues of the dispute. The kindly spirit with which Mr. Gandhi was received during the course of the second Round-table Conference by the cotton spinners of Lancashire, whom his boycott had impoverished, is proof of the social and moral efficacy of this spiritual non-violence. It was one of the great triumphs of his method.

One of the most important results of a spiritual discipline against resentment in a social dispute is that it leads to an effort to discriminate between the evils of a social system and situation and the individuals who are involved in it. Individuals are never as immoral as the social situations in which they are involved and which they symbolise. If opposition to a system leads to personal insults of its representatives, it is always felt as an unjust accusation. William Lloyd Garrison solidified the south in support of slavery by the vehemence of his attacks against

---

[6] Quoted by Clarence M. Case, *Non-Violent Coercion*, p. 364.
[7] Quoted by Andrews, *op. cit.*, p. 297.

slave-owners. Many of them were, within the terms of their inherited prejudices and traditions, good men; and the violence of Mr. Garrison's attack upon them was felt by many to be an evidence of moral perversity in him. Mr. Gandhi never tires of making a distinction between individual Englishmen and the system of imperialism which they maintain. "An Englishman in office," he declares, "is different from an Englishman outside. Similarly an Englishman in India is different from an Englishman in England. Here in India you belong to a system that is vile beyond description. It is possible, therefore, for me to condemn the system in the strongest terms, without considering you to be bad and without imputing bad motives to every Englishman."[8] It is impossible completely to disassociate an evil social system from the personal moral responsibilities of the individuals who maintain it. An impartial teacher of morals would be compelled to insist on the principle of personal responsibility for social guilt. But it is morally and politically wise for an opponent not to do so. Any benefit of the doubt which he is able to give his opponent is certain to reduce animosities and preserve rational objectivity in assessing the issues under dispute.

The value of reducing resentments to a minimum in social disputes does not mean that resentment is valueless and wholly evil. Resentment is, as Professor Ross observed, merely the egoistic side of the sense of injustice.[9] Its complete absence simply means lack of social intelligence or moral vigor. A Negro who resents the injustice done his race makes a larger contribution to its ultimate

[8] *Ibid.*, p. 242.   [9] E. A. Ross, *Social Control*, p. 37.

emancipation than one who suffers injustice without any emotional reactions. But the more the egoistic element can be purged from resentment, the purer a vehicle of justice it becomes. The egoistic element in it may be objectively justified, but, from the perspective of an opponent in a social dispute, it never seems justified and merely arouses his own egotism.

Both the temper and the method of non-violence yield another very important advantage in social conflict. They rob the opponent of the moral conceit by which he identifies his interests with the peace and order of society. This is the most important of all the imponderables in a social struggle. It is the one which gives an entrenched and dominant group the clearest and the least justified advantage over those who are attacking the *status quo*. The latter are placed in the category of enemies of public order, of criminals and inciters to violence and the neutral community is invariably arrayed against them. The temper and the method of non-violence destroys the plausibility of this moral conceit of the entrenched interests. If the non-violent campaign actually threatens and imperils existing arrangements the charge of treason and violence will be made against it none-the-less. But it will not confuse the neutral elements in a community so easily. While there is a great deal of resentment in Britain against the Indian challenge of its imperial dominion, and the usual insistence upon "law and order" and the danger of rebellion by British imperialists, it does not have quite the plausible moral unction which such pretensions usually achieve.

Non-violent coercion and resistance, in short, is a type

of coercion which offers the largest opportunities for a
harmonious relationship with the moral and rational factors in social life. It does not destroy the process of a
moral and rational adjustment of interest to interest completely during the course of resistance. Resistance to self-
assertion easily makes self-assertion more stubborn, and
conflict arouses dormant passions which completely obscure the real issues of a conflict. Non-violence reduces
these dangers to a minimum. It preserves moral, rational
and co-operative attitudes within an area of conflict and
thus augments the moral forces without destroying them.
The conference and final agreement between Mr. Gandhi
and the Viceroy Lord Irwin, after the first Round-table
Conference, was a perfect example of the moral possibilities of a non-violent social dispute. The moral resources and spiritual calibre of the two men contributed
to its success. But it would have been unthinkable in a
dispute of similar dimensions carried on in terms of violence. It was a telling example of the possibility of preserving co-operative and mutual attitudes within an area
of conflict, when the conflict is conducted with a minimum of violence in method and spirit.

The differences between violent and non-violent methods of coercion and resistance are not so absolute that it
would be possible to regard violence as a morally impossible instrument of social change. It may on occasion,
as Mr. Gandhi suggests, be the servant of moral goodwill. And non-violent methods are not perfect proofs of
a loving temper. During the War one sect of the pacifist
Doukhobors petitioned the Canadian Government to
withdraw the privileges of conscientious objectors from

another sect which had disassociated themselves from it, "for no reason other than to satisfy the feeling of ill-will towards their brothers."[10] The advantages of non-violent methods are very great but they must be pragmatically considered in the light of circumstances. Even Mr. Gandhi introduces the note of expediency again and again, and suggests that they are peculiarly adapted to the needs and limitations of a group which has more power arrayed against it than it is able to command. The implication is that violence could be used as the instrument of moral goodwill, if there was any possibility of a triumph quick enough to obviate the dangers of incessant wars. This means that non-violence is a particularly strategic instrument for an oppressed group which is hopelessly in the minority and has no possibility of developing sufficient power to set against its oppressors.

The emancipation of the Negro race in America probably waits upon the adequate development of this kind of social and political strategy. It is hopeless for the Negro to expect complete emancipation from the menial social and economic position into which the white man has forced him, merely by trusting in the moral sense of the white race. It is equally hopeless to attempt emancipation through violent rebellion.

There are moral and rational forces at work for the improvement of relations between whites and Negroes. The educational advantages which have endowed Negro leaders to conduct the battle for the freedom of their race have come largely from schools established by philanthropic white people. The various inter-race commissions

10 See Case, *op. cit.*, p. 162.

have performed a commendable service in eliminating misunderstandings between the races and in interpreting the one to the other. But these educational and conciliatory enterprises have the limitations which all such purely rational and moral efforts reveal. They operate within a given system of injustice. The Negro schools, conducted under the auspices of white philanthropy, encourage individual Negroes to higher forms of self-realisation; but they do not make a frontal attack upon the social injustices from which the Negro suffers. The race commissions try to win greater social and political rights for the Negro without arousing the antagonisms of the whites. They try to enlarge, but they operate nevertheless within the limits of, the "zones of agreement." This means that they secure minimum rights for the Negro such as better sanitation, police protection and more adequate schools. But they do not touch his political disfranchisement or his economic disinheritance. They hope to do so in the long run, because they have the usual faith in the power of education and moral suasion to soften the heart of the white man. This faith is filled with as many illusions as such expectations always are. However large the number of individual white men who do and who will identify themselves completely with the Negro cause, the white race in America will not admit the Negro to equal rights if it is not forced to do so. Upon that point one may speak with a dogmatism which all history justifies.

On the other hand, any effort at violent revolution on the part of the Negro will accentuate the animosities and prejudices of his oppressors. Since they outnumber him hopelessly, any appeal to arms must inevitably result in a terrible social catastrophe. Social ignorance and economic interest are arrayed against him. If the social ignorance is challenged by ordinary coercive weapons it will bring forth the most violent passions of which ignorant men are capable. Even if there were more social intelligence, economic interest would offer stubborn resistance to his claims.

The technique of non-violence will not eliminate all these perils. But it will reduce them. It will, if persisted in with the same patience and discipline attained by Mr. Gandhi and his followers, achieve a degree of justice which neither pure moral suasion nor violence could gain. Boycotts against banks which discriminate against Negroes in granting credit, against stores which refuse to employ Negroes while serving Negro trade, and against public service corporations which practice racial discrimination, would undoubtedly be crowned with some measure of success. Non-payment of taxes against states which spend on the education of Negro children only a fraction of the amount spent on white children, might be an equally efficacious weapon. One waits for such a campaign with all the more reason and hope because the peculiar spiritual gifts of the Negro endow him with the capacity to conduct it successfully. He would need only to fuse the aggressiveness of the new and young Negro with the patience and forbearance of the old Negro, to rob the former of its vindictiveness and the latter of its lethargy.

There is no problem of political life to which religious imagination can make a larger contribution than this problem of developing non-violent resistance. The discovery of elements of common human frailty in the foe and, concomitantly, the appreciation of all human life as possessing transcendent worth, creates attitudes which transcend social conflict and thus mitigate its cruelties. It binds human beings together by reminding them of the common roots and similar character of both their vices and their virtues. These attitudes of repentance which recognise that the evil in the foe is also in the self, and these impulses of love which claim kinship with all men in spite of social conflict, are the peculiar gifts of religion to the human spirit. Secular imagination is not capable of producing them; for they require a sublime madness which disregards immediate appearances and emphasises profound and ultimate unities. It is no accident of history that the spirit of non-violence has been introduced into contemporary politics by a religious leader of the orient. The occident may be incapable of this kind of non-violent social conflict, because the white man is a fiercer beast of prey than the oriental. What is even more tragic, his religious inheritance has been dissipated by the mechanical character of his civilisation. The insights of the Christian religion have become the almost exclusive possession of the more comfortable and privileged classes. These have sentimentalised them to such a degree, that the disinherited, who ought to avail themselves of their resources, have become so conscious of the moral confusions which are associated with them, that the insights are not immediately available for the social struggle in the Western world. If they are not made available, Western civilisation, whether it drifts toward catastrophe or gradually brings its economic life under social control, will suffer from cruelties and be harassed by animosities which destroy the beauty of human life. Even if justice should be achieved by social conflicts which lack the spiritual elements of non-violence, something will be lacking in the character of the society so constructed. There are both spiritual and brutal elements in human life. The perennial tragedy of human history is that those who cultivate the spiritual elements usually do so by divorcing themselves from or misunderstanding the problems of collective man, where the brutal elements are most obvious. These problems therefore remain unsolved, and force clashes with force, with nothing to mitigate the brutalities or eliminate the futilities of the social struggle. The history of human life will always be the projection of the world of nature. To the end of history the peace of the world, as Augustine observed, must be gained by strife. It will therefore not be a perfect peace. But it can be more perfect than it is. If the mind and the spirit of man does not attempt the impossible, if it does not seek to conquer or to eliminate nature but tries only to make the forces of nature the servants of the human spirit and the instruments of the moral ideal, a progressively higher justice and more stable peace can be achieved.

CHAPTER TEN

THE CONFLICT BETWEEN INDIVIDUAL AND SOCIAL MORALITY

A REALISTIC analysis of the problems of human society reveals a constant and seemingly irreconcilable conflict between the needs of society and the imperatives of a sensitive conscience. This conflict, which could be most briefly defined as the conflict between ethics and politics, is made inevitable by the double focus of the moral life. One focus is in the inner life of the individual, and the other in the necessities of man's social life. From the perspective of society the highest moral ideal is justice. From the perspective of the individual the highest ideal is unselfishness. Society must strive for justice even if it is forced to use means, such as self-assertion, resistance, coercion and perhaps resentment, which cannot gain the moral sanction of the most sensitive moral spirit. The individual must strive to realise his life by losing and finding himself in something greater than himself.

These two moral perspectives are not mutually exclusive and the contradiction between them is not absolute. But neither are they easily harmonised. Efforts to harmonise them were analysed in the previous chapter. It was revealed that the highest moral insights and achievements of the individual conscience are both relevant and necessary to the life of society. The most perfect justice cannot be established if the moral imagination of the in-

[257]

dividual does not seek to comprehend the needs and interests of his fellows. Nor can any non-rational instrument of justice be used without great peril to society, if it is not brought under the control of moral goodwill. Any justice which is only justice soon degenerates into something less than justice. It must be saved by something which is more than justice. The realistic wisdom of the statesman is reduced to foolishness if it is not under the influence of the foolishness of the moral seer. The latter's idealism results in political futility and sometimes in moral confusion, if it is not brought into commerce and communication with the realities of man's collective life. This necessity and possibility of fusing moral and political insights does not, however, completely eliminate certain irreconcilable elements in the two types of morality, internal and external, individual and social. These elements make for constant confusion but they also add to the richness of human life. We may best bring our study of ethics and politics to a close by giving them some further consideration.

From the internal perspective the most moral act is one which is actuated by disinterested motives. The external observer may find good in selfishness. He may value it as natural to the constitution of human nature and as necessary to society. But from the viewpoint of the author of an action, unselfishness must remain the criterion of the highest morality. For only the agent of an action knows to what degree self-seeking corrupts his socially approved actions. Society, on the other hand, makes justice rather than unselfishness its highest moral ideal. Its aim must be to seek equality of opportunity for all life. If this equality and justice cannot be achieved without the assertion of interest against interest, and without restraint upon the self-assertion of those who infringe upon the rights of their neighbors, then society is compelled to sanction self-assertion and restraint. It may even, as we have seen, be forced to sanction social conflict and violence.

Historically the internal perspective has usually been cultivated by religion. For religion proceeds from profound introspection and naturally makes good motives the criteria of good conduct. It may define good motives either in terms of love or of duty, but the emphasis is upon the inner springs of action. Rationalised forms of religion usually choose duty rather than love as the expression of highest virtue (as in Kantian and Stoic morality), because it seems more virtuous to them to bring all impulse under the dominion of reason than to give any impulses, even altruistic ones, moral pre-eminence. The social viewpoint stands in sharpest contrast to religious morality when it views the behavior of collective rather than individual man, and when it deals with the necessities of political life. Political morality, in other words, is in the most uncompromising antithesis to religious morality.

Rational morality usually holds an intermediary position between the two. Sometimes it tries to do justice to the inner moral necessities of the human spirit rather than to the needs of society. If it emphasises the former it may develop an ethic of duty rather than the religious ethic of disinterestedness. But usually rationalism in morals tends to some kind of utilitarianism. It views human conduct from the social perspective and finds its ultimate standards in some general good and total social harmony. From that viewpoint it gives moral sanction to egoistic as well as to altruistic impulses. justifying them because they are natural to human nature and necessary to society. It asks only that egoism be reasonably expressed. Upon that subject Aristotle said the final as well as the first authoritative word. Reason, according to his theory, establishes control over all the impulses, egoistic and altruistic, and justifies them both if excesses are avoided and the golden mean is observed.

The social justification for self-assertion is given a typical expression by the Earl of Shaftesbury, who believed that the highest morality represented a harmony between "self-affections" and "natural affections." "If," said Shaftesbury, "a creature be self-neglectful and insensible to danger, or if he want such a degree of passion of any kind, as is useful to preserve, sustain and defend himself, this must certainly be esteemed vicious in regard of the end and design of nature."[1]

It is interesting that a rational morality which gives egoism equality of moral standing with altruism, provided both are reasonably expressed and observe the "law of measure," should again and again find difficulty in coming to terms with the natural moral preference which all unreflective moral thought gives to altruism. Thus Bishop Butler begins his moral theorising by making conscience the balancing force between "self-love" and "benevolence." But gradually conscience gives such a preference to benevolence that it becomes practically identified

---

[1] Third Earl of Shaftesbury, *An Inquiry Concerning Virtue or Merit*, Bk. II, Part I, sec. III.

with it. Butler is therefore forced to draw in reason (originally identified with conscience) as a force higher than conscience to establish harmony between self-love and conscience.[2]

The utilitarian attempt to harmonise the inner and outer perspectives of morality is inevitable and, within limits, possible. It avoids the excesses, absurdities and perils into which both religious and political morality may fall. By placing a larger measure of moral approval upon egoistic impulses than does religious morality and by disapproving coercion, conflict and violence more unqualifiedly than politically oriented morality, it manages to resolve the conflict between them. But it is not as realistic as either. It easily assumes a premature identity between self-interest and social interest and establishes a spurious harmony between egoism and altruism. With Bishop Butler most utilitarian rationalists in morals believe "that though benevolence and self-love are different . . . yet they are so perfectly coincident that the greatest satisfaction to ourselves depends upon having benevolence in due degree, and that self-love is one chief security of our right behavior to society."[3] Rationalism in morals therefore insists on less inner restraint upon self-assertion than does religion, and believes less social restraint to be necessary than political realism demands.

The dangers of religion's inner restraint upon self-assertion, and of its effort to achieve complete disinterestedness, are that such a policy easily becomes morbid, and that it may make for injustice by encouraging and permit-

2 *Cf.* Joseph Butler, *Fifteen Sermons on Human Nature.*
8 Butler, *op. cit.*, Sermon 1.

ting undue self-assertion in others. Its value lies in its check upon egoistic impulses, always more powerful than altruistic ones. If the moral enterprise is begun with the complacent assumption that selfish and social impulses are nicely balanced and equally justified, even a minimum equilibrium between them becomes impossible.

The more the moral problem is shifted from the relations of individuals to the relations of groups and collectives, the more the preponderance of the egoistic impulses over the social ones is established. It is therefore revealed that no inner checks are powerful enough to bring them under complete control. Social control must consequently be attempted; and it cannot be established without social conflict. The moral perils attending such a political strategy have been previously considered. They are diametrically opposite to the perils of religious morality. The latter tend to perpetuate injustice by discouraging self-assertion against the inordinate claims of others. The former justify not only self-assertion but the use of non-rational power in reinforcing claims. They may therefore substitute new forms of injustice for old ones and enthrone a new tyranny on the throne of the old. A rational compromise between these two types of restraint easily leads to a premature complacency toward self-assertion. It is therefore better for society to suffer the uneasy harmony between the two types of restraint than to run the danger of inadequate checks upon egoistic impulses. Tolstoi and Lenin both present perils to the life of society; but they are probably no more dangerous than the compromises with human selfishness effected by modern disciples of Aristotle.

If we contemplate the conflict between religious and political morality it may be well to recall that the religious ideal in its purest form has nothing to do with the problem of social justice. It makes disinterestedness an absolute ideal without reference to social consequences. It justifies the ideal in terms of the integrity and beauty of the human spirit. While religion may involve itself in absurdities in the effort to achieve the ideal by purely internal discipline, and while it may run the peril of deleterious social consequences, it does do justice to inner needs of the human spirit. The veneration in which a Tolstoi, a St. Francis, a crucified Christ, and the saints of all the ages have been held, proves that, in the inner sanctuary of their souls, selfish men know that they ought not be selfish, and venerate what they feel they ought to be and cannot be.

Pure religious idealism does not concern itself with the social problem. It does not give itself to the illusion that material and mundane advantages can be gained by the refusal to assert your claims to them. It may believe, as Jesus did, that self-realisation is the inevitable consequence of self-abnegation. But this self-realisation is not attained on the level of physical life or mundane advantages. It is achieved in spiritual terms, such as the marytr's immortality and the Saviour's exaltation in the hearts of his disciples. Jesus did not counsel his disciples to forgive seventy times seven in order that they might convert their enemies or make them more favorably disposed. He counselled it as an effort to approximate complete moral perfection, the perfection of God. He did not ask his followers to go the second mile in the hope that those who

[263]

had impressed them into service would relent and give them freedom. He did not say that the enemy ought to be loved so that he would cease to be an enemy. He did not dwell upon the social consequences of these moral actions, because he viewed them from an inner and a transcendent perspective.

Nothing is clearer than that a pure religious idealism must issue in a policy of non-resistance which makes no claims to be socially efficacious. It submits to any demands, however unjust, and yields to any claims, however inordinate, rather than assert self-interest against another. "You will meekly bear," declared Epictetus, "for you will say on every occasion 'It seemed so to him.'" This type of moral idealism leads either to asceticism, as in the case of Francis and other Catholic saints, or at least to the complete disavowal of any political responsibility, as in the cast of Protestant sects practicing consistent non-resistance, as, for instance, the Anabaptists, Mennonites, Dunkers and Doukhobors. The Quakers assumed political responsibilities, but they were never consistent non-resisters. They disavowed violence but not resistance.

While social consequences are not considered in such a moral strategy, it would be shortsighted to deny that it may result in redemptive social consequences, at least within the area of individual and personal relationships. Forgiveness may not always prompt the wrongdoer to repentance; but yet it may. Loving the enemy may not soften the enemy's heart; but there are possibilities that it will. Refusal to assert your own interests against another may not shame him into unselfishness; but on occasion it has done so. Love and benevolence may not lead to complete mutuality; but it does have that tendency, particularly within the area of intimate relationships. Human life would, in fact, be intolerable if justice could be established in all relationships only by self-assertion and counter-assertion, or only by a shrewd calculation of claims and counter-claims. The fact is that love, disinterestedness and benevolence do have a strong social and utilitarian value, and the place they hold in the hierarchy of virtues is really established by that value, though religion may view them finally from an inner or transcendent perspective. "The social virtues," declares David Hume, "are never regarded without their beneficial tendencies nor viewed as barren and unfruitful. The happiness of mankind, the order of society, the harmony of families, the mutual support of friends, are always considered as a result of their gentle dominion over the breasts of men."[4] The utilitarian and social emphasis is a little too absolute in the words of Hume, but it is true within limits. Even the teachings of Jesus reveal a prudential strain in which the wholesome social consequences of generous attitudes are emphasised. "With what measure you mete, it shall be measured to you again." The paradox of the moral life consists in this: that the highest mutuality is achieved where mutual advantages are not consciously sought as the fruit of love. For love is purest where it desires no returns for itself; and it is most potent where it is purest. Complete mutuality, with its advantages to each party to the relationship, is therefore most perfectly realised where it is not intended, but love

[4] David Hume, *An Enquiry Concerning the Principles of Morals*, Part 2, sec. II.

is poured out without seeking returns. That is how the madness of religious morality, with its trans-social ideal, becomes the wisdom which achieves wholesome social consequences. For the same reason a purely prudential morality must be satisfied with something less than the best.

Where human relations are intimate (and love is fully effective only in intimate and personal relations), the way of love may be the only way to justice. Where rights and interests are closely interwoven, it is impossible to engage in a shrewd and prudent calculation of comparative rights. Where lives are closely intertwined, happiness is destroyed if it is not shared. Justice by assertion and counter-assertion therefore becomes impossible. The friction involved in the process destroys mutual happiness. Justice by a careful calculation of competing rights is equally difficult, if not impossible. Interests and rights are too mutual to allow for their precise definition in individual terms. The very effort to do so is a proof of the destruction of the spirit of mutuality by which alone intimate relations may be adjusted. The spirit of mutuality can be maintained only by a passion which does not estimate the personal advantages which are derived from mutuality too carefully. Love must strive for something purer than justice if it would attain justice. Egoistic impulses are so much more powerful than altruistic ones that if the latter are not given stronger than ordinary support, the justice which even good men design is partial to those who design it.

This social validity of a moral ideal which transcends social considerations in its purest heights, is progressively weakened as it is applied to more and more intricate, indirect and collective human relations. It is not only unthinkable that a group should be able to attain a sufficiently consistent unselfish attitude toward other groups to give it a very potent redemptive power, but it is improbable that any competing group would have the imagination to appreciate the moral calibre of the achievement. Furthermore a high type of unselfishness, even if it brings ultimate rewards, demands immediate sacrifices. An individual may sacrifice his own interests, either without hope of reward or in the hope of an ultimate compensation. But how is an individual, who is responsible for the interests of his group, to justify the sacrifice of interests other than his own? "It follows," declares Hugh Cecil, "that all that department of morality which requires an individual to sacrifice his interests to others, everything which falls under the heading of unselfishness, is inappropriate to the action of a state. No one has a right to be unselfish with other people's interests."[5]

This judgment is not sufficiently qualified. A wise statesman is hardly justified in insisting on the interests of his group when they are obviously in unjust relation to the total interests of the community of mankind. Nor is he wrong in sacrificing immediate advantages for the sake of higher mutual advantages. His unwillingness to do this is precisely what makes nations so imprudent in holding to immediate advantages and losing ultimate values of mutuality. Nevertheless it is obvious that fewer risks can be taken with community interests than with individual interests. The inability to take risks naturally results in a

[5] Hugh Cecil, *Conservatism*, p. 182.

[267]

benevolence in which selfish advantages must be quite apparent, and in which therefore the moral and redemptive quality is lost.

Every effort to transfer a pure morality of disinterestedness to group relations has resulted in failure. The Negroes of America have practiced it quite consistently since the Civil War. They did not rise against their masters during the war and remained remarkably loyal to them. Their social attitudes since that time, until a very recent date, have been compounded of genuine religious virtues of forgiveness and forbearance, and a certain social inertia which was derived not from religious virtue but from racial weakness. Yet they did not soften the hearts of their oppressors by their social policy.

During the early triumphs of fascism in Italy the socialist leaders suddenly adopted pacifist principles. One of the socialist papers counselled the workers to meet the terror of fascism with the following strategy: "(1) Create a void around fascism. (2) Do not provoke; suffer any provocation with serenity. (3) To win, be better than your adversary. (4) Do not use the weapons of your enemy. Do not follow in his footsteps. (5) Remember that the blood of guerilla warfare falls upon those who shed it. (6) Remember that in a struggle between brothers those are victors who conquer themselves. (7) Be convinced that it is better to suffer wrong than to commit it. (8) Don't be impatient. Impatience is extremely egoistical; it is instinct; it is yielding to one's ego urge. (9) Do not forget that socialism wins the more when it suffers, because it was born in pain and lives on its hopes. (10) Listen to the mind and to the heart which advises you that the working people should be nearer to sacrifice than to vengeance."[6] A nobler decalogue of virtues could hardly have been prescribed. But the Italian socialists were annihilated by the fascists, their organisations destroyed, and the rights of the workers subordinated to a state which is governed by their enemies. The workers may live "on their hopes," but there is no prospect of realising their hopes under the present regime by practicing the pure moral principles which the socialistic journal advocated. Some of them are not incompatible with the use of coercion against their foes. But inasfar as they exclude coercive means they are ineffectual before the brutal will-to-power of fascism.

The effort to apply the doctrines of Tolstoi to the political situation of Russia had a very similar effect. Tolstoi and his disciples felt that the Russian peasants would have the best opportunity for victory over their oppressors if they did not become stained with the guilt of the same violence which the czarist regime used against them. The peasants were to return good for evil, and win their battles by non-resistance. Unlike the policies of Gandhi, the political programme of Tolstoi remained altogether unrealistic. No effort was made to relate the religious ideal of love to the political necessity of coercion. Its total effect was therefore socially and politically deleterious. It helped to destroy a rising protest against political and economic oppression and to confirm the Russian in his pessimistic passivity. The excesses of the terrorists seemed to give point to the Tolstoian opposition to violence and resistance. But the terrorists and the

* Quoted by Max Nomad, *Rebels and Renegades*, p. 294.

pacifists finally ended in the same futility. And their common futility seemed to justify the pessimism which saw no escape from the traditional injustices of the Russian political and economic system. The real fact was that both sprang from a romantic middle-class or aristocratic idealism, too individualistic in each instance to achieve political effectiveness. The terrorists were diseased idealists, so morbidly oppressed by the guilt of violence resting upon their class, that they imagined it possible to atone for that guilt by deliberately incurring guilt in championing the oppressed. Their ideas were ethical and, to a degree, religious, though they regarded themselves as irreligious. The political effectiveness of their violence was a secondary consideration. The Tolstoian pacifists attempted the solution of the social problem by diametrically opposite policies. But, in common with the terrorists, their attitudes sprang from the conscience of disquieted individuals. Neither of them understood the realities of political life because neither had an appreciation for the significant characteristics of collective behavior. The romantic terrorists failed to relate their isolated acts of terror to any consistent political plan. The pacifists, on the other hand, erroneously attributed political potency to pure non-resistance.

Whenever religious idealism brings forth its purest fruits and places the strongest check upon selfish desire it results in policies which, from the political perspective, are quite impossible. There is, in other words, no possibility of harmonising the two strategists designed to bring the strongest inner and the most effective social restraint upon egoistic impulse. It would therefore seem

better to accept a frank dualism in morals than to at·
tempt a harmony between the two methods which
threatens the effectiveness of both. Such a dualism would
have two aspects. It would make a distinction between
the moral judgments applied to the self and to others;
and it would distinguish between what we expect of individuals and of groups. The first distinction is obvious
and is explicitly or implicitly accepted whenever the
moral problem is taken seriously. To disapprove your
own selfishness more severely than the egoism of others
is a necessary discipline if the natural complacency toward the self and severity in the judgment of others is to
be corrected. Such a course is, furthermore, demanded
by the logic of the whole moral situation. One can view
the actions of others only from an external perspective;
and from that perspective the social justification of self-
assertion becomes inevitable. Only the actions of the self
can be viewed from the internal perspective; and from
that viewpoint all egoism must be morally disapproved.
If such disapproval should occasionally destroy self-assertion to such a degree as to invite the aggression of others, the instances will be insignificant in comparison with
the number of cases in which the moral disapproval of
egoism merely tends to reduce the inordinate self-assertion of the average man. Even in those few cases in
which egoism is reduced by religious discipline to such
proportions that it invites injustice in an immediate situation, it will have social usefulness in glorifying the
moral principle and setting an example for future generations.

The distinction between individual and group morality is a sharper and more perplexing one. The moral obtuseness of human collectives makes a morality of pure disinterestedness impossible. There is not enough imagination in any social group to render it amenable to the influence of pure love. Nor is there a possibility of persuading any social group to make a venture in pure love, except, as in the case of the Russian peasants, the recently liberated Negroes and other similar groups, a morally dubious social inertia should be compounded with the ideal. The selfishness of human communities must be regarded as an inevitability. Where it is inordinate it can be checked only by competing assertions of interest; and these can be effective only if coercive methods are added to moral and rational persuasion. Moral factors may qualify, but they will not eliminate, the resulting social contest and conflict. Moral goodwill may seek to relate the peculiar interests of the group to the ideal of a total and final harmony of all life. It may thereby qualify the self-assertion of the privileged, and support the interests of the disinherited, but it will never be so impartial as to persuade any group to subject its interests completely to an inclusive social ideal. The spirit of love may preserve a certain degree of appreciation for the common weaknesses and common aspirations which bind men together above the areas of social conflict. But again it cannot prevent the conflict. It may avail itself of instruments of restraint and coercion, through which a measure of trust in the moral capacities of an opponent may be expressed and the expansion rather than contraction of those capacities is encouraged. But it cannot hide the moral distrust expressed by the very use of the instruments of coercion. To some degree the conflict between the purest individual morality and an adequate political policy must therefore remain.

The needs of an adequate political strategy do not obviate the necessity of cultivating the strictest individual moral discipline and the most uncompromising idealism. Individuals, even when involved in their communities, will always have the opportunity of loyalty to the highest canons of personal morality. Sometimes, when their group is obviously bent upon evil, they may have to express their individual ideals by disassociating themselves from their group. Such a policy may easily lead to political irresponsibility, as in the case of the more extreme sects of non-resisters. But it may also be socially useful. Religiously inspired pacifists who protest against the violence of their state in the name of a sensitive individual conscience may never lame the will-to-power of a state as much as a class-conscious labor group. But if their numbers grew to large proportions, they might affect the policy of the government. It is possible, too, that their example may encourage similar non-conformity among individuals in the enemy nation and thus mitigate the impact of the conflict without weakening the comparative strength of their own community.

The ideals of a high individual morality are just as necessary when loyalty to the group is maintained and its general course in relation to other groups is approved. There are possibilities for individual unselfishness, even when the group is asserting its interests and rights against other communities. The interests of the individual are related to those of the group, and he may therefore seek advantages for himself when he seeks them for his group. But this indirect egoism is comparatively insignificant beside the possibilities of expressing or disciplining his egoism in relation to his group. If he is a leader in the group, it is necessary to restrain his ambitions. A leadership, free of self-seeking, improves the morale of the whole group. The leaders of disinherited groups, even when they are avowed economic determinists and scorn the language of personal idealism, are frequently actuated by high moral ideals. If they sought their own personal advantage they could gain it more easily by using their abilities to rise from their group to a more privileged one. The temptation to do this among the abler members of disinherited groups is precisely what has retarded the progress of their class or race.

The progress of the Negro race, for instance, is retarded by the inclination of many able and educated Negroes to strive for identification and assimilation with the more privileged white race and to minimise their relation to a subject race as much as possible. The American Labor Movement has failed to develop its full power for the same reason. Under the influence of American individualism, able labor men have been more ambitious to rise into the class of owners and their agents than to solidify the laboring class in its struggle for freedom. There is, furthermore, always the possibility that an intelligent member of a social group will begin his career in unselfish devotion to the interests of his community, only to be tempted by the personal prizes to be gained, either within the group or by shifting his loyalty to a more privileged group. The interests of individuals are, in other words, never exactly identical with those of their communities. The possibility and necessity of individual moral discipline is therefore never absent, no matter what importance the social struggle between various human communities achieves. Nor can any community achieve unity and harmony within its life, if the sentiments of goodwill and attitudes of mutuality are not cultivated. No political realism which emphasises the inevitability and necessity of a social struggle, can absolve individuals of the obligation to check their own egoism, to comprehend the interests of others and thus to enlarge the areas of co-operation.

Whether the co-operative and moral aspects of human life, or the necessities of the social struggle, gain the largest significance, depends upon time and circumstance. There are periods of social stability, when the general equilibrium of social forces is taken for granted, and men give themselves to the task of making life more beautiful and tender within the limits of the established social system. The Middle Ages were such a period. While they took injustices for granted, such as would affront the conscience of our day, it cannot be denied that they elaborated amenities, urbanities and delicate refinements of life and art which must make our age seem, in comparison, like the recrudescence of barbarism.

Our age is, for good or ill, immersed in the social problem. A technological civilisation makes stability impossible. It changes the circumstances of life too rapidly to incline any one to a reverent acceptance of an ancestral order. Its rapid developments and its almost daily changes in the physical circumstances of life destroy the physical symbols of stability and therefore make for restlessness, even if these movements were not in a direction which imperil the whole human enterprise. But the tendencies of an industrial era are in a definite direction. They tend to aggravate the injustices from which men have perennially suffered; and they tend to unite the whole of humanity in a system of economic interdependence. They make us more conscious of the relations of human communities to each other, than of the relations of individuals within their communities. They obsess us therefore with the brutal aspects of man's collective behavior. They, furthermore, cumulate the evil consequences of these brutalities so rapidly that we feel under a tremendous urgency to solve our social problem before it is too late. As a generation we are therefore bound to feel harassed as well as disillusioned.

In such a situation all the highest ideals and tenderest emotions which men have felt all through the ages, when they became fully conscious of their heritage and possible destiny as human beings, will seem from our perspective to be something of a luxury. They will be under a moral disadvantage, because they appear as a luxury which only those are able to indulge who are comfortable enough to be comparatively oblivious to the desperate character of our contemporary social situation. We live in an age in which personal moral idealism is easily accused of hypocrisy and frequently deserves it. It is an age in which honesty is possible only when it skirts the edges of cynicism. All this is rather tragic. For what the individual conscience feels when it lifts itself above the world of nature and the system of collective relationships in which the human spirit remains under the power of nature, is not a luxury but a necessity of the soul. Yet there is beauty in our tragedy. We are, at least, rid of some of our illusions. We can no longer buy the highest satisfactions of the individual life at the expense of social injustice. We cannot build our individual ladders to heaven and leave the total human enterprise unredeemed of its excesses and corruptions.

In the task of that redemption the most effective agents will be men who have substituted some new illusions for the abandoned ones. The most important of these illusions is that the collective life of mankind can achieve perfect justice. It is a very valuable illusion for the moment; for justice cannot be approximated if the hope of its perfect realization does not generate a sublime madness in the soul. Nothing but such madness will do battle with malignant power and "spiritual wickedness in high places." The illusion is dangerous because it encourages terrible fanaticisms. It must therefore be brought under the control of reason. One can only hope that reason will not destroy it before its work is done.

INDEX

INDEX

Aidos, 38 f.
Allport, Floyd, *Introduction*, xvii.
American Federation of Labor, 185.
Amos, the Prophet, 66.
Andrews, C. F., 243 *n.*, 244, 248 *n.*
Aquinas, Thomas, on relation of religion and ethics, 69.
Asceticism, 53–57, 71.
Asquith, Herbert, 208 f.
Augustine, Saint, on relation of the religious and secular, 69; view of this world, 70.

Barthianism, conception of God in, 64; doctrine of man and sin in, 68.
Beard, Charles, 114 *n;* Charles and Mary, 107 *n.*, 136 *n.*
Beecher, Henry Ward, 79.
Bell, Clive, 127.
Bentham, Jeremy, 44, 45 *n.*
Bernstein, Eduard, 181, 186, 204, 220 f.
Bismarck, 208.
Blunt, Wilfrid Scawen, 93.
Bonn, M. J., 165 *n.*
Boucher, Jonathan, 133.
Boudin, L. B., 182.
Bousset, J. B., 56 *n.*
Bowers, Claude, 132 *n.*
Briand, A., 224 ff., 228.
Briffault, Robert, 31 *n.*, 143.
British Empire, the, political sense and moral pretensions of, 108 f.; policy in Egypt, 103 f.; policy in India, 109 f., 249 f.
Broad, C. D., 37 *n.*
Brooks, Adam, 135.
Brown, William Adams, *Introduction*, xxi f.
Bryan, W. J., 133–6.
Bukharin, N., 195 f.
Bülow, von, 17 *n.*
Butler, Bishop J., 260 f., 261 *n.*

Case, Clarence M., 248 *n.* *See also Introduction*, xviii.
Cecil, Hugh, 267.

Celsus, *see* Origen.
Channing, W. E., 59 *n.*
Childs, John, *Introduction*, xv.
Choate, Joseph, 136.
Christian Ethic, the, 57. *See also* Love.
Christianity, apocalyptic element in, 82; liberal, confusion of, *Introduction*, xxi f.
Churchill, Winston, 93.
Coercion, 3 ff., 173 f.; always present in history, 192; covert forms in existing peace, 233; justifiable pragmatically, 234 ff.; violent and nonviolent types, 240–8, 250 ff., 254 ff. *See also* Chap. 7, *Justice through Revolution. See also* Chap. 8, *Justice through Political Force. See also* Violence.
Combination Act (1875), 207 f.
Communism, dream of equalitarian society in, 61; emphasis upon catastrophe, 62; eschatological element in, 222; religious absolutism of, 222 f. *See also* Marxism.
Condorcet, M. J., 24.
Coolidge, Calvin, 106.
Cunow, Heinrich, 229.

D'Abernon, Lord, 83 *n.*
Davis, Carless, 122 *n.*, 131 *n.*, 138.
DeMan, Henry, 160, 186.
De Mandeville, B., 55 *n.*
Democracy, 12; rise of modern, 5 f., 14; power in, 15; Marxist estimate of, 148 ff.; belief of workers in democratic state, 203 f.
Dewey, John, 35, 212. *See also Introduction*, xiii ff.
Dibelius, Wilhelm, 87 *n.*, 109.
Dicey, Edward, 84.
Dickinson, G. Lowes, 93 *n.*
Didache, 74.
Diodorus Siculus, 12 *n.*
Dorman, M. R. P., 137 *n.*
Douglas, Paul, 218 *n.*
Dwight, Timothy, 123 f.

INDEX

Eckardt, von, Hans, 140 *n.*
Education, universal, 120–3; illusions of educators, 212 ff. *See also Introduction,* xii–xxiv.
Edwards, Jonathan, on sin, 67.
Engels, F., 145–8, 190.
England, progress of social change in, 187, 190; conservative reaction in, 189, 210, 215 f.; Socialism in, 204 ff.; Fabianism in, 204 f.
Epictetus, 264.
Eucken, Rudolf, 98.

Fabianism, 204 f.
Farm revolt of the West, 133–6.
Farmer, the, his place in revolutionary socialism, 182; as conservative factor in parliamentary socialism, 216; conservative and individualistic nature, 217 f.
Fénelon, F., de la M., 55 *n.*
Force, 20, as morally redemptive, 110. *See* Violence and Coercion. *See also* Chap. 8, *Justice through Political Force,* and *Introduction,* xxiii.
Foreign Policy Association, *Can we have a planned economy?* 213 *n.*
Foster, William Z., 195.
Frank, Waldo, 43 *n.,* 65 *n.,* 197 f.
Freisinger, Otto, 126 *n.*

Gandhi, 172, 269; as exponent of non-violence, 241–9, 251 f., 254.
Garrison, William Lloyd, 248–9.
Germany, conditions in, 112; attitude of workers in Revolution, 151, 204; Socialist theory in, 181; course of social change in, 182–191; Catholic party in, 183 ff.; State control in, 207; Fascism in, 210, 215 f.
Giddy, Mr., 118.
Gladstone, William Ewart, 103 f.
Godkin, E. L., 133 ff.
Gurian, Waldemar, 193 *n.*
Guyon, Madame, 56 *n.*

Haller, Johannes, 84 *n.*
Hamilton, A., Hamiltonian and Jeffersonian dispute, 131 f.
Harnack, Adolf, 97 f.
Hart, Hornell, *Introduction,* xvii.

Hay, Secretary, 101, 124 f.
Hegel, 126 *n.*
Heiler, F., 64 *n.*
Helvetius, 44 *n.*
Hermes, Gertrude, 163.
Hobhouse, L. T., 29 *n.,* 159 *n.*
Hocking, W. E., 53 *n.*
Holmes, Oliver Wendell, 136.
Holy Alliance, Treaty of, 104 f.
Hughes, Secretary, 106.
Hume, David, 141, 265.
Hypocrisy, of individuals, 99; of groups, 8; of nations, 95–109; of privileged classes, 117–141.

Ibsen, Henrik, 160.
India, 87, 96, 109 f., 138 f.
Inequality, 89, 127, 165, 192; basis of class division, 114; basis of disproportion of power, 167; to be destroyed in Communist theory, 194 f.; inequality of reward in modern Russia, 197 f.
Injustice, 31; obscured by sentimentality of religion, 80.
Isaiah, 61.
Italy, 191, 210; character of Socialist opposition to Fascism in, 268 f.

Japan, militant class in, 7, 114.
Jaurés, Jean, 203, 226, 228.
Jefferson, Thomas, Jeffersonian and Hamiltonian dispute, 131 f.
Jesus, sayings of, 56 *n.,* 58, 71, 162; teaching of, 263 ff.
Jews, the, religious and millennial hope of, 61.

Kant, Immanuel, 29, 37, 58.
Kautsky, Karl, 186, 204, 211.
Kellogg Pact, 79. *See also Introduction,* xxi.
Kingdom of God, Gospel conception of, 61.
Kirk, K. E., 56 *n.*

Laidler, Harry, 190 *n.*
Laissez faire, 33.
Laski, Harold, 3, 80 *n.,* 188 *n.*
League of Nations, 19, 79, 110 f. *See also Introduction,* xxi f.

INDEX